Greenwich Village

A Primo Guide to Shopping, Eating, and Making Merry in True Bohemia

Robert Heide

John Gilman

ST. MARTIN'S GRIFFIN / NEW YORK

12 31 1997
Doug
Van
Valkenburgh

Previous page: Washington Arch

On May 30, 1890, a year after a temporary wooden arch was erected for the centennial celebration of George Washington's inauguration as President (April 30, 1789), Henry G. Marquand, chairman of the Washington Arch Memorial committee, stated at a cornerstone-laying ceremony for a permanent marble arch: "This is the arch of peace and goodwill to men. It will bring rich and poor together in one common bond of patriotic feeling."

The formal dedication of the permanent arch on May 4, 1895, was attended by President Grover Cleveland, who was escorted by the governor and an imposing military pageant down Fifth Avenue to the square. There, other high-level officials and their glittering escorts joined the cheering crowds while marching regiments and blaring bands contributed to the festive celebration.

Previous page, below: Detail, 32 Washington Square West

Page i: Washington Square, circa 1960

Street paintings and celebrity portraits: Thomas G. Lohre, Jr., Greenwich Village artist

Philip Cohen, chief photographer

Other photos: Ken Bachtold: 184 (top). Timothy Bissell: v, 27. Charles Caron: 167. (bottom). Steve Cooper: i, 48 (bottom), 68. Jim Fitzgerald: 11. John Gilman: 75 (bottom), 135. Tim Goetz: 50 (bottom), 60, 61, 99, 101, 102, 103, 105, 107, 108, 109, 111, 112 (top), 115, 117, 118, 137, 153, 174, 176, (bottom right), 182, 189. James D. Gossage: 26, 163. George Haimsohn: 162 (top). Billy Name: 22, 98, 164 (top). David Schmidlapp: 114 (both). Anita and Steve Shevett: 167. Stephen Eric Shore: 19, 20, 21. Alan B. Tepper: 164 (bottom). Joel Warren: 50 (top). Bill Yoscary: 23.

Line drawings: Charles T. Dougherty I: 72 (right), 86.

Note: Stores, restaurants, theaters, nightclubs, and coffeehouses sometimes move to another location or close altogether. Please do not blame the authors. As of this printing everything was where it was. Things change. Just go on to the next place in the book.

Design by Maura Fadden Rosenthal

Library of Congress Cataloging-in-Publication Data

Heide, Robert.
    Greenwich Village : a primo guide to shopping, eating, and
making merry in true Bohemia / Robert Heide and John Gilman.
      p. cm.
    ISBN 0-312-11868-6 (pbk.)
    1. Greenwich Village (New York, N.Y.)—Guidebooks. 2. New York
(N.Y.)—Guidebooks. I. Gilman, John.   II. Title.
   F128.68.G8W45   1995
   917.47' 10443—dc20   94-46638
                                         CIP

First St. Martin's Griffin Edition: April 1995
10 9 8 7 6 5 4 3 2 1

*This book is dedicated to Buster,
the Christopher Street Dog,
who has walked—and sniffed—
all of these streets many times*

Acknowledgments

Edward Albee, Alexandra Anderson-Spivey, Kenneth Anger, George Barteni-eff, Sheyla Baykal, Timothy Bissell, Victor Bokris, Angelina Boone, David Bourdon, Robert Bryan, Mary Claire Charba, Jeff and Jacky Clyman, Philip Cohen, Jacque Lynn Colton, Chuck Corbett, Jane Cronin, John Reid Cur-rie, Robert Dahdah, John DiSalvo, Magi Dominic, Bob Dylan, Norma Edgar, John Epperson, Linda Eskenas, Marianne Faithfull, Crystal Field, Farrar Fitzgerald, James Fitzgerald, Jim Fitzgerald, Zoe Fitzgerald, Manuel Garza, Jeffrey Geiger, Timothy Goetz, Mary Goldie, Dwight Goss, Steve Gould, Ben Green, Evie Greenbaum, Uta Hagen, John Hammond, Ann Harris, Nescha and Joe Henderson, John Heyes, Robin Hirsch, William M. Hoffman, Donald Howarth, Nancy Keller, H. M. Koutoukas, Paul Leiber, Bruce Levine, Carson Link, Ron Link, Wendy Lipkind, Tom Lohre, Adam Lowstetter, Don Madia, Judith Malina, Helen Mathews, Chris Mathewson, Larry Myers, Lee Paton Nagrin, Billy Name, Jeremiah Newton, Tom O'Hor-gan, Rochelle Oliver, Jerry Pagano, John Paterson, Clayton Patterson, Allen Perry, Albert Poland, Elvira Poppe, Everett Quinton, Lawrence J. Quirk, Mike Reardon, Ruby Rims, Helen Rogers, David Schmidlapp, William Schoell, Martha Seymour, Michael Smith, Adele and George Speare, Kim Stanley, Lady Hope Stansbury, Rita Brue Stanziani, Walter Steding, Ellen Stewart, Shirley Stoler, Lise Beth Talbot, Tiny Tim, Gwenn Victor, Michael Wallis, Suzanne Fitzgerald Wallis, Chris Weidner, Colin Wilson, Marguerite Young.

At the *Village Voice*: Guy Trebay, Michael Feingold, Lynn Yaeger, Jeff Weinstein, Ross Wetzsteon, and Richard Kopperdahl.

Thanks to the following authors and editors: Richard Alleman (*The Movie Lover's Guide to New York*, 1988), Alexandra Anderson and B. J. Archer (*Anderson & Archer's SoHo*, 1979), Sally Banes (*Greenwich Village 1963*, 1993), Rick Beard and Leslie Cohen Burlowitz (*Greenwich Village Culture and Counterculture*, 1993), Anna Alice Chapin (*Greenwich Village*, 1917), George Chauncey (*Gay New York*, 1994), Edmund T. Delaney (*New York's Greenwich Village*, 1967), Martin Duberman (*Stonewall*, 1993), R. Bruce Gaylord (*Gaylord's Guides Presents Greenwich Village*, 1984), Joyce Gold (*From Trout Stream to Bohemia*, 1988), Fred W. McDarrah (*Greenwich Village*, 1963), Fred W. McDarrah and Patrick J. McDarrah (*The Greenwich Village Guide*, 1992), Terry Miller (*Greenwich Village and How It Got That Way*, 1990), Joseph Mitchell (*Joe Gould's Secret*, 1965), Mary Peacock (*Voice Guide to Manhattan's Hottest Shopping Neighborhoods*, 1987), Rosetta Reitz and Joan Geisler (*Where to Go in Greenwich Village*, 1961), Vicki Rovere (*Worn Again Hallelujah!*, 1993), Caroline F. Ware (*Greenwich Village 1920–1930*, 1935).

Contents

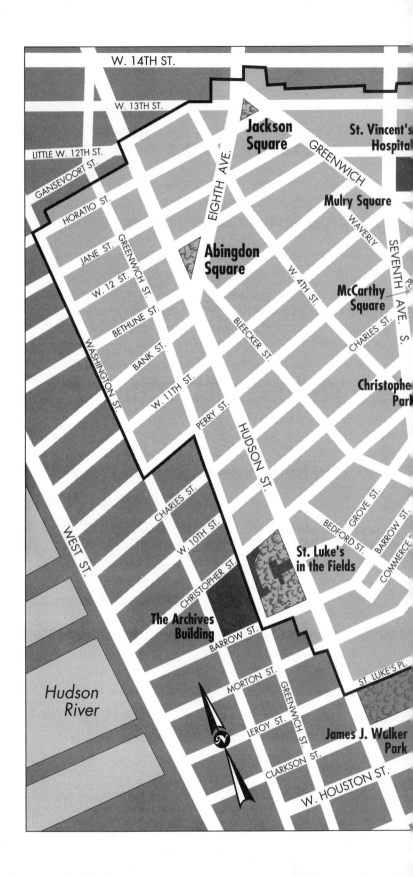

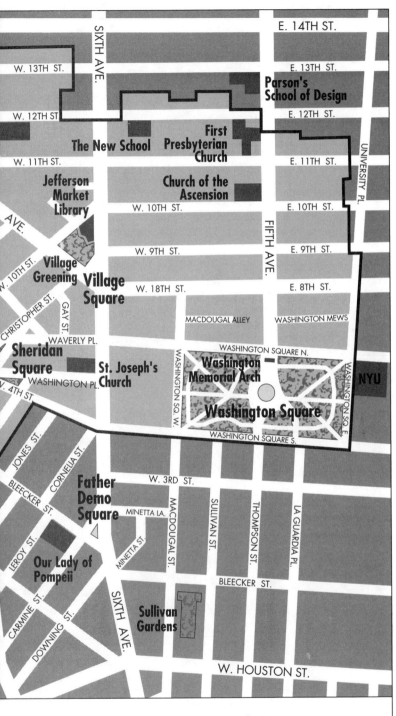

Greenwich Village Historic District

The Village—The Way It Was, A Historic View

*T*he Dutch bought Manhattan Island from the Indians in 1626. At that time the area that we now know as Greenwich Village was primarily a woodland in which deer, elk, woodchuck, and other four-footed species roamed. Pheasants, wild turkeys, owls, crows, and other large birds commingled with smaller varieties like cardinals, robins, and sparrows, the latter still populating the Village today. The Village acreage west of Minetta Brook was called *Bossen Bouwerie* (meaning farm in the woods) and became known as the best tobacco plantation in the colony. Under the direction of the Dutch West India Company, tobacco plantations flourished in Manhattan. The Sapokanican Indians, who lived in their own tiny village on the banks of the Hudson River, first cultivated this fertile land fed by Minetta Brook's off-shoot creeks, and they fished for trout and striped bass.

In 1633, the Dutch West India Company made one Wouter Van Twiller general director of the colony. Taking over the whole of what was then called the Minetta Basin, he developed it into his own farm. A map created by Van Twiller himself outlines the original Sapokanican Tribe pathways on his estate, one of which would become Christopher Street. Banking the tobacco profits for himself, instead of giving the monies over to the colony, he was ousted by 1638. A 1795 map indicates that the house Van Twiller had built and lived in was still standing then. It is believed that the house was torn down in 1825 to make way for the laying-out of MacDougal Street.

After the British captured Nieuw Amsterdam in 1664, a commander of a fleet of English warships named Sir Peter Warren eventually purchased, in 1733, a large portion of the Village tobacco plantation that would comprise three hundred acres. Sir Peter and his wife and three daughters lived in a beautiful mansion overlooking the mighty Hudson River. Before returning to England where he died (leaving his family to live on in the New World), the old commander planted an orchard and created farmland that he called Greenwich. The house that came to be known as Greenwich House and later Warren House, located in the Village at the vicinity of Perry and West Fourth Streets, was a festive annual gathering place for neighboring residents and their children. In the 1750s and 1760s, the Greenwich country-side attracted well-to-do families who constructed stalwart homes reflecting their social status as well as their conservative religious backgrounds. One of these fine houses, compact and simple compared to later Victorian era architectural styles, was called Richmond Hill and was used as a military headquarters by General George Washington in 1776. John Adams and Aaron Burr also occupied this house at different times. A country manor house owned by William Bayard was the site of Alexander Hamilton's death. Shot and mortally wounded by Aaron Burr in Weehawken, New Jersey, Hamilton was rowed across the river and taken to the Bayard House, where he died in bed.

During the smallpox and yellow fever epidemics that ravaged the population of New York in 1822, families moved from the Battery north to avoid "The Path of the Plagues." They settled in the country village on the Hudson that eventually developed into Greenwich Village. Many of them felt that "the good clean air" and the proximity of the river were healthier for their families in times of plague. As schools and banks opened, along with shops and new businesses, Greenwich Village became a vital link to the city as a whole. Many of the brick Federal buildings from this period still stand on the Village's winding streets. By 1850 the Washington Square–lower Fifth Avenue area became the place where successful merchants built their grand townhouses. This gentrification changed the area from a small country village into a thriving town.

By the end of the nineteenth century, however, wealthier residents began moving uptown to the latest fashionable areas, while residential buildings in the Village were largely neglected by some absentee landlords. Eventually the rents for this dilapidated housing came down, attracting artists, radicals, and intellectual rebels who came for the "free life" and saw the Village as America's Paris. To be sure, the search for a freer lifestyle had already attracted the likes of Henry James, who wrote about those New York aristocrats who led stifled lives in novels such as *Washington Square*, as well as the psychologist and philosopher William James (Henry's brother), Ralph Waldo Emerson, Washington Irving, Edgar Allan Poe, who was the master of dark tales, brothers Augustus and Louis Saint-Gaudens, Walt Whitman, who hung out at Pfaff's Beer Hall at Broadway and Bleecker, Stephen Crane, Edith Wharton, Willa Cather, Lafcadio Hearn, Bret Harte, Winslow Homer, John La Farge, and E. Leutz, who painted *Washington Crossing the Delaware*. Noted Village visitors and/or habitués included the Prince of Wales (later Edward VII), Jerome Bonaparte (Napoleon's brother), opera singers Enrico Caruso, Nellie Melba, Lillian Nordica, and Jenny "The Swedish Nightingale" Lind, and actresses Sarah Bernhardt, Lola Montez, Ada Clare, and Adah Isaacs Menken. Robert Louis Stevenson stayed in the Village at the Albert Hotel, still standing on East Eleventh Street.

Double-decker busses going through Washington Square Arch in the 1920s

During the First World War, the Village began to symbolize the repudiation of traditional values. Those who lived and congregated in the Village were fleeing the emptiness they felt was at the core of what some called "overbearing social controls." Freudian psychoanalysis was then coming into fashion in the Village for those who could afford to have their unconscious—and their ego-libido—set free.

The Village during the 1890s and at the turn of the century was primarily populated by Italian, Irish, and German immigrants and their offspring. These groups mixed with the more libertine Villagers, who usually tried to pay little or no attention to people they regarded as lower-class foreigners. The Irish and Italians, dominated by the Catholic Church, viewed the showgirls, poets, artists, and novelists as living without morals. The values of the Church were shunned by Bohemians. Village types smoked openly on the streets, and their concept of free love shocked the repressed immigrant class. Homosexuality was taboo even as a subject of discussion. Nevertheless, early Village Bohemia accepted "experimentation" and welcomed "lavender lads" and "Isle of Lesbos" women into their circles. Village thinkers and radicals preached against the idea of making money for its own sake, speaking out in public against bourgeois values and for the liberation of women.

The Village Bohemian crowd of this period often gathered in groups, with some living in communes for practical purposes; but all were fiercely independent and highly individualistic. Villagers, 70 percent of whom did not attend church, regarded the immigrants as ignorant and downright medieval, while the immigrants looked upon Villagers as atheists who were steeped in sin. Adding to the friction was the fact that most of these Bohemians had been raised as Protestants or Jews.

There was also enmity between the immigrant groups. Irish gangs were formed to protect their turf against the Italians, and the Italians—Sicilians and Genoese for the most part—took over blocks and corners they regarded as their territory. Violent clashes and fights would ensue. The younger men would get drunk and look for fights. Villagers and Bohemians who wrote poetry and produced art were usually not the targets of this hostility. In a sense, they were patronized by the more conventional immigrant classes as naughty children who, when push came to shove, deserved to be protected. Also, the Bohemians ate in Italian and German restaurants and drank McSorley's Irish Ale, and so were permitted their space. To top it off, the immigrant families were in bed by nine or ten while the Village Bohemians drank and partied all night. A "live and let live" attitude seemed to prevail in the Village just as it does today.

St. Vincent's Hospital

The Greenwich Village Hospital and Medical Center occupies several buildings along Seventh Avenue South and on West Eleventh Street and West Twelfth Street. It is the largest Catholic medical center in the eastern United States and is a catchment area for the Village, offering medical, psychiatric, and alcoholic services and related programs. In the mid-nineteenth century, Sister Mary Xavier Megegan, Sister Mary Ulrica O'Reilly, Sister Mary Angela Hughes, and Sister Mary Agnes Hancock, four Sisters of Charity, were assigned to establish an infirmary in New York to provide medical and spiritual care to the sick poor of the city. On November 1, 1849, they rented a house on East Thirteenth Street where they set up beds. Initially, Sister Mary Angela Hughes supervised the other three sisters who toiled twenty-four hours a day, seven days a week. Drinking and bathing water had to be carried in from a nearby well; and the sanitary conditions were primitive by today's standards. Part of their charitable work was in conjunction with the Prince Street Orphan Asylum. These four devoted caretakers of the sick eventually became seventeen nursing sisters who led St. Vincent's into the twentieth century as the excellent hospital it is today.

Sheet music for Greenwich Village Follies, *M. Witmark & Sons, 1922*

In 1916, John Reed, Marcel Duchamp, John Sloan, and a few others, after a night of drinking in local taverns, decided to hike up to the top of the Washington Square Arch, using a staircase behind a small door at the base of the arch's western plinth. On reaching their destination, they continued drinking and cavorting, declaring as loudly as possible that the Village was henceforth a free republic, a new Bohemia! They refused to come down until the Mayor promised he would do everything he could to bring this about. Thus Greenwich Village became known across the country as "Little Bohemia." The brooding playwright Eugene O'Neill felt at home in the rundown bars of the Village and the Bowery. These later became the inspiration for the setting of *The Iceman Cometh*, which takes place in a bar filled with drunks who live on booze and pipe dreams until one day their illusions are shattered. In an earlier O'Neill play entitled *Diff'rent*, one character confronts another with the line "You said you were diff'rent, but you're just like all the rest," reflecting O'Neill's disillusionment with the Bohemian life around him. The teens and twenties in the Village were the time of the "coldwater flat," apartments that had no heat and cold water only. Water could be heated on a gas, wood, or coal stove. But in the winter artists and writers like O'Neill would gather at places like The Hell Hole to warm up on shots of whiskey as they sat around a coal stove waiting for spring to arrive.

Edna St. Vincent Millay wrote about loneliness, drink, and despair in her Village book *Second April*, after winning the Pulitzer Prize for *Renascence*. The red-haired Irish lass who also wrote the play *Aria da Capo* (produced at the Provincetown Playhouse) moved to the Village in 1923. John Dos Passos, Frank Norris, Theodore Dreiser, Will Irwin, Diego Rivera, Thomas Hart Benton, Alexander Calder, Edward Hopper, Rockwell Kent, Everett Shinn, Paul Manship, and Edward Arlington Robinson are but a handful of the writers and artists who came to the Village in quest of greatness. Later it would be poet Dylan Thomas, who died after a night of drinking at the White Horse Tavern, and e.e. cummings, John Masefield, Djuana Barnes, Anais Nin, and others who were drawn to the Bohemian life in the Village.

The 1940s, 1950s, and 1960s in the Village are now regarded as the final days of Bohemian life. In the 1950s, Beat poets and coffeehouse existentialists inter-mingled with a new breed of intellectually oriented rebel actors who studied the "Method" with Lee Strasberg at the Actor's Studio. To some, Marlon Brando and Montgomery Clift and James Dean, who was dead by the mid-1950s, were interchange-

Sheridan Square, circa 1950 (note Stonewall Inn sign and Mother Hubbard's on right)

able with Jack Kerouac, Allen Ginsberg, and Gregory Corso, poets who arrived in the Village via San Francisco, Paterson, New Jersey, Florida, and other places. All represented a certain outré glamour to Villagers. Intellectual—and fashion—styles were set in Paris's Left Bank, where philosophers Sartre and Camus expounded existential-ism to the sad, sometimes angry street songs of Edith Piaf and Juli-ette Greco. The MGM musical *Funny Face* (1956), which starred Audrey Hepburn and Fred Astaire, featured Hep-burn as a skinny, doe-eyed Beatnik working in a Greenwich Village bookstore. In the film, Hep-burn goes to Paris, where she studies "empathi-calism" with a Sartre-like guru, meeting him and his followers at coffeehouses and in his bachelor digs. Hepburn, dressed in a black sweater, black pedal pushers, and pancake-flat ballerina slippers, dances to a jazz quartet in a Left Bank dive and thus helped make Beatnik fashion popular. But the "real" Beats offered more than a fashion statement. They helped revive spirits that had been beaten down by World War II, McCarthyism, the specter of the A-Bomb, and fifties conformity and materialism. Angry Beat poets and rebel ac-tors who wanted to be more than cogs in the show business machine gave others hope of a way out of their apathy and disillusionment.

With the assassinations of President John Fitzgerald Kennedy, Martin Luther King, Jr., and Bobby Kennedy, the logical place for a new

Audrey Hepburn, as a Greenwich Village book clerk in Funny Face, *wore this all-black, beatnik-style outfit in the movie. The "Audrey look" and the black ensemble became an existential fashion* must *in the Village of the 1950s.*

Night scene on Eighth Street, circa 1950

counterculture to appear was the Village. The unpopular Vietnam war and student radicals such as Abbie Hoffman contributed to the unrest. Bob Dylan, Joan Baez, Peter, Paul and Mary, Eric Anderson, and others developed a new folk music of protest, politics, and outrage. Rock 'n' roll hit the Village with a vengeance in the mid-to-late sixties. Dylan abandoned folk music to become the guru-poet of rock with his hit song "Just Like a Rolling Stone," and Jimi Hendrix, Janis Joplin, and Jim Morrison were familiar figures in both the West and East Village, doing drugs and screaming out their rage at America and the rest of the world. Village clubs like the Night Owl introduced groups such as the Lovin' Spoonful and the Mamas and the Papas.

The Rolling Stones and other British "invasion" groups, including Herman's Hermits, the Dave Clark Five, and the Moody Blues, performed at the Academy of Music on Fourteenth Street (now the Paladium) to thunderous screams and applause. The East Village Fugs, popular with Villagers, were the irreverent underground counterpart to the pre-"Sergeant Pepper" Beatles. The off-off Broadway theaters run by Joe Cino, Ellen Stewart, Al Carmines, and others created a dynamic new playwrights' movement. The hippie-nudie rock musical *Hair*, directed by Tom O'Horgan, originally produced in the Village, moved uptown where it shook up the Broadway theater. O'Horgan also directed Paul Foster's *Tom Paine* and *Futz* by Rochelle Owens, a play about a farmer who is persecuted and killed by townsfolk for having sex with his pig whom he lovingly refers to as Amanda.

The counterculture continued to thrive in the Village into the 1970s, when the so-called sexual revolution took place. Out of this new sexual freedom would emerge women's liberation as well as gay liberation. The freedom to be who and what you are in terms of one's sex or sexuality was always a prerogative of Village life. But in the seventies sexual freedom was taken to new, excessive heights at Village places like the primarily heterosexual Hellfire Club, and the Anvil, which was frequented by gay men. The seventies after-hours bar-discos with their dark, dingy backrooms for sex were compared by some writers to the infamous sex clubs of Germany's Weimar Republic. The director Werner Fassbinder, whose films include *Fox and His Friends* and *Veronica Voss*, used to fly in from Germany just to have wild weekends of sex and drugs at the Anvil. Performers like the "Amazing Yuba" set her/himself on fire at the Anvil during a wild dance, while "Mr. Slit" danced nude in the dark guided by the light in his coal miner's hat. Ruby Rims, a flamboyant drag queen who resembled an overweight version of singer Bernadette Peters, lip-synched the song "It Should Have Been Me" to the great delight of customers at the Anvil, who were high on amyl-nitrate fumes wafting through the club. The Mine Shaft, the Toilet, and the Cell Block were other notorious gay clubs in the Village where almost anything might happen—and usually did.

The seventies was also a decade in which people took a nostalgic look back at decades like the 1920s and the 1930s. Hippies and intellectuals flocked to underground cinemas, many "stoned" on one drug or another, to watch the Busby Berkeley musical films *Gold Diggers of 1933*, *Footlight Parade*, *42nd Street*, or *Gold Diggers of 1935*. They were captivated by the films' dance sequences, in which the human form rotated in a kaleidoscopic whirligig of psychedelic motion. Writer Susan Sontag had coined the word *camp* in one of her essays. A "camp sensibility" embraced puritanical or conformist attitudes in an absurdist tongue-in-cheek way, exaggerating conventions to the point of turning them inside out. Women in 1930s or 1940s makeup resembled men in drag, and this brought forth the artifice of bending gender with a vengeance, and with a new hilarity in town . . . and this included the high-tenor singing of Dick Powell and clunky tap-dancing of Ruby Keeler. Nostalgia films featuring such greats as Ginger Rogers and Fred Astaire, Carole Lombard, Clark Gable, Myrna Loy, Humphrey Bogart, Bette Davis, and other stars of Hollywood's Golden Era found new audiences in the mid-1970s at Theater 80 St. Marks in the East Village. Flea markets and Salvation Army stores sold blue mirrored coffee tables and overstuffed mohair living room sets and other Art Deco artifacts that the previous Mom-and-Pop generation had thrown away. Hippies wore Mickey Mouse watches, got high and went to screenings of *Fantasia*, reading new meaning into the Disney film that was unsuccessful in its initial release in the early 1940s. With the newfound popularity of overly made-up movie stars like Jean Harlow and Claudette Colbert, drag could finally come out of the closet; and Candy Darling, Jackie Curtis, and Divine became cinematic camp superstars. Divine, Miss Edie, Mink Stole, and the other members of director John Waters's artistic family created a trash movement in cult "midnight-show-only" films such as

Bedford Street

Commerce Street

Pink Flamingos, Female Trouble, and *Multiple Maniacs* that took "excess" a giant step further. The late 1960s saw Jackie Curtis's *Glamour, Glory and Gold*. This off-off Broadway comedy featured Melba La Rose and Candy Darling and was directed by Ron Link. It also introduced Robert De Niro, a Village actor who appeared in plays by Shelley Winters and Julie Bovasso at the Actor's Playhouse on Seventh Avenue South and the Manhattan Theater Club, respectively. Jackie Curtis, who resembled a blowsy, glittery Barbara Stanwyck, and Candy Darling, a dead ringer for Carole Lombard, went on to become Warhol film stars in the 1970s. De Niro achieved stardom in *Godfather II*. Another Village actor, Al Pacino, who used to recite Shakespeare at the Caffe Cino, also found fame in *The Godfather*, *Godfather II*, and other films.

In the 1980s, the co-op and condo conversion craze hit the Village, which endangered reasonable housing for artists and other Villagers. Rental units in the Village, along with other areas, jumped sky-high, driving struggling artists to abandon ship and move elsewhere. Some said it was as if a group of bankers in a boardroom had got together and declared, "Let's get 'em where it hurts!" Railroad flats with a bathtub in the kitchen that were $40 to $60 in the sixties or $125 in the seventies shot up to $900 and more by the 1980s. There was an influx of "young upwardly mobile" professional men and women into the Village. The Yuppies or Guppies (gay upwardly mobile) did not question the economic shifts of the Reagan years. Businesses were also affected. A store on Christopher Street that rented for $250 in 1978 jumped to $2,000 at the beginning of the

Christopher and Bleecker

1980s, and rents doubled by the end of the eighties. New immigrants who came to the Village included Arabs, Israelis, Indians, Pakistanis, and Koreans. Hard-working, many opened newspaper kiosks, cigarette shops, and delis, in the process changing the ethnic makeup of the neighborhood. The Greeks, Italians, Irish, and other immigrants who had come to the Village before took all of this in stride with little animosity.

Homelessness increased in the 1980s and hit the Village particularly hard. Nonetheless people felt sheltered by the tolerance of this community. Beggars asked for money more aggressively than the sixties flower-children, who had stood on street corners asking passersby "Got any strange change?" "Money for food" became the catchphrase of eighties street people, some of whom slept in subways, in doorways, over sidewalk grates, and in makeshift cardboard dwellings. Yuppies passed the homeless on Village streets everyday—recipients of the eighties' economic prosperity and privation.

The early eighties also witnessed the emergence of a strange new disease, with some of the earliest cases showing up at St. Vincent's Hospital. Since most of the initial victims were gay men, it was called GRID (Gay-Related Immune Deficiency Syndrome) and was said to have originated in Africa from the green monkey. Eventually, scientists discovered that the virus infected not just gay men but potentially anyone, and the acronym changed to AIDS (Acquired Immune Deficiency Syndrome). This terrible plague took its toll on many in the Village, to such an extent that some began to refer to the "EIGHTIES" as the "AIDIES." Unfortunately, AIDS continues to spread and take lives in the nineties, although the practice of safe sex through the use of condoms has helped check the epidemic somewhat.

Many pseudo- and real artists, writers, and actors who could indulge in life and artistic experimentation from the 1900s through the 1970s could, by the 1980s, no longer afford to live in the Village unless they had a rent-controlled apartment or were of independent means. Some migrated to the East Village, even homesteading in Alphabet City; the abandoned buildings and desolate empty lots, the drug pushers and homeless people creating a frightening "Third World" no-man's-land east of First Avenue. Loisaida (Avenue C between Houston and East Fourteenth Street), populated by Hispanic-Americans, emerged as a vibrant "new" neighborhood. Rents in the East Village skyrocketed too, though less rapidly; and the SoHo lofts occupied by artists in the seventies were quickly becoming the property of only the superrich or of movie stars.

In the East Village, an eighties storefront gallery movement nurtured a new generation of artists. Keith Haring first drew his cartoon-like "nuclear babies" on sidewalks and subway station walls. Haring's free-form graffiti style offered some relief from Andy Warhol's deadpan, frozen-in-time Pop-art images. Haring's youthful ebullience was in vivid counterpoint to Warhol's cold, mechanistic art, particularly his endless lithos of show-off show-biz personalities like Liza Minnelli or Mick Jagger. Unfortunately, Warhol died in 1987 and Haring in 1990, a victim of AIDS at age thirty-one.

Though the West Village in the 1990s is still a charming and historic neighborhood in which to live and visit, some of the color and dash of its original Bohemian style and culture have shifted to the East Village, which offers new rock clubs like the Pyramid, the Continental, and C.B.G.B.'s and oddball shops like Little Rickie and Atomic Passion. In addition, independent and used bookstores, once a staple of the West Village, are now mostly located on the east side. Inexpensive thrift shops and restaurants also thrive in the East Village. Under-thirty, do-nothing Gen-X types abound in the East Village along with rebellious, get-back-at-your-parents skinheads. Styles now run the gamut from shaved heads to fuchsia-dyed spiked hair, and eyebrow, cheek, nose, and navel rings are as fashionable as earrings. The color black once again signifies rebellious youth, having come full circle from the Beatnik period. Black shirts and pants, skirts and dresses, stockings and shoes are in—as are, yes, white socks.

The West Village, the heart of the Greenwich Village Historic District, is on the rebound. Stylish new jazz clubs and sparkling new espresso bars are opening all the time. Some optimists even predict that rents will come down and Little Bohemia will return—after the year 2000, that is!

Village residents with participants at Wigstock, 1994

The Way We Were–Albee, Warhol, Edie, Dylan, and Cino in the Village: A Personal Reminiscence by Robert Heide

My initial forays into Greenwich Village took place when I was in my teens and living with my family in the small town of Irvington, New Jersey. Before that time I remember as a child standing on a hilltop near my house and looking out in wonder at the tall Manhattan buildings that scraped the sky. It all seemed to be so near and yet at the same time so distant, appearing from that viewpoint almost as a mirage. There were, to be sure, always those Gotham trips made with my parents to see a Broadway musical, to Radio City or to the Roxy, followed by a visit to the Automat on Times Square, where for a few nickels put into a slot you could, upon turning a knob, receive from a glass-encased "pop-open" compartment a sandwich on a plate or a small crock of baked beans.

One day in the mid-1950s, an English teacher took a group of teenaged boys, including myself, by bus into the Village to tour the sites, the historic buildings, and the Village art show in the streets around Washington Square. This was to be my first glimpse of what was then referred to as "Little Bohemia," and the long-haired artists, some of whom were handing out political pamphlets and calling for revolution, seemed fascinating in their intensity. Later I found my way back into the Village, sometimes borrowing my father's Chevy coupe and sometimes going along with two school friends, Dick and Gloria, who drove in from New Jersey in a 1950 scarab-shaped chartreuse Lincoln convertible. Dick was a classmate of mine at the Carteret School for Boys—a college prep school—and Gloria, who later changed her name to Gilbey, was a platinum-haired debutante who lived on posh Wyoming Avenue in South Orange, New Jersey. If nobody's family car was available for such a jaunt, there was always the Springfield Avenue bus, which deposited us at Penn Station in Newark where a PATH train—then called the Hudson Tubes—would leave us at Christopher Street or Ninth Street for just one nickel.

Though we sometimes went to a nightclub at Number One Fifth Avenue, Dick and Gloria and I preferred to hang out at an infamous cellar dive at 183 West Tenth Street between West Fourth Street and

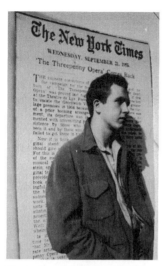

Young playwright Robert Heide

Seventh Avenue South called Lenny's Hideaway. Though we were not of drinking age, none of that seemed to matter too much in those days; and the liquor was always flowing. The surly German bartender at Lenny's, an ex-ballet dancer named Robbie, concocted and served a special deadly drink he called "der clinker," a mixture of apricot brandy, straight brandy, vodka, and apricot nectar, served in a cup, which left those who drank it more than slightly punch-drunk. Some regulars who imbibed this mixture would nod out after just one, while others kept on drinking into the night. A Village character named Ian Orlando Macbeth, who dressed imperiously in the style of the Renaissance, with a hat, long, billowing capes, tights, and curl-point felt slippers, always ordered a clinker; after gulping down his second he would spout poetry in exquisite iambic pentameter, sometimes shouting in a grand fury and at other times sobbing away in some deep remorseful state of melancholia. With pink hair and a pink beard, he sometimes came in with a screeching cockatoo perched on his shoulder. At Lenny's I encountered what I then thought, from my prep school perspective, to be a truly decadent, artistic Village crowd. Later I learned that some of these characters whom I believed were geniuses were often the least inclined to practice their "art," preferring mostly to hang out in local saloons or taverns, posturing as flamboyant artistes manqués. Some acquaintances and friendships I made at Lenny's included Edward Albee and his composer friend William "Bill" Flanagan, composer Ned Rorem, Tom Eyen (later the author of *Dreamgirls*), H. M. Koutoukas, who called himself a chamber dramatist, the old-time actress Peggy Joyce, and director Ron Link, who was then a stage manager for the off-Broadway musical *Leave It to Jane*. Rorem and Flanagan were protégés of Virgil Thompson, who sponsored musical evenings at Carnegie Hall for these two gifted composers. At that time Albee was writing poetry and had an afternoon job delivering telegrams. Rorem, Flanagan, and Albee all drank heavily.

During this time I liked to go in the afternoons to the Village coffeehouses, which were mostly on Bleecker or MacDougal Streets, just as they are today. An article in *Whisper* or *Confidential Magazine* that made a strong impression on Dick, Gloria, and me described the sloppy Bohemian-style Village apartment shared by Wally Cox, the intellectually effete TV star of "Mr. Peepers" fame, and Marlon Brando. The article reported Brando's predilection for cruising around town dressed in a black leather jacket riding a motorcycle. This rebel-let-all-hell-run-wild attitude appealed to my desire to experience

James Dean

new freedoms in the same way that James Dean's tortured psyche had evolved into a more virulent, almost psychotic dimension as expressed by the teenage character called Jim Stark he so brilliantly portrayed in the 1955 film *Rebel Without a Cause*. I had also read in a magazine that James Dean, who was an idol of mine, liked to prowl around the Village in his early New York acting days. One of his haunts was the Rienzi, a coffeehouse that has long since disappeared, at 107 MacDougal between Bleecker and Third Streets. When I first went to the Rienzi, an exhibit on the walls by photographer Roy Schott featured portraits of a neurotic, unshaven James Dean, looking intensely into the camera lens or gazing forlornly into space. The young men who were sometimes Dean actor-lookalikes sat under the photographs sipping espresso; they wore scowls and spent long hours reading Kierkegaard's *Fear and Trembling—The Sickness Unto Death* or some other existentialist book by Nietzsche or Heidegger. I remember one particular day when H. M. Koutoukas and I, at separate tables, were both wearing identical black turtleneck sweaters and black trousers while trying to decipher "the meaning" or "non-meaning" of Jean Paul Sartre's big philosophical tome, *Being and Nothingness*. This was the Beat period in the Village and black clothing was then the fashion just as it is once again in the East Village. Just across the street from the Rienzi at a coffee shop called the Gaslight, some of us sat and listened to the poetry of Gregory Corso, Ted Jones, Taylor Mead, Jack Micheline, Allen Ginsberg, and Jack Kerouac. Ginsberg and Kerouac were just in from San Francisco and startled listeners with what was then referred to in a somewhat cynical way as "automatic-poetry," which meant that most of it was written at a heated temperature of the mind, rather than being heartfelt or clever in the manner of more Romantic poets like Keats, Shelley, or Edna St. Vincent Millay.

I left the diversions of Greenwich Village to study at Northwestern University in Evanston, Illinois, and in some sense, with the intention of trying to clean up my act. The dissolution I had been emulating had caught up with me and my parents were insisting that I do something with my life. Instead, once I got to Northwestern, I was drawn into the more arty theater department at the School of Speech by a teacher named Alvina Krause and was soon acting in college productions of *Major Barbara* and *Romeo and Juliet*. Trying to create a sense of the Bohemian in my fraternity house room, I hung a plastic mobile from the ceiling and pictures of Edgar Allan Poe or Arthur Rimbaud or Jean Cocteau on the wall, much to the chagrin of my more conservative "brothers," who always seemed to be drinking beer and throwing cottage cheese "snowballs" at frat members in the Alpha Delta Phi house dining room. Soon schoolroom boredom and nostalgic yearnings for the Village I had left behind combined to drive me to the "El" (elevated railway), which took me from the college campus in Evanston to Chicago's equivalent to the Village, the Near North Side. Here I eagerly sought out the characters on Bughouse Square—poets, radicals, and outright crazies—and at a place called the College of Complexes, I met a woman who called herself Clark Street Mary, famous for her song which included the lyric:

> *. . . now you live on Lake Shore Drive*
> *and you don't know that I'm alive.*
> *Don't try to Clark Street me.*
> *I remember the time when you bargained for a dime.*
> *Don't try to Clark Street me.*

It was not surprising that, between visits to the Near North Side and spring and Christmas breaks and summer vacations spent in Greenwich Village, conflicts arose and my studies in the history of the Far East and other subjects suffered. Miraculously, despite the pressures of conformity versus nonconformity, I somehow completed my courses and got my diploma.

After my stint at Northwestern came to an end, my parents announced that they were leaving Irvington and moving to a ranch house in Point Pleasant, New Jersey. My older sister Evelyn had married and was living in nearby Bricktown and my older brother Walter, who was also married, moved to Orangevale, California. I saw all of this as my permanent chance to escape from my parents and suburbia to—where else?—Le Village. I signed up to study dramatics with Stella Adler and with the help of my father I made the big move to the Village, just two blocks from my old watering hole—Lenny's Hideaway. I renewed my friendship with Edward Albee, who by then was having fights with William Flanagan, now the music critic at the *Herald Tribune*. They still shared an apartment on West Fourth Street, but Edward, who had inherited money from RKO Albee, no longer had to go door-to-door delivering telegrams, a job he had taken in any case as a sort of joke. He had just completed a play called

The Zoo Story and was trying to have it produced in the Village. He was also writing poetry and we both were reading our poetry with another writer, my upstairs neighbor, Dick Higgins. This was at a coffeehouse called Pandora's Box on West Fourth Street on Sheridan Square, right next to the old Circle-in-the-Square Theater and the historic Louie's Tavern, all demolished to make way for a massive, cheaply constructed apartment building. Another neighbor was Sally Kirkland, who was the youngest member of the Actor's Studio. After work at the Caffe Figaro, where she was a waitress, she would come home and listen to the music of Edith

Edward Albee in the early 1960s

Piaf, Francoise Hardy, and Sylvie Vartan, thinking she was in the more romantic Left Bank of Paris along with Brigitte Bardot and Jeanne Moreau. Dick Higgins, the heir to the Worcester steel mills, became a disciple of Gurdjief and the composer John Cage, and later was a founding member of the art movement Fluxus. Albee detested Higgins's experimentalist poetry and Higgins referred to Albee's writings as "poims," meaning that they were too romantic and not mechanistic enough for his tastes. My own poems were somewhat in the middle. One of them, called "Statue," went:

> *I dreamt*
> > *last night*
> *I held*
> > *your head*
> *in my hands.*
> *It was strangely*
> > *detached.*
> *The hands*
> *that held it were*
> > *—amputated.*

Robert Heide at the Cino with "Statue" mask

Albee liked to go drinking all night, and I would hop around with him from bar to bar, sometimes continuing after hours at the apartment of a cohort or a stranger or at Edward's place, where fights fueled by liquor would ensue into the wee hours of the morning. Some of the angry, bitter dialogue exchanged between Albee and Flanagan later turned up verbatim in the play *Who's Afraid of Virginia Woolf?* I remember in a kind of hazy way a pub crawl with Brendan Behan and Edward Albee, which started at the White Horse Tavern, eventually winding up at the Ninth Circle and then Julius on West Tenth Street. Behan was practically incoherent at this point due to the progression of his alcoholism, but he seemed to be having a great time, sometimes laughing uproariously and sometimes singing jolly Irish ditties in a boisterous manner. An early sixties photo of Albee in a crewcut still hangs on the wall of Julius alongside the photos of boxers and sports figures. Often I would meet Albee at Village Drugs on Seventh Avenue South, right next to the Actor's Playhouse, at around four in the afternoon for a walk around the Village. Usually he was having a bromo-seltzer, which he followed with a black and white ice-cream soda. The counter at this drugstore, like the one that used to be at Bigelow's Drugs, on Sixth Avenue, served hamburgers, eggs, and sandwiches and displayed a fresh, roasted turkey every day. Actors, writers, and artists hung out there, sometimes all day long. Marguerite Young and Anais Nin often were discussing literature or their careers over coffee at Village Drugs. Another late afternoon "breakfast" spot was Jack and Jill's on Bleecker where for forty cents you could have a glass of juice, two doughnuts, and a cup of coffee.

Downtown theater and cabaret people used to go to Clara's Pam Pam, a ham-and-eggery (now Pennyfeathers and still serving eggs, ham, and coffee) or Mother Hubbard's (on Seventh Avenue South at Sheridan Square, where the Down Beat jazz club is now), run by a woman named Adele Speare, who resembled Joan Crawford in *Mildred Pierce* in her platform high heels and shoulder-padded dresses. Like Mildred Pierce, Adele always wore a fox-fur chubby coat and baked the best apple pies this side of Mom's Kitchen. A Mother Hubbard "Big 3" included a hamburger, a piece of apple pie, and coffee for ninety-five cents. The cooks, who now run the Pink Teacup on Grove Street, learned it all at Mother Hubbard's place. One of the waiters who served pie there early on was Harry Belafonte.

During this time I studied with Stella Adler, then Uta Hagen, and then Harold Clurman, with some vague idea that I might be the next Brando or, at the very least, a second-lead type like Dennis Hopper. As the sixties progressed, Edward, with the successes of *The Zoo Story*, *The American Dream*, and *The Death of Bessie Smith*, had joined the ranks of Arthur Kopit, Jack Gelber, and Jack Richardson, who were referred to in *Esquire* magazine collectively as "four on a new wave," the American counterparts to European absurdists like Ionesco, Beckett, and DeGhelderode. The English kitchen drama of Osborne, Orton, Wesker, and others was just coming into play and Albee, with *Who's Afraid of Virginia Woolf?* as a big Broadway hit starring Uta Hagen, had left the absurdists behind to become America's angriest playwright. When the *New Yorker* featured a portrait of Albee as a new angry young man and success-phenomenon-deluxe, they wrote about his favorite Village bar, which was the San Remo on MacDougal and Bleecker Street (now defunct). The Friday night after the article appeared, the Remo was jammed not just with regulars but with celebrities like Leonard Bernstein, Simone Signoret, Tennessee Williams, and others who wanted to catch a glimpse of the new cause celeb at his special haunt.

Albee had created a fervor for the one-act play form; and it seemed writers who had been actors or poets or something else were suddenly writing one-act plays. A young writer named Terrence McNally moved in with Edward at his new floor-through apartment on West Tenth Street. Flanagan was out after nine years. Friends thought he had subjugated his own talent to Edward's and had become a victim of Edward's success. A few years later he died of some kind of overdose following a heavy drinking binge. Arriving in the Village, as if by the busload, were new actor/writers like Sam Shepard, John Guare, Lanford Wilson, and a score of others who joined in on the exploding sixties coffeehouse experimental theater movement, which later came to be known as "off-off Broadway." Many writers, actors, and directors could not find work either on Broadway in the commercial theater or off-Broadway, which was becoming increasingly costly in the area of production. Where off-Broadway had previously thrived on a shoestring, now big bucks were required to mount a production because of unions and other rising costs. Many of these theater hopefuls and other actors, directors, and writers had studied with Strasberg, Adler, or Meisner, or had done their theater academic studies at universities like Northwestern's School of Speech or the Yale School of Drama and were anxious to find places to practice and develop their work.

Joe Cino

The father and "little theater saint" of the off-off Broadway movement was Joe Cino, a large, burly Italian with an abun-

Andy Warhol filming The Bed

dant, humanistic, and all-embracing hopeful attitude, whose Caffe Cino in a storefront at 31 Cornelia Street became the first to produce original plays, mostly one-acters by the aforementioned young writers and others like Doric Wilson, Robert Patrick, William M. Hoffman, Don Kvares, Storey Talbot, Tom Eyen, Leonard Melfi, David Starkweather, and Paul Foster, with actors like Al Pacino, Harvey Keitel, and Bernadette Peters (who starred in *Dames at Sea*, first produced at the Cino) joining in the fun. H. M. Koutoukas was called the quintessential Cino playwright because his campy, poetic plays with titles like *Tidy Passions* and *With Creatures Make My Way* assaulted the audience with a convoluted humor that mixed up concepts with ideologies to produce eerily horrific insights into the complexities of the human dilemma. Death and life were interchangeable to "Harry," as we called him, who always lived just this side—or just on the edge—of madness.

At this juncture I also began to try my hand at the playwriting game. My play *Hector*, influenced by Beckett's *Krapp's Last Tape*, received a good production at the Cherry Lane Theater along with Jean Cocteau's *Marriage on the Eiffel Tower* and poet Kenneth Koch's play *Pericles*. Another play of mine, *West of the Moon*, was an encounter between a hustler and a religious fanatic, two young men each on the verge of a nervous breakdown, one in an agitated state of free-floating paranoia while the other is withdrawing into a nonverbal catatonic web of conflicts bordering on hysteria and suicide. The play, set in a doorway on a rainy night on Christopher Street in the Village, was produced by Lee Paton (later known as the East Village performance artist Lee Nagrin) at a theater called New Playwrights on West Third Street. Eventually the theater, which was an off-Broadway house, fell into economic hard times and Lee ran off with the lighting man named Billy Hollywood who was shooting heroin. On the bill with *West of the Moon* was *The Blood Bugle* by Harry Tierney, Jr., starring James Cahill and Jerry Pagano. Jerry was the real-life inspiration for Albee's character Jerry in *The Zoo Story*. The counterculture of the mid-sixties was in full force, including the folk-rock scene led by Bob Dylan and new rock 'n' rollers like the Lovin' Spoonful and the Mamas and the Papas, both groups appearing at the Nite Owl (now Bleecker Bob's record store on Third Street). With plenty of mescaline, LSD, and marijuana to go around, everyone seemed to be having a good time. Rents were under one hundred dollars and money was wherever you found it. Mostly, no one needed much money to live on the fringes, and Joe Cino, for one, was always good for a provolone sandwich and a cup of cappuccino. Paul Simon and Art Garfunkel were singing about their thirty-dollar Village rent in the song "Bleecker Street," also recorded by Peter, Paul and Mary. Mary Travers

Robert Heide at Warhol filming in November 1965

today recalls that the rent on her coldwater flat was about the same when the group first started singing folk music in the Village.

Eventually I started to make the Caffe Cino my second home. Joe Cino was a father figure to a great many who looked up to him as a kind of Stromboli puppeteer who could make you dance, sing, act, or write plays with the pull of a string. People who were part of Joe's "family" included Charles Stanley, Johnny Dodd, John Torrey, Magie Dominic, Charles Loubier, Michael Smith, Kenny Burgess, and Bob Patrick. Lady Hope Stansbury, the Cino waitress for a time, went on to perform off-Broadway with Divine in *Women Behind Bars* and played Divine's daughter in *Neon Woman*. Both were written by Tom Eyen, who also wrote *Why Hannah's Skirt Won't Stay Down* with Helen Hanft and Steve Davis. Top plays that premiered at the Cino include:

> *Icarus' Mother* by Sam Shepard
>
> *The Madness of Lady Bright*, *Ludlow Fair*, and *This Is the Rill Speaking* by Lanford Wilson
>
> *Hurrah for the Bridge* by Paul Foster
>
> *Something I'll Tell You Tuesday* and *The Loveliest Afternoon of the Year* by John Guare
>
> *War* by Jean Claude van Italie
>
> *The Haunted Host* and *The Warhol Machine* by Robert Patrick
>
> *Thank You Miss Victoria*, *Goodnight, I Love You*, and *Saturday Night at the Movies* by William M. Hoffman
>
> *Cobra Invocations* and *With Creatures Make My Way* by H. M. Koutoukas
>
> *A Funny Walk Home* by Jeff Weiss
>
> *Sometime Jam Today* by Storey Talbot (starring his wife LiseBeth)
>
> *The White Whore and the Bit Player* by Tom Eyen
>
> *Dames at Sea or Gold Diggers Afloat* by George Haimsohn, directed by Robert Dahdah

James Jennings and Larry Burns in The Bed

One night Joe Cino's partner, John Torrey, in a drunken rage, burned down the Caffe Cino, and later director Ron Link and Ellen Stewart, who developed La Mama, her own coffeehouse theater modeled after the Cino, gave benefits to raise money for rebuilding in a variety of places. I wrote a play called *The Bed* for one of the Cino fundraisers held at the Sullivan Street Theater. It was an existential drama in which two men are trapped in an apartment on a big slab of a bed drinking booze and taking drugs with no way out. Joe identified with this precarious situation and invited me to bring *The Bed* to the Cino when it reopened.

The Bed, directed by Robert Dahdah at the Caffe Cino, was a big hit, and Elanore Lester of the *New York Times* did a piece in the magazine section about it along with a detailed account of the plays of Sam Shepard, Robert Patrick, Lanford Wilson, and others. After this *Times* article, the Cino was descended upon by those who saw it as a new, happening place. The noted English philosopher/writer Colin Wilson saw my play and explained to me what it was about from a purely existential point of view. Andy Warhol, whom I had met on previous occasions through the photographer Edward Wallowitch, came several times, giving me a quote about "pure emptiness" that I used on the poster, along with this one from Bob Dylan: "I know there're some people terrified of the bomb. But there are other people terrified to be seen carrying a *Modern Screen* magazine. Experience teaches that silence terrifies people the most." Warhol decided

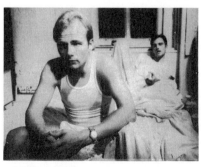

The Bed, *as filmed by Andy Warhol*

to film *The Bed* and set up his cameras in Richard Bernstein's Bowery loft. After the actors James Jennings and Larry Burns did their work on stage at the Cino, they would go to the loft for Andy's multiple shoots—the movie, the first of Warhol's to use a split-screen technique, was shown first at the 41st Street Theater and at the Cinemateque. I started hanging out with Andy at this time at his silver factory in the west forties and introduced him to some of his superstars like On-

Left to right: Louis Waldon, Taylor Mead, Andy Warhol, 1968

dine and Billy Name. One night we went to the Caffe Bizarre on Third Street to see the Velvet Underground led by Lou Reed, a group that Andy was thinking of signing up. When he did sign them, he brought Nico to join them in a light-show extravaganza at the Dom on St. Marks Place. Andy felt Nico's blond beauty and super-cool attitude brought something elegant into the otherwise grungy look of the group. The Velvet Underground was presented as part of what Andy called "The Plastic Exploding Inevitable." The Underground's first album with a Warhol peel-off banana on the cover turned out to be among the most innovative rock 'n' roll albums of all time. Rock 'n' roll disc jockeys objected to Lou Reed's song "Heroin," which they felt might influence some of their youthful listeners to use the drug. Album sales were initially hurt by lack of air play, but it didn't seem to bother Andy or anyone else if the album was a success or not. It was not considered "cool" or "Zenlike" among Warholites to worry about things like that.

After having dinner one evening at Bobo Rockefeller's house with David Rockefeller, Fleur Trujillo, the daughter of the dictator, and Edie Sedgwick (then labeled the "Girl of the Year" by major newspapers and important fashion magazines), who was always to be found at Andy's side, Warhol asked me if I would write a film script for Edie in which she commits suicide at the end. I said I would think about it. After all the partying with the uptown Rockefeller crowd I accompanied Andy back to the Factory. He seemed to be in a little-boy-lost state and as we relaxed on his couch, which itself was the subject of a Warhol film called *The Couch*, he asked, "What do you think it all means?"

"I don't know," I said, which seemed to me to be just the right answer to such a profound question.

"What do you think we should do next?" he asked, staring blankly at me through wire-rim, rose-colored glasses. By this time gray light was coming in through the factory windows.

"Well, Andy, I think you should just keep doing the same thing."

"What do you mean?" he asked.

"Well," I explained, "you're into this Zen repetition of images thing . . . just change around the colors—a purple and green Campbell's Soup can, for instance, a Marilyn Monroe with fuchsia hair and a yellow face . . ."

"Oh . . ." Andy whined. "Gee . . ."

And so not too far off in the future Andy went into full production at the Factory, changing the colors of his Marilyns, Elizabeth Taylors, Campbell Soup cans, and other images. At one point he promised me that I could have one of these silk-screened canvases but I never collected.

At around that time I noted that there was some kind of power struggle going on between Andy and Bob Dylan over Edie, whom Dylan was enamored of. It was said that he wrote "Just Like a Woman" for Edie. Supposedly the song "Here Comes Your Nine-teenth Nervous Breakdown," recorded by the Rolling Stones, was also written for Edie, who, like a twenties flapper, relished a life of ex-cess—partying every night, swilling liquor, popping pills, and even shooting amphetamines directly into her veins. Dylan, who was su-percool but had meaning and depth, hated Andy's icy-cold "it's-all-empty" routine. Once, after Andy filmed a still life of Dylan sitting in a chair staring into a camera, a bored and restless Dylan, occasionally scratching his nose, got up, picked out a bigger-than-life-size Elvis "two-gun" silk-screen canvas, and walked with it into the freight ele-vator. As the doors closed, Dylan said to Andy in a matter-of-fact tone, "I think I'll just take this for payment, man." Andy, usually blank and cool, was floored, and his milk-white skin turned tomato-soup red. No one had ever asked Andy for anything, at least not with that kind of directness.

I decided the right script for Edie would be *The Death of Lupe Velez*. In the book *Hollywood Babylon*, Kenneth Anger writes about a bizarre suicide in which the Mexican spitfire movie actress swallows Seconal, which causes her to throw up her Mexi-spice dinner all over the bed and floor of her Hollywood hacienda home. Rather than the beautiful death she had planned surrounded by Tuberoses, she was found dead with her head in a toilet bowl by the news media. I told this story to Edie one day while we were riding all over town in her limousine, which I later discovered belonged to Dylan. Edie, who looked especially beauti-

Andy Warhol and Robert Heide at a Village art happening

ful and radiant as a flower in full
bloom that day, loved riding
around with charge cards or just
popping into restaurants like the
Ginger Man and signing her
name to the check after drinking
double-vodka Bloody Marys. I
gave Andy the script for *The
Death of Lupe Velez* (later called
Lupe) and he filmed it in color
the same day, although Edie was
too stoned to remember her
lines. I did not watch these pro-

Edie Sedgwick

ceedings but that night over the phone Andy asked me to meet him at
the Kettle of Fish on MacDougal Street (now moved, intact, to Third
Street). When I arrived at the Kettle, as it was called, Edie was there
but Andy had not yet shown up. Edie, out of it as usual, had tears in
her eyes.

"What's happening?" I asked.

"I try to get close to him but I just can't get through," Edie said,
staring now at the front door, adding quickly, "Oh, here he is . . ."

At that moment Andy came in dressed in a matching black leather
ensemble consisting of tight-fitting pants and a jacket inlaid with
chromium studs. Andy had purchased several custom-made outfits
from the Leather Man on Christopher Street, some in blue suede
and others in black or gray leather. Usually Andy only wore dirty
black dungarees with striped T-shirts, but this night he was wearing
one of his splashier outfits. He ordered a soda and then excused himself to check in at the Factory by telephone.

"What's happening with the *Lupe* film?" I asked Edie, who
seemed to be in a catatonic trance.

"Oh . . ." she said in a faraway voice. "We already filmed that."

At the same time Andy returned to the table, a black Cadillac
stretch-limo pulled up in front of the bar, and in a flash Bob Dylan,
looking spidery-thin, dressed all in black and wearing shades, sat
down with us. His brown-blond Afro haircut was perfectly coiffed,
with not a hair out of place. Edie perked up, turning on her little-girl
Marilyn Monroe-cum-Judy Garland charm, purring like a kitten at
the rock superstar, who just stared angrily at the table.

"Oh, hi . . . uh . . ." Andy murmured.

After a long, tense period in which no one said a word, Dylan
grabbed Edie by the arm and with a snarl demanded she leave with
him.

"Let's split," he exclaimed, and almost dutifully Edie followed
him out the door and into the waiting limousine, which sped off into

the night. The story around town was that Dylan and his manager wanted to handle Edie as a property, although no one seemed too sure what she could do, least of all Edie herself, who showed little interest in acting, singing, or anything else. She once thought she could become a weathergirl on TV, but that notion was always treated as a joke.

With Dylan and Edie off somewhere, Andy asked if we could walk over to Fourth Street and Cornelia to look at the building (5 Cornelia) where Freddie Herko the dancer had committed suicide. Freddie had been in the fifth-floor walk-up apartment of Johnny Dodd, the lighting designer at the Caffe Cino, performing a nude dance to a recording of Mozart's *Coronation Mass* playing at full blast when he took a ballet leap out the window, plunging to his death. Staring up at the window, Andy muttered softly, "When do you think Edie will commit suicide? I hope she lets us know when she's gonna do it, so we can film it." I looked at Andy, but as usual there was little or nothing to say. An Edie lookalike minus Edie's charm, grace, and style who was called Ingrid Superstar (named by mentor Andy himself) was waiting in the wings at the Silver Factory hoping to take over the number-one spot if something "happened" to Edie. My one appearance in a Warhol film (my fifteen minutes of fame) was opposite underground filmmaker Jack Smith, who played the title role in *Dracula*, also called *Batman Dracula*. This two-hour black-and-white film was made in 1964 by Warhol actually prior to his filming *The Bed* and was documented by the Andy Warhol Film Project at the Whitney Museum of American Art in 1994. In it I am wearing a hat with the word *suicide* printed on it. Until recently I did not recall making this film. Billy Name, who took still pictures during the shooting of the movie, said to me at the Whitney screening, "We were all so strung out . . . on drugs . . . or whatever. Who could remember?"

Bob Dylan

Hippie-street crazies started hanging out at the Factory and some carried guns, often inviting people to play Russian roulette. An atmosphere of danger and drugs permeated the scene, and I started going back to the Cino, which by then was not much better. The drug scene by 1966 had come home to roost at the Cino, and some of the people shooting up amphetamines there were from the Warhol crowd: Pope

Ondine, Soren Agenoux, and others. I wrote a play for the Cino called *Moon* about a young couple living on the edge who are menaced in their apartment by another couple they met at a party the night before. A young actor named John Gilman played an artist living upstairs from the couple who spends his time painting circles and baking bread. His peace offering of homemade bread quiets things down and for a time breaks the tension, managing to defuse the underlying rage kept under control by the other characters in the play. *Moon* was produced in several theaters around town, including the Manhattan Theater Club and the Cherry Lane, and I subsequently wrote another play about two hippies called *At War with the Mongols* for John and *Moon*'s lead actress, Linda Eskenas. Linda was a brilliant actress and had a reputation as a reigning Lower East Side slum goddess. John had been in a William M. Hoffman play called *Goodnight, I Love You*. Hoffman, a seminal Cino playwright, would later hit Broadway with the first AIDS play, *As Is*.

Ellen Stewart of La Mama also produced a play of mine, *Why Tuesday Never Has a Blue Monday*, directed by Ron Link. The subject of the play was a one-hour psychoanalytic session with a therapist-seducer who tries to help a neurotic Method actress make a distinction between her real-life roles and her stage roles. I had written the play for the Actors Studio with Kim Stanley and Jason Robards in mind, but Marilyn Roberts and Patrick Sullivan, who were not box-office names, wound up in the play instead.

On Friday night, March 31, 1967, Joe Cino was inside his caffe on Cornelia Street; he had taken drugs and was performing a wild Greek dance with a knife. Though there was no audience, an upstairs neighbor named Josie swears she heard "voices" in the theater daring Joe to "do it," which he finally did, stabbing himself in several places and carving a circle in his abdominal area. Rushed to St. Vincent's Hospital, he died there on Sunday, April 2, 1967, of multiple self-inflicted wounds. One year prior to this exactly, Joe's companion John Torrey had accidentally died from an electrical shock while screwing a light bulb into a theater lamp. Charles Stanley, an actor who took on male and female parts, presided over the Cino, and under his auspices, and later *Village Voice* theater critic Michael Smith's, it survived for just one more year. We returned to do

John Gilman (left), Robert Frink (right) in Robert Heide's play Moon, *at the Caffe Cino, 1967*

Robert Heide and John Gilman on Commerce Street in the Village in 1982

Moon again, but things were never the same. Other plays brought in that last year after Joe's untimely death included those by H. M. Koutoukas, Robert Patrick, and Tom Eyen. The very last play performed there was called *Monument*, written by the poet/dramatist Diane Di Prima.

The Caffe Cino and the pioneer spirit of Joe Cino were honored as the first off-off Broadway theater by a glittering exhibition in the Vincent Astor Gallery in the New York Public Library for Performing Arts at Lincoln Center, March 5 through May 11, 1985. The Cino had lasted for almost ten years. It spent its first year in 1958 on MacDougal Street, and the other nine at 31 Cornelia Street. The Cornelia Street Cafe at 29 Cornelia Street, just next door to where the old Cino had been, continues the tradition of coffee shops that promote the reading of new poetry, readings from first novels as well as the performance of some musical events and plays. Each year on the anniversary of Joe Cino's death, a group of the Cino regulars and friends of Joe Cino as well as visiting celebrities, curiosity seekers, and Village historians gather to pay their respects. At the meeting in 1994, attended by Quentin Crisp, Jacque Lynn Colton, and others, poet Magie Dominic wrote the following poem:

Cappuccino at the Cino

Once upon a time—Joe Cino at the coffee machine—
Bells, magic, glitter, twinkle lights and Italian pastries,
Birthday books, wobbly chairs, comic books, opera and Moon.
These things, all in one small room once, on Cornelia.

I was invited by Edward Albee and Richard Barr, Edward's producer, to become a member of the New Playwrights Unit Workshop at the Village South Theater on VanDam Street headed by Albee, Barr, and Clinton Wilder. Its members included LeRoi Jones, Sam Shepard, Terrence McNally, Paul Zindel, Emmanuel Peluso, Mart Crowley (*The Boys in the Band*), Larry Osgood, Harvey Perr, and Derek Washburn. Richard Barr bragged about his "stable of playwrights just ready to let loose on the public," and he and his friend actor Donald Davies of *Krapp's Last Tape* fame hosted parties at Richard's digs on MacDougal Alley and later on Eighth Street, where playwrights and actors could meet the likes of Noel Coward and John Gielgud, at usually all-male cocktail parties.

I continued to write plays in the 1970s and 1980s. *Suburban*

Two Greenwich Village Ghosts

For some time we had heard many stories about Greenwich Village ghosts such as the one who is said to haunt the Cherry Lane Theater. Actors, directors, and writers have all felt a strange presence at this old off-Broadway theater. Some have seen a blue-white glow at the top of the stairs leading up from the tiny lobby or at the end of the corridor that leads to the dress-

ing rooms. Village lore has it that this is the ghost of Aaron Burr, though some say it is the restless spirit of Tom Paine. Certainly both were personages that were connected to this particular Village area in a significant way. Not only has the ghost of the Cherry Lane played pranks upon the actors on stage there: it seems to take a hand in a production's fate. If the ghost does not care for a play, it closes in a big hurry. An in- *visible wall is thrown up between the au-*

Thomas Paine

dience and cast as if some force intended to interrupt the flow of the action. Perverse or absurdist dramas like Beckett's Endgame *or Joe Orton's* Entertaining Mr. Sloane *seem to get the go-ahead, as opposed to those that are regarded as too light or frothy, like* Blown Sideways Through Life.

We were once guests, with a few other people, in the attic rooms of a house at 7 Leroy Street. The actor Tom Ellis was living there in two separate areas that had been converted into one apartment. The rear room had two small windows that looked out on a small courtyard garden beyond which was a small house not visible from the street. Ellis often held afternoon tea parties in his charming apartment and regaled his guests with stories about Tallulah Bankhead, whom he had worked with on Broadway in a short-lived production called Eugenia *by Randolph Carter. He had also worked in summer stock shows with the hilarious Tallulah. On this particular afternoon in late spring, as we sipped darjeeling tea and ate Sutter's cookies (Sutter's was a bakery/coffee shop on Tenth Street and Greenwich Street which was famous as a place to rendezvous in the Village), a sudden loud crash*

Tremens and *Increased Occupancy* were done at Westbeth; *American Hamburger, Mr. Nobody, Tropical Fever in Key West,* and *Crisis of Identity* were produced at Theater for the New City. I also began writing books with John Gilman on American popular culture. The first of these was *Dime-Store Dream Parade,* published in

---

found a small glass chandelier on the floor with all of its cut-glass inserts and globes shattered. Without a word, Ellis fetched a small whiskbroom and a metal dust tray, swept up the broken glass and deposited it into a trash bin. He picked up the metal parts of the chandelier, then put them on a sidetable. "Oh, well," he sighed. Following this incident, which no one made too much of, two doors of an old hutch cabinet flew open; they swiftly slammed shut and then swung again, back and forth, several times. This was repeated over and over again.

"What is it? What is going on here?" someone asked, extremely perturbed.

"Oh, it's Elsbeth," Ellis calmly replied. "I'd better open the windows." On opening both of the back windows, he laughed aloud, declaring, "She probably felt trapped! She likes to fly in and out of the windows."

"Who is Elsbeth?" asked another tea party guest, visibly upset and ashen.

"Oh, she was the chambermaid of this house—over a hundred years ago," Ellis explained. "She was murdered, strangled and

drowned, in Minetta Creek by her mistress, who caught her in bed with the master of the house. Elsbeth is still hovering about, in a state of unrest, I guess." Ellis added that he talked to Elsbeth at times and did not feel there was anything unusual about conversing with a ghost. "Ghosts are all over the Village—so what else is new?" Ellis concluded, adding, "Would anyone like a scone with some apricot jam? More tea?" Just another mad tea party in Greenwich Village.

Cherry Lane Theater on Commerce Street

Jazz Age Gay Bars

Gay bars became a mainstay in the Village after the early days of Prohibition, which began in 1919. One of the first was Paul and Joe's Bar on Ninth Street and Sixth Avenue. During the First World War, it was crowded with soldiers, prostitutes, and the occasional homosexual, all in search of an evening's pleasure. By 1922 this bar was regarded as the main rendezvous in the Village for homosexuals and transvestites. Since the word "gay" was not in use, it was referred to in those days as a "pansy place," even by the Bohemian crowd, many of whom did not want their concept of "free love" to include "queer" behavior by the time the twenties rolled around. One Broadway columnist of the day described Paul and Joe's as "a hangout for the underworld, stage and movie celebrities, operatic divas, dainty elves and stern women."

Another 1920s gay club was the Jungle on Cornelia Street where special events and parties were quite the thing. A Polish-Jewish lesbian named Eva Kotchever who changed her name to Eve Adams (after the Biblical Adam and Eve) was known as "The Queen of the Third Sex," and she ran a gay tea room called the Black Rabbit, where theater people mingled with butch lesbians who dressed like working-class men and drank straight rum. Adam's Tea Room was another gay bar on MacDougal Street in the Prohibition era, and these so-called tea rooms (serving whiskey in tea cups to thwart the law) were the first enclaves for gay culture in a still solidly middle-class community. These earliest gay clubs, which were constantly under the scrutiny of of-

1979 by E. P. Dutton. We haunted flea markets in search of things from Lost America, mostly pop artifacts like Coca-Cola store signs, bottles of Hopalong Cassidy Hair Trainer, Mickey Mouse toothbrush holders, Charlie McCarthy radios and dolls, and Aunt Jemima salt and pepper shakers. Like Andy Warhol, and many others, who collected everything from fine Art Deco to cookie jars to discarded diamond engagement rings, we were seeking the "real" Pop art, which was the mass-produced stuff originally sold at dime-stores. These items took on an almost tribal significance in the late sixties and the decades that followed. The America we

ficials who deemed them to be "degenerate" hangouts, gave Greenwich Village the reputation across America as a "peculiar place." The Flower Pot on Christopher Street and the Red Mask on Charles Street were other tea rooms and one, the Pirate's Den on Christopher Street, evolved from a tea room into a popular nightclub.

Village "masquerade" balls were popular events where gay and straight Bohemians could easily mix in the teens and twenties. These occurred as often as twice a week. One perpetual party place was Webster Hall, a community center on East Eleventh Street and Third Avenue. Some of these festive occasions gave lesbians and gay men the opportunity to dress in their favorite "drag," be it historical or contemporary. Costume balls were popular specialty events on holidays and in particular on New Year's

Eve, Valentine's Day, and Halloween. They often utilized imaginative titles like "The Kit Kat Ball," "The Playboy's Carnival," or the straightforward "Village Artists Bohemian Costume Ball." On October 11, 1994, Webster Hall presented "The Dada Ball" (a re-creation of their 1917 "Blindman's Ball"), a benefit to support Housing Works and Visual AIDS.

"Sheet music": a 1923 song very popular with the Village jazz-age gay crowd

knew seemed to be vanishing and this memorabilia was an archaeological treasure-trove to be saved for God-knows-what or for whom. In any case, a new century was just over the horizon, and we thought that whatever we collected might be of significance to future generations. Many young people today now ask of sixties survivors, "What was it like in the sixties? Why is Stonewall such a big deal? What happened at Woodstock? Who was Joe Cino?" and sometimes, unbelievably, the question is asked, "Who were the Beatles?"

Fool Moon in the Village–People, Places, and Extraordinary Characters

*G*reenwich Village has existed since the 1900s as a unique area where the unusual and outrageous are seen as commonplace. The lore and legends of the old Village combine with the new in a tapestry of the sometimes strange and artistically extraordinary. Village Bohemians and characters as well as Village ghosts abound. The famous, infamous, dissolute, and bizarre inhabitants traverse the winding streets of their chosen place, which is often a long distance from their original hometowns, both in place and in spirit. Some of these "characters" seem to be drawn to the Village in search of the elusive, wandering from bar to bar, coffee shop to tea room, never actually finding what it is they thought they were looking for in the first place. Dark rathskellers, rundown candlelit dens, extravagant clubs, and all-night parties were an integral part of the excitement and experiment of the Village before the more conservative, money-minded 1980s and 1990s brought an influx of trendy restaurants and chic designer coffee-counters. But if you look hard enough, you will still be able to find traces of what is left of life in the underground of Little Bohemia, a name that is seldom used today to describe Greenwich Village. High real-estate prices and high rents seem to have buried the concept of Bohemianism.

Some of the places now remembered by only a few have become part of the mythology of "those fun-filled days of the Village." The Pirate's Den, converted from a stable, at 10 Sheridan Square was one of the most popular clubs of the Prohibition era. The interior of the Pirate's Den, with its dark wooden beams, stained glass, hanging ship lanterns, ships' cannons, racks with old guns, candlelight on the tables, and real shrieking parrots, made for a fantasy-environment. Doormen and waiters were dressed as pirates who could break into staged swordfights and pistol duels at a moment's notice. The Village "eerie pubs" of today, including Jekyll and Hyde, the

Walt Whitman

Henry James

Slaughtered Lamb, and Jack the Ripper, most resemble the Pirate's Den. The nightclub in the film *Greenwich Village* (1944), in which Carmen Miranda entertains, had an interior like a pirate ship. Other night spots in the 1920s included the Wigwam, a place where the staff, wearing scanty clothing, impersonated Sapokanican Indians, the original inhabitants of the Village.

The Village in the 1920s seemed unaffected by Prohibition, with many taverns, bars, tea rooms, and clubs continuing as speakeasies. The Greenwich Village Inn at 5 Sheridan Square was another watering hole that persisted during the days of bathtub gin and wild flappers who danced the Black Bottom and the Charleston into the night. Expanding into a basement at 6 Sheridan Square, the club prospered, offering entertainment and liquor without too many brushes with the law. "Protection" was widespread by the early 1920s, with money flowing into the hands of politicians and the police, all of whom frequented many of the thirty thousand speakeasies that operated in New York City.

The original Nut Club opened in 1919 at 99 Seventh Avenue South in the building that in the late 1950s was the Sheridan Square Playhouse. There, the revival of *Leave It to Jane* was a big hit, with Kathleen Murray as Jane, Dorothy Greener, George Segal, and Lainie Kazan. The Circle Repertory staged new plays for many years in the original digs of the old Nut Club. Another famous barroom was the Golden Swan, an Irish bar that was in business prior to World War I. Located at Sixth Avenue and Fourth Street, it was torn down in 1928 to make way for the building of the Sixth Avenue subway. A rundown place with sawdust on the floor, the Swan attracted derelicts and vagrants, most of them of Irish descent. Regulars referred to this gloomy dive as "The Hell Hole" and the name stuck throughout its existence. A twenty-seven-year-old bum named Eugene O'Neill, who declared himself a regular and "resident" of the bar in 1915, used this place and some of his other haunts as the inspiration for the searing barroom drama *The Iceman Cometh*. When this four-hour-plus play was successfully revived by director Jose Quintero in the 1950s at the Circle-in-the-Square, which was on Sheridan Square on Fourth Street (where Sloan's supermarket is now), the theater was right next to Louie's Tavern, a place similar to the Hell Hole, where O'Neill liked to get drunk. In the 1950s actor

James Dean drank at Louie's Tavern and Julius on Tenth Street.

In O'Neill's time, intellectuals would reminisce about the "old" Village, which featured such luminaries as James Fenimore Cooper, who in 1832 resided on Bleecker Street just west of Broadway, or William Dunlap, a post-Revolutionary painter and writer with the distinction of being called the "first American playwright" who also adapted many German and French plays for American audiences. In 1835, at his residence at

Eugene O'Neill—in the early Provincetown Theater days

15 Greenwich Avenue, he articulated his philosophy in a book entitled *American Life History of the Rise of the Arts in the United States*. Washington Irving, before moving to Tarrytown, stayed for a time with his sister at 15 Commerce Street, and it was here that in 1816 he wrote "The Legend of Sleepy Hollow." The dark, brooding Edgar Allan Poe lived with his child-wife Virginia on Carmine Street in 1837. After moving to Sixth Avenue near Waverly Place, he penned *The Fall of the House of Usher*. Because of financial woes, Poe later moved into a boarding house on Waverly Place, eventually going to Philadelphia to try his luck. In 1844, he returned to the Village, living at 15 Amity Street (now West Third Street), where he finished *The Raven*, the work that earned him world acclaim.

By the 1830s, a book called *Scènes de la Vie de Bohème*, a dramatic account of an erudite group of Paris Bohemians, had an influence in the Village, and this book also provided the basis for the opera by Puccini, *La Bohème*. The term *Bohemia* originated in Paris to describe "the artistic life" and found its way into the lexicon of nineteenth-century Village thinkers who were quick to adopt Parisian attitudes. The connection between the Village and Paris's Left Bank became one of long standing. Nineteenth-century iconoclasts who rebelled against the prudery of the Victorian age included Henry Clapp, who in 1858 founded a radical and opinionated weekly journal that for nine years extolled the "free spirit" of Bohemian life. Clapp's journal, the *Saturday Press*, challenged outdated attitudes about sexuality. It also championed Walt Whitman's *Leaves of Grass* with its exalted and romantic visions of homosexual love, published in 1850 amid cries of public outrage. The *Press*'s reviewer was Thomas Bailey Aldrich, who also helped to introduce Mark Twain to the East by covering Twain's "The Jumping Frog." Aldrich would later become editor of the *Atlantic Monthly*.

In the last decades of the nineteenth century, Greenwich Village was the place to be if you were an aspiring artist or writer. Henry James, who often traveled abroad, always considered Washington Square his home base, and it was in 1881 that *Washington Square* was cited by critics to be the first novel of importance to be written about New York City. Contrary to popular belief, James did not actually live on Washington Square. Born in 1843 just east of the square on Washington Place, James also lived for a time at 58 West Fourteenth Street.

Stephen Crane wrote *The Red Badge of Courage* at 61 Washington Square South, a book that brought him instant fame. O'Henry lived at 49 East Ninth Street, on Waverly Place, and on Washington Square South at various times after 1902. Mark Twain was another who moved into a number of dwellings in the Village, including 3 Fifth Avenue, 21 Fifth Avenue, and 14 West Tenth Street. Edith Wharton, who followed the literary style established by Henry James, wrote *The House of Mirth* in 1905 while living on Washington Square, before she left for France in 1907. Theodore Dreiser was known as a Village Bohemian who practiced "free love" as well as portraying loose sexual alliances in novels such as *Sister Carrie* and his semi-autobiographical *The Genius*. He lived at 16 St. Luke's Place. By 1910 *The Masses*, a journal edited by Max Eastman, had become the central nerve of the Bohemian cult. The staff of *The Masses* lived at the Liberal Club at 133 MacDougal Street, and it was here that new dramatists such as Sherwood Anderson first read their plays. Anderson, Eugene O'Neill, D. H. Lawrence, Theodore Dreiser, Carl Sandburg, Walter Lippman, and Robert Frost all contributed to another influential publication geared to a new society called *Seven Arts*, which was founded in 1916 by James Oppenheim and Waldo Frank. These writers also frequented the most famous of all the literary salons hosted by heiress Mabel Dodge at 23 Fifth Avenue. A friend and patron of struggling artists, Ms. Dodge held court on Wednesday evenings with a Bohemian crowd who gladly socialized with her wealthy, curiosity-seeking uptown friends, some of whom were in search of an artist or artiste-manqué they could adopt. The uptown-lowdown rich-and-poor chase was often the subject of plays and of silent movies of the day.

Maxwell Bodenheim

Mabel Dodge started her salon when she moved to the Village in 1912. One of her amours was John Reed, who had coproduced a play by his friend Eugene O'Neill in the

Village on MacDougal Street. Reed was to play a part in the Russian Revolution; his book *10 Days that Shook the World*, chronicling his experiences in Russia, was written in two months and published by Horace Liveright in March 1919 to great acclaim. Reed returned to Russia, where he died of typhus on October 17, 1920. He was the only American to be buried in the Kremlin wall. Soon after his death, his legend flourished in the United States and in the Soviet Union. Reed's experiences were the subject of Warren Beatty's epic film, *Reds*.

Another wealthy arts patron was Gertrude Vanderbilt Whitney, who opened a studio on MacDougal Alley to show the works of new American artists. In 1931, Whitney's "ashcan school" gained acceptance with the opening of the Whitney Museum of American Art at 8 West Eighth Street (now located uptown on Madison Avenue and Seventy-fifth Street).

Villagers who were on summer vacation on Cape Cod in 1916 returned in the fall to form the Provincetown Players at 139 MacDougal Street (between West Fourth and West Third Streets). Eugene O'Neill's *Bound East for Cardiff* was its first hit; and O'Neill became the Provincetown's resident playwright, also writing *The Long Voyage Home* and *Diff'rent*. Some of his earlier plays attracted a following among adventurous theatergoers. The early players involved with "experimental" drama at the Provincetown included Miriam Hopkins, Bette Davis, and writer Edna St. Vincent Millay. In 1924, Millay and a handful of others opened the Cherry Lane Theater on Commerce Street to stage dramas less realistic, psychological, and commercial, and more mystical and poetic. One of the actors at the Cherry Lane was the young John Barrymore. Another theater group of note at this time was Eva La Gallienne's Civic Repertory, which operated on Fourteenth Street.

In 1921, after two successful seasons on Sheridan Square, the *Greenwich Village Follies* moved to the Shubert Theater uptown, bringing worldwide fame to what was once a tiny Village musical review. "Come to Bohemia" was one of the production's popular songs.

Most people who came to hang out in the Village in the 1920s and 1930s wanted to have a good time, particularly on weekends. The sideshows they sought were found in what old-time Bohemians regarded as vulgar tourist traps. Yet many nighttime regulars were amused by

John Wallowitch—cabaret singer, composer, and pianist

Barbra Streisand in her "Bon Soir" days in the Village

the ongoing stampede of the bourgeoisie, who needed to escape the trap of their own daily existence. Bruno's Garret at 58 Washington Square South was a popular spot for tourists, who had to pay a small fee to get in to see and to commingle with the Village characters. Romany Marie catered to the likes of Duchamp and O'Neill at 133 Washington Place, later moving her tea room to Grove Street. Romany Marie (a.k.a. Marie Marchand), a native of Moldavia, wore gypsy skirts and blouses to please the tourist trade. She also read tea leaves and palms as well. The Mad Hatter, one of the first of the Village tea rooms, was on the site of the Washington Square Coffee Shop at 150 West Fourth Street. Its wooden facade, visible from Sixth Avenue, is still intact. Village hangouts and rendezvous clubs included the Black Parrot on Sheridan Square, Swart's TNT, the Golden Swan, the Pirate's Den, the Pepper Pot, the Purple Pup, the Little Sea Maid, Polly Holliday's, and Puss-in-Boots. The Crumperie at 6-1/2 Sheridan Square, a tea room run by Mary Alletta Crump and her aged mother, catered to an artistic and theatrical clientele. These Bohemian restaurants and tea rooms were painted in brilliant shades of vermilion, violet, sunburst-yellow, acid-green, electric-blue, magenta, and other "violent" colors, sometimes in zigzag combinations with stripes and lightning bolts as design elements. (Bright "psychedelic" colors became popular again in the 1960s in Village hippie hangouts.) Poets read their "purple poetry" by candlelight in the smoke-filled interiors, and bad art depicting the winding streets of the historic Village was barely visible under the dim lights.

The Candy Man was a character named Tiny Tim (not to be confused with the later songster, Tiny Tim), who worked as a hawker at many Bohemian dens in Greenwich Village, including the Pepper Pot, selling "soul candies" with snippets of his own psychological verse written on the wrappings. Sonia, the Cigarette Girl, called herself a Slavic soothsayer. Born Ella Breistein, she became Eleanor Brandt when she moved to the Village and opened her smoke shop on West Fourth Street. Here, as "Sonia, the Cigarette Girl," she sold hand-rolled cigarettes made with the most potent tobacco she could find, as well as her own special love potions, Village knickknacks, art prints, and "soul" books. In 1921, Sonia the Cigarette Girl wrote a letter to a friend describing her new pseudo-self-invented Village personality as empty and meaningless. Villagers, however, loved Sonia and her "strange outfits."

The stock market crash in October 1929 brought the Great Depression to the Village, affecting its residents just as it did the rest of America. The song "Brother, Can You

Tiny Tim began his career at Page 3

Spare a Dime," the bitter anthem of the Depression, originated in the Greenwich Village revue *Americana* as a response to FDR's campaign theme song, "Happy Days Are Here Again." Writers and artists, many starving even prior to the Depression, found it difficult to make even a thin dime with poetry, short stories, novels, plays, or drawings and paintings; "art" was considered a luxury in the hard times following the Wall Street collapse. When Roosevelt was inaugurated in 1933, new hope for some Village writers and artists came when federal monies were poured into WPA theater and arts projects. The first open-air art market was established in and around Washington Square in 1932 to raise money for "down-on-their-luck" artists, and continues to the present as an annual event.

Many of the clubs, tea rooms, and bars continued through the 1930s, through the war years of the 1940s and even into the 1950s. During the 1940s, many young aspiring Village artists, writers, and actors found themselves getting haircuts and uniforms from Uncle Sam to win the battles against Germany and Japan. Village actresses doubled their theater or waitress jobs by working for free "uptown at the Stage Door Canteen." The all-star movie *Stage Door Canteen* (1943) depicts a group of girls living in a Village rooming house who dance with servicemen right alongside Tallulah Bankhead, Helen Hayes, Katherine Cornell, and Lynn Fontanne.

Following World War II, New York University began to "revitalize" Washington Square, and from 1950 through the 1970s many high-rise luxury apartment buildings were constructed. This was done at the expense of many historic buildings, and the demolition action accelerated the formation of the Greenwich Village Historic District by the City of New York Landmarks Preservation Commission in 1969. The Association of Village Home Owners, Manhattan Community Board #2, and other organizations encouraged this protection for the area that had over one thousand buildings built before the Civil War. The commission stated in its "purpose of designation": "From the totality of Greenwich Village emanates an appearance and even more a spirit and character of old New York which no single block thereof and no individual Landmark could possibly provide. It is this collective emanation which distinguishes an Historic District, and particularly Greenwich Village, from a Landmark and gives it a unique aesthetic and historical value." Two thousand and thirty-five buildings stand in the District, which includes almost all of the West Village from Fifth Avenue to Hudson Street. Unfortunately, the designation did not include the blocks west of Hudson (Greenwich Street, Washington Street, Weehawken Street). Before historic designation, New York University constructed the starkly modern Washington Square Village apartments over the foundations of several historic blocks of small, mid-nineteenth-century homes south of Washington Square. Following his term in office, ex-Mayor Edward I. Koch moved into another eyesore luxury high-rise building at 2 Fifth Avenue. This monstrous, twenty-story building constructed in 1952 blocked the row of small row houses that were once stables on MacDougal Alley from their previously direct line to Greenwich Mews on the east side of Fifth Avenue. Jefferson Market Courthouse was ready to be blasted until a group of concerned Village citizens saved it for use as a branch of the New York Public Library in 1961.

In 1959, Presidential candidate John F. Kennedy made a campaign speech in front of the Cafe Reggio on MacDougal Street, the same area where Kerouac, Ginsberg, Orlovsky, Burroughs, Ferlinghetti, Corso, and others were proclaiming their Beat philosophy and railing against American politics and the American way of life. The Fat Black Pussy Cat Theater and restaurant attracted these poets and others, including folksingers, into its realm. Two bona-fide characters from a previous era who still wandered Village streets and who continued to fr quent bars and coffeehouses in the MacDougal Street area into the 1950s were Joe Gould and Maxwell Bodenheim. Gould, a 1911 graduate of Harvard, hung out mostly at places like the Kettle of Fish and the Minetta Tavern (still at 113 MacDougal

Street), where he cadged drinks and dinner from tourists, by entertaining them with stories of the old Village. "Professor Seagull," as he was called, was writing *The Oral History of the World*, which was supposedly a manuscript of several thousand pages. Some of these pages were given to gullible landlords or rooming-house matrons in lieu of rent owed, and these were primarily verbatim conversations Gould listened to in bars or on the streets of the Village. When he died in August 1957, no manuscript was found, and some wondered if the *Oral History* was a hoax. However, years later, many manuscript pages of the work were discovered in a file drawer by Israel Young, owner of the Folklore Center. The consensus of those who have read it is that this was not the "masterpiece" Gould had always claimed it to be. When the short, bearded Gould charmed a potential big spender, bartender, or restaurateur out of a couple of drinks and/or dinner, he convinced them that fame and riches were waiting for him just around the corner. Portraits of Joe Gould still hang on the walls of the Minetta Tavern and the Kettle of Fish.

Poet, novelist, lecturer, and liberal Maxwell Bodenheim came to the Village in 1923 but by the 1950s had become a combination Village character and derelict. The dissolute, idiosyncratic Bodenheim was a gaunt ghost of his former self, a Southern gentleman who spoke in a charming "Old South" manner. He ended up selling his hand-written poetry for a drink at his second "home," the legendary San Remo bar and restaurant run by the Santini family on MacDougal and Bleecker, just across from the Caffe Borgia. His picture hung at the Remo in the 1950s and he was regarded there as a relic of days gone by. Back in the mid-1920s, Bodenheim had written a book called *Replenishing Jessica*, an account of a nymphomaniacal girl who could not control her sexual urges. Originally banned in some cities, its first-year sales totaled thirty thousand, a good amount in the publishing marketplace of the time. Bodenheim's success and his darkly handsome looks attracted a number of women, each of whom fell madly in love with him. Bodenheim was twenty-eight when he met an eighteen-year-old named Gladys Loeb who had literary aspirations Bodenheim quickly squelched. Gladys tried to commit suicide, turning on the gas in the kitchen of her fifth-floor walk-up, but was rescued at the last moment by her landlady. After that incident, her father brought her back to the Bronx and forbade her from seeing Bodenheim or ever going to the Village again. Virginia Drew, another Bodenheim lover, did not get off so easily. She was found dead in the Hudson River, strangled, and though the police questioned Bodenheim, who was the last person seen with her, her murderer was never found. The blind street wanderer known as Moondog, a poet musician who carried a staff and wore Biblical robes, recited a verse supposedly about this affair:

> *Had his will*
> *Had his fill*
> *And strangled her.*

(Though this was not intended as a direct reference to Bodenheim, many felt it was.) Moondog was everywhere to be seen in New York in the 1940s, 1950s, and 1960s but now seems to have disappeared off the face of the earth. Another girlfriend to whom Bodenheim wrote passionate love letters was one of sixteen people killed in a freak subway accident in 1928. Bodenheim continued to write books with titles like *A Virtuous Girl*, *Georgie May*, *Sixty Seconds*, *Duke Herring*, and *Ninth Avenue* but after the Crash of '29 he descended into a life of drink and despair. His reputation was somewhat salvaged when he wrote his Village memoirs in *My Life and Loves in Greenwich Village*. This personal chronicle of Little Bohemia is thought to have influenced Armistead Maupin's *Tales of the City*. Bodenheim and his common-law wife, Ruth Fagan, were brutally stabbed to death by a psychotic seaman in a cheap Bowery flophouse on February 6, 1954.

Once an embarrassment to the Beat poets who found his poetry sentimental and stifling, Bodenheim was posthumously honored by them as a symbol of the Village and the free life. Bodenheim himself had become cynical about the Village in his latter days, referring to it as a Coney Island of the mind and a tourist zoo. Beats Neal Cassady and Jack Kerouac, though more literate than Bodenheim, emulated his path to self-destruction. Both were dead from the ravages of drug and alcohol abuse by the end of the sixties.

Other characters who were known as San Remo-ites included Winnie, a large black woman who spoke fluid French and, after a few drinks, cursed at passersby and tourists in a loud, raucous manner. Once a group of tourists on a bus tour of the Village stared in shock and disbelief when Winnie, standing in front of the San Remo, took off all her clothes and shouted, "Anybody want to fuck a star?" The police were called in, and they took Winnie to Bellevue for observation. The next day she was out and carrying on her wild routines. Another heavy drinker and regular at the Remo was poet Bob Mitchell, who, after a few bourbons, would begin spouting Gaelic poetry in a loud voice. He was thrown out of the bar on several occasions when he was seen pushing jukebox buttons with his penis—to the dismay of some customers and the delight of others. Actress Shirley Stoler, the red-haired star of *Honeymoon Killers* and *Seven Beauties*, beams with delight when she reminisces about the days and nights she spent at the Remo "intoxicated on life."

"The San Remo is considered the last of the great Bohemian bars," says Jerry Striker, a writer who frequented the place in the 1950s and remembers a crowd of boisterous heavy drinkers. Weegee, the famed photographer, made the Remo his home base along with Maxwell Bodenheim, but Weegee also went often to Louie's Tavern and the Kettle of Fish. The poet Jake Spencer, after a few pints of beer and a couple of boilermakers at the Remo or the White Horse,

would stand on the bar and recite his verse. Striker recalls
that at the White Horse Tavern
you could buy two steins of
beer served in a white crockery
mug for a quarter, and at other
places a draft beer was ten or
fifteen cents. The San Remo,
which was at 93 MacDougal
Street, printed NO RADIO—
NO TELEVISION on its à la
carte menu, which offered
cheap Italian dinners served at
lightning-fast speed in the separate dining room.

*Candy Darling—transvestite Village
performer and Warhol superstar*

"The bartenders at the
Remo were tough SOB's,
though," Striker says. "Occasionally they would beat up drunk customers—just for the hell of it. The food at the Remo—Italian pastas
and salads—was dirt cheap. Carmine De Sapio went there. He liked
Village artists and poor tenants. He helped them in their fights with
landlords . . . and then along came Koch. We thought he was a liberal. After him—and Ronald Reagan too—it all changed. It's all
memory, like Proust . . . remembrances of things past. We had fun
there, at the Remo." At the San Remo, customers would occasionally
smash their glasses on the floor in a fit of rage but no one, including
the bartenders, paid any mind. Another who frequented the Remo in
its heyday, though he lived in the East Village, was poet W. H. Auden.
The Beat poet Jack Micheline, who read poetry with Ginsberg, Kerouac, and Orlovsky, wrote the following poem:

Greenwich Village 1955

Walking down MacDougal Street
Past San Remo
Past Kettle of Fish
Shirley Stoler and Weegee
walking hand in hand

A nightspot that was popular during the 1950s was the Village
Barn, which had flourished for many years before. The space for
the bar had been excavated one hundred feet below street level to
create the Barn, which had a hayseed ambience that gave city slick-
ers and the tourists who frequented it the feeling of actually being
in the country. Haystacks, along with fake cows and chickens,

added to this barnyard atmosphere, as did the hillbilly singers and waiters.

The cabaret scene that is still a happening thing in the Village was as its zenith in the 1950s and 1960s. Jan Wallman's Upstairs at the Duplex, when it was still on Grove Street (now on Christopher Street across from Christopher Park), first introduced comics Woody Allen, Joan Rivers, JoAnn Worley, and Rodney Dangerfield to the public as well as first-rate cabaret singers like Joanne Beretta and Lovelady Powell, each of whom developed a following there in the late fifties and early sixties. Lovelady Powell brought Hal Holbrook as Mark Twain to the Duplex, after which he went on to become a Broadway, movie, and TV star. Composer-pianist John Wallowitch appeared often at the Duplex; he also played piano at the Showplace on West Fourth Street, where Barbra Streisand sang and the waitress was then Cass Elliot. Wallowitch was known in the Village for the legendary salon he hosted in his seven-room apartment at 8 Barrow Street, where singers like Pat Brooks, Rosemary O'Reilly, Alice Ghostly (the latter two were introduced in Leonard Sillman's *New Faces of 1952* along with Eartha Kitt), and Lee Wiley performed, with John at the piano, for invited guests who were served special double martinis by John's roommate, playwright Neil Karrer. Christopher Plummer, Marion Winters, Edgar De'Evia, Ted Mann, Jose Quintero, and Andy Warhol were regulars at these drop-in affairs. Wallowitch kept everyone amused with his piano-playing, songs, gossip, and bawdy jokes, and is still doing it on cable TV and in cabarets.

Another popular cabaret was the Bon Soir, at 40 West Eighth Street, which has become a legend because of the people who first played there. In the 1950s, Felicia Saunders, whose hit recordings were "The Song from Moulin Rouge" and "Fly Me to the Moon," developed an almost cult following among sophisticated and smart gay men, who stood at the bar in suits and ties or sat at tiny tables in the small, intimate basement room. They could make or break a new performer by responding with wild, vociferous enthusiasm or a deadly silence. But the brilliant Saunders could do no wrong and her nightclub act is still regarded as the pinnacle of cabaret performance art by those who saw her. Another was Portia Nelson, whom the crowd treated with great respect, not just for her fine lyric soprano voice but for her warmth and the depth of meaning she gave a lyric.

Village artist Don Madia, who was a busboy at the Bon Soir, recalls an audition by a newcomer named Barbra Streisand at the club. "This was a strange-looking woman, believe me. Not pretty at all. But what a talent. When she was hired she was paid seventy-five dollars a week for one show a night and two on weekends. On opening night here was this kind of Beatnik from Brooklyn wearing this bizarre beehive hairdo, a sheath dress, a silver lamé vest over it, and pointy George Washington–style shoes with buckles. A mess! But when she opened her mouth—that talent—God knows where it came from. The first songs she sang were 'Sleeping Bee' from the Truman Capote Broadway show *House of Flowers*, 'Lover Come Back to Me,' and a knockout, slow-build version of the Depression song 'Happy Days Are Here Again.' Barbra played over eleven weeks and was an instant hit at the Bon Soir, which was considered a tough room. But she was tough too. She was really a Beatnik, though—and still is—she does not want to live by any-one else's rules. Everyone came down to hear this new 'superstar'—be-fore the word was invented. One night Judith Anderson and Lillian Gish arrived from uptown to see Barbra. Henry Fonda came several times. From there she went on to appear in *I Can Get It for You Whole-sale* on Broadway, then a contract with Columbia Records—you know the rest. I remember hearing 'The Coloring Book' song at Lenny's Hideaway on the jukebox by Kitty Kallen. Soon Barbra's version was just pushed on everywhere—and no more Kitty. She had come a long way from the Lion [a gay bar at 62 West Ninth Street], where she first sang for her supper. She lived then in the Village right across from the Lion at 69 West Ninth Street. I really liked her. She was . . . is . . . a real person. Direct. No nonsense. And she really knew what she wanted. It was no big thing. She just sang but—wow!"

Joan Rivers followed the same path, according to her biography *En-ter Laughing*, first playing at the Lion and then doing a stint on the same bill with Barbra Streisand, who, like Joan, also appeared at the Duplex. Don Madia also remembers that Elaine May and Mike Nichols were turned down after they auditioned at the Bon Soir. Some others who began there include Phyllis Diller, Woody Allen, Morgana King, Kaye Ballard (the cousin of Paul Bellardo, who owns a well-known Christopher Street boutique), Jeri Sothern, who was making a comeback but was visibly drunk most nights according to Madia, Rose "Chee-Chee" Murphy, Sylvia Symms, and a lip-synching drag act called Tony and Eddy. Mabel Mercer, known as the queen of cabaret, who had played at Bricktop's in Paris and whom Frank Sinatra said he learned phrasing from, sang often at the Bon Soir.

Cafe Society during the late 1930s and 1940s (it closed in 1950) was a racially integrated nightclub frequented by radicals, intellectu-als, and gays. Billie Holiday sang "Strange Fruit" here and Lena Horne also performed at the Society. In the audience at Cafe Society you might find Eleanor Roosevelt rubbing elbows with Paul Robeson and Canada Lee. Other regulars included Lillian Hellman, Budd Schulberg, and S. J. Perelman. Cafe Society could only have emerged out of Roosevelt's New Deal; it became known as a place where leftists and blacks could meet and discuss their general disillu-sionment with American political life. Integrated bands played here, and the Boogie-Woogie first caught on at Cafe Society. A

backer of the club, Benny Goodman led the first nationally inte-grated band.

The Village Vanguard first opened in a Village basement in 1935 on Charles Street under the aegis of Max Gordon. One year later, it moved to the basement on Seventh Avenue where it is still found. Judy Holliday and Betty Comden and Adolph Green performed here from 1939 to 1941, and the Vanguard was also home to early black folksingers like Leadbelly (Huddie Ledbetter) and Josh White, who appeared there in the 1940s. The Weavers also performed at the Van-guard before it became primarily a jazz club.

Eighth Street in the 1950s and 1960s was also the scene of most of the gay bars in the Village, including Mary's, the old Colony, Main Street, and Mona's Royal Roost at 28 Cornelia Street. Two others, Carr's, which catered to older gentlemen, and Lenny's Hideaway, a more Bohemian-theatrical hangout, were on Tenth Street. Dirty Dick's on Christopher Street and West Street, which became Bad-lands (in recent years replaced by a XXX video shop), was another oldtime gay watering hole. Joel Heller's Club on Eighth Street in the mid-1960s was the first to feature go-go boys right in the window dancing in cages. Drag bars were the 82 Club next to La Mama's at 82 East Fourth Street and the notorious El Chico, which became the Moroccan Village. These bars were primarily frequented by tourist couples who wanted to see a drag show in the Village. Two other pop-ular drag bars were called the Tenth of Always on Third Street and the Crazy Horse Café, at 149 Bleecker Street. A well-known lesbian nightclub called Page 3 on Seventh Avenue South between Tenth Street and Charles Street (where Woody's is now located) introduced Tiny Tim (before "Tiptoe Through the Tulips" and Miss Vicki), whose falsetto versions of obscure 1920s and 1930s songs were a de-light to audiences. Page 3 attracted tourists as well as lesbians and gay men, all of whom were charmed by the host/hostess with the mostest—Jackie "Mr. Rhythm" Howe, who wore her 1950s "D.A." (short for duck's ass) platinum-blond hair slicked down with Vitalis. Tom O'Horgan, the director of *Hair*, *Jesus Christ Superstar*, and *Lenny*, recalls a really weird club at 21 East Eighth Street, at the corner of University, called Frankie's Tropical Bar. It was here that O'Horgan directed his drag version of *Little Me* calling it *Big Me*. Tom O'Horgan also reminisced about gallivanting around the Village in a gorilla suit just for the fun of it.

Frank Thompson Galleries on Cornelia Street was one of the latter-day bastions for Bohemia. A painter in the pre-Raphaelite style, Thompson with his Liberace–Shirley Temple goody-two-shoes manner and thick golden hair, held court in his crowded little gallery, regaling customers with stories about wild sexual days and nights in old Greenwich Village. Thompson died in 1994, and many of his friends, including Lady Hope Stansbury, another Cornelia Street resident, wept at the passing of this insipid jolly elfin man who was regarded along with Quentin Crisp as one of the pioneers of liberal gay politics.

Jeremiah Newton, the writer, film critic, and NYU teacher/scholar, remembers that in 1966 the police tried to close off large sections of the Village because parents' groups were complaining about their runaway children disappearing into Village communes and being turned on to LSD and other drugs in Washington Square. This curtailment exercise lasted exactly three days. Newton met Jimi Hendrix at the Cock and Bull (now the Olive Tree) on MacDougal Street through a "speed freak" girlfriend named Jonah. Hendrix was working as a security guard and bouncer at Salvation II (now home of the Ridiculous Theater). The three of them were sitting at a table at the Cock and Bull when a U.S. Marine approached and asked them how to get around the Village. The Marine, joining them at the table, said, "I can't stand to be around Village queers," whereupon Hendrix grabbed Newton (whom he had just met) around the waist and, holding his hand, said to the Marine, "Well, man, we're lovers," prompting the young Marine to bolt for the door. Newton subsequently would run into Hendrix at the Cafe Feenjon, which was also on MacDougal. Hendrix, who wore lavender silk shirts and crushed velvet culottes with matching boots, also hung out at the Electric Circus on St. Marks Place. When he achieved fame as a rock star, Hendrix built his Electric Lady Sound Studio on Eighth Street next to the Eighth Street Theater (a now-defunct movie house) in the same basement that had once housed the old Village Barn.

Another place on MacDougal Newton recalls was the Lost Coin, operated by a Sister Faye who was a religious fanatic. She served cookies and coffee free of charge to the young acid-freak runaways hanging out on MacDougal Street in the sixties. Newton and Candy Darling, the drag Warhol superstar, were permanently banned from the shop when Candy blurted out a joke to one of the religious helpers: "Jesus was on the cross and sees the Virgin Mary walking by and says, 'Hi, Mary,' and Mary, looking up, says, 'Hi, Grace!' " Other nightclub/bar/restaurants of days gone by in the Village were Nick's on Seventh Avenue South and Tenth Street, which was decorated with elk and moose heads, dark wood ceiling beams and stained glass, a leftover of the days when it was a rathskeller (it later became Your Father's Moustache, a Dixieland club), and Jack Delaney's on Grove Street at Sheridan Square. Delaney's animated neon sign had jockies on horseback jumping over fences, and the sign as well as the restaurant were regarded as Sheridan Square landmarks for many years. Trudy Heller's famous club on the corner of Sixth Avenue and Ninth Street (now a pizza joint) booked early engagements for the Manhattan Transfer and comebacks for the likes of Big Mama Thornton.

Memories of people and places still pour forth from those who remember the way the Village was. There was Stanziani's famous restaurant on the corner of Fourth Street and Tenth Street, where owner Joe Stanziani served the best pizza and Italian food in the Village, according to the many who went there. Photographs of Joe, who was a hero in the Italian Army during World War I, were all over the walls. When he died, his wife, Rita, who was the chief cook and waitress, closed the place. Later she took her maiden name, Rita Brue, and returned to her sculpting, exhibiting her work at places like the Salmagundi Club. When new owners wanted to rent the space occupied by Stanziani's, Rita Brue demanded that they call it Formerly Joe's, which they did. A favorite Village watering hole and restaurant, Formerly Joe's is now also closed. Aldo's at 340 Bleecker Street was another good Italian restaurant and bar. Older Villagers also like to reminisce about Sutter's Bakery on West Tenth Street and Greenwich Avenue, a pastry shop deluxe that made the best croissants and peach-star pastries anywhere. This bakery was a favorite place to shop and eat for celebrities such as Bette Midler and Joan Sutherland, who were often seen there (not together), eating Sutter's cookies, which were delicious—and addictive.

Village characters of the 1960s, 1970s, and 1980s included Baldwin Stegman, the tarot card reader and disciple of Ouspensky and Gurdjieff, who held court at Riker's on Sheridan Square. This Riker's delivered your eggs on a plate on a conveyor belt, which in turn took the dishes away, as did the Riker's on Eighth Street. Other popular chain eateries frequented by Village Bohemia included the Waldorf Cafeteria, Nedick's, Howard Johnson's, and Chock Full O' Nuts, all located on Sixth Avenue between Washington Place and Eighth Street. Bickford's on Fourteenth Street and Seventh Avenue was a white-tiled favorite for a cheap meal. Ian Orlando MacBeth,

the Renaissance street costume artist and painter; Marguerite Young, the author
who dressed in the manner of
a Bohemian gypsy and took
over twenty years to write her
masterpiece, *Miss MacIntosh
My Darling*, sometimes taking one month to write just
one sentence; Rollerina, the
drag queen, who roller-skated
down Christopher Street in a
blue ballroom gown; Ruth
Truth, a bearded drag who
sometimes dressed as the

*Bette Midler—lived on Barrow
Street in her Village days*

Statue of Liberty; and John Eric Broaddus, a costume artist who
went everywhere in elaborate hats and artfully designed outfits, his
nostrils and inner ears made up with lipstick and paint, were among
the more colorful characters often seen walking around Village streets
and sitting on stools and in booths for hours at a time in chain restaurants and coffee shops.

Intoxicated but idiosyncratic street derelicts on Sheridan Square
who were also regulars on Christopher Street included leather-clad and
chain-bound Stagger Lee, toeless Boston John, Blond-ragamuffin
John John, and Bambi, who ordered Riker's hamburgers by shouting
into a Christopher Street parking meter outside in a loud Bette Davis
voice. A favorite character was "Mother" Douglas, who owned a small
bakeshop on West Fourth Street (now Chez Claude, the French bak-

ery), where for hours on end
she would entertain cus-
tomers with her stories of the
old Village. Her bright yellow hair and red-rouge
cheeks gave her the appearance of a comic-strip character, and her delicious
Southern-style baked goods
had customers lining up
around the block. There was
Ivor and his Magic Black
Cape, a ne'er-do-well
philosopher who was said to
have flown out of a sixth-
floor apartment window on
Grove Street, landing on the

*Ian Orlando MacBeth, street
costume artist*

sidewalk below without a scratch, and Maurice the Newspaper Man, who looked like the reincarnation of Walt Whitman and who regularly hung out at the Lion's Head. Maurice collected newspapers and magazines from the 1920s onward, storing them in lockers he kept all over the city. He would sell some of these as souvenirs to tourists on the streets or in Village bars. Black Marsha was another favorite Village character always to be found on Christopher Street, usually in haphazard partial drag, reminiscing about hitting a policeman over the head with a bottle at the Battle of Stonewall (1969). Marsha was an internationally acclaimed entertainer with Hot Peaches Review, an Andy Warhol model, Anvil bar icon, and a legendary lady of the evening. Marsha P. Johnson (a.k.a. Malcolm Michaels) was fished out of the Hudson River at Christopher Street on July 6, 1992, her unflagging good cheer and dazzling smile extinguished forever. Black Marsha is now referred to as "The Saint of Christopher Street" or "The Saint of the Stonewall."

Jackie, a witchlike street person who wore her hair piled up in a rat's nest, covering it with a kerchief and a plastic Baggie, begged for "money for food" all over the Village. According to Jeremiah Newton, a drunk knocked her down outside a Village bar, breaking her neck and killing her. It was later discovered that she owned several properties, including the Old Mills Hotel on Bleecker Street, and had a large bank account.

Another "Jackie" was Jackie Curtis, the Warhol superstar who one day thought he was Barbara Stanwyck and the next James Dean. Jackie was always out on the streets and in the bars of the East and West Village until he overdosed on drugs one night. At his East Side funeral, he was laid out in an open casket, covered with glitter, and friends tucked three "joints" (marijuana cigarettes) into the casket, thinking that Jackie would need to get high in the next life. A writer and stage and film actor, Jackie had many plays on the boards in the Village, and he was a grandson of Slugger Ann's, who operated a bar that for many years was a popular spot at 192 Second Avenue (at Twelfth Street) in the East Village. Today it is called Dick's Bar. One of the more infamous characters

John Eric Broaddus, costume and book artist

in the Village is H. M. Koutoukas, sometimes called just Harry. Koutoukas, who is renowned for his Gothic chamber plays and camp-operas, created the term *Cobra Jewels* (actually borrowed from Maria Montez, who spoke the line "Giff me doze Cobrah chewels!" in the film *Cobra Woman*), and he wears a great many of them, some designer pieces, on his capes or flowing gold lamé or crepe outfits. His search for the one Cobra Jewel that belonged to a long-dead Egyptian princess, and is said

H. M. Koutoukas wearing his cobra ring

to contain the secret to the mystery of existence, has led Harry all over the world in an endless search for serenity. He is always drawn back to Sheridan Square, where he is sure he will find the lost jewel somewhere.

Judith Malina and Julian Beck were an integral part of Village life, particularly in the 1960s when their Living Theater on Fourteenth Street and Sixth Avenue was in full swing, presenting plays such as Jack Gelber's *The Connection* (a jazz-junkie play) in which Martin Sheen (then a James Dean lookalike) made his first appearance, William Carlos Williams's *Many Loves*, Pirandello's *Tonight We Improvise*, Ken Brown's *The Brig*, and Bertolt Brecht's *Man Is Man*, which starred Joe Chaiken.

The East Village also has had its share of characters, including performance artist Penny Arcade, known as a "Slum Goddess Extraordinaire," whose one-woman show *Bitch, Dyke, Fag-Hag, Whore* played to packed houses for over two years at the Village Gate on Bleecker Street. The underground off-off Broadway theater is alive and well at P.S. 122 (150 First Avenue at Ninth Street); Theater for the New City (155 First Avenue at Tenth Street), run by Crystal Field and George Barteni-eff, who continuously present new plays, street theater, and special events; the ongoing

Quentin Crisp, celebrated writer and East Village resident

La Mama (74A East Fourth Street), run by Ellen Stewart; and the Public Theater. Playwrights continue to address new problems and issues. The AIDS plays of Larry Kramer (*The Normal Heart*), Harry Kondolean (*Zero Positive*), and William M. Hoffman (*As Is*) opened the doors of awareness to this devastating illness that has attacked so many in all fields of endeavor. The Ridiculous Theatrical Company, having lost its leader, Charles Ludlam, to AIDS, continues to operate under Everett Quinton, presenting hilarious drag plays that keep audiences rolling in the aisles with laughter. All over the East and West Village, new gender-bender performance people continue to emerge out of clubs like the Pyramid, the Wonder Bar, and the Boy Bar. The brilliant Lypsinka (John Epperson) is one of these new artists, as are lesser known "stars" of the underground such as Hedda Lettuce, Anita Cocktail, Della Katessen, and Esther Egg. International Crisis, now deceased, Cherry Vanilla, and Lady Bunny set the stage for Ru-Paul to become the first major rock 'n' roll drag star to come out of the Village.

Lypsinka (a.k.a. John Epperson)

People and places are always in flux, disappearing and reappearing, and change is the name of the game. What is here today is gone tomorrow. Some who came to the Village found the fame they were seeking, while others found the fame-game to be elusive. The playwright Rochelle Owens, who wrote *Futz*, *Bechlch*, and other experimental plays, once said to an aspiring hopeful, "Never try to court the Bitch Goddess Success. [In Greek mythology, 'success' is ruled by a Bitch Goddess.] The bitch will turn her back on you. If you just do your work, do your own life. That's it. Then, the bitch might take you for a ride, but she might drop you back down again too." Joe Cino of the Caffe Cino put it simply when he said to an annoying playwright who was asking him too many questions about life, love, and the theater, "Look, just do your own thing."

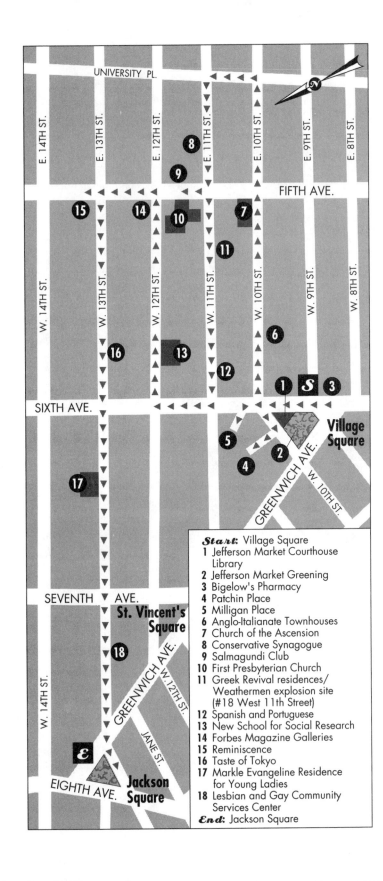

Start: Village Square
1 Jefferson Market Courthouse Library
2 Jefferson Market Greening
3 Bigelow's Pharmacy
4 Patchin Place
5 Milligan Place
6 Anglo-Italianate Townhouses
7 Church of the Ascension
8 Conservative Synagogue
9 Salmagundi Club
10 First Presbyterian Church
11 Greek Revival residences/ Weathermen explosion site (#18 West 11th Street)
12 Spanish and Portuguese
13 New School for Social Research
14 Forbes Magazine Galleries
15 Reminiscence
16 Taste of Tokyo
17 Markle Evangeline Residence for Young Ladies
18 Lesbian and Gay Community Services Center
End: Jackson Square

Greenwich Village Walks

Village Square to Jackson Square

START: *The Village Square, Sixth Avenue, Greenwich Avenue, and Christopher Street*

*T*he Jefferson Market Courthouse is the notable landmark in this traditional center of the Village, built in 1876 in high Victorian Gothic style in the triangle block bounded by Tenth Street, Sixth Avenue, and Greenwich Avenue. It is all that remains of a complex that included a police court, a prison, an octagonal watchtower and fire station, and a teeming produce market. The building was saved from developers, who wanted to tear it down to build an apartment house in the 1960s, by outraged Villagers led by Lewis Mumford, e. e. cummings, and others. Its exterior and interior were restored by Giorgio Cavaglieri in 1967 and became a branch of the New York Public Library. The Women's House of Detention, an Art Deco prison located on the southern (Greenwich Avenue) side of the courthouse, was torn down in 1973 and the land was converted into a volunteer-run community viewing garden called the Jefferson Market Greening. The prison, built in 1929 and designed by Sloan and Robertson Associates, who were also the architects of the Graybar Building on Lexington Avenue, was a fourteen-story monument to modernity accommodating 429 prisoners. Through its ornate bronze and marble lobby

Jefferson Market Courthouse

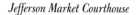

53

marched Dorothy Day in 1957 (arraigned for civil disobedience) and Angela Davis in 1970 (for extradition to California on murder and kidnapping charges). On the east side of the Village Square across Sixth Avenue is Bigelow's Pharmacy, an 1890s Romanesque Revival building featuring one of the Village's last remaining 1930s neon signs, which spells out in blue and orange: C. O. BIGELOW, INC. EST. 1838.

Behind the Jefferson Market Courthouse Library on the north side of Tenth Street (between Sixth Avenue and Greenwich Avenue) is Patchin Place, a secluded dead-end street with only ten houses, all built as boardinghouses in 1848. Theodore Dreiser, John Masefield, John Reed, and e. e. cummings all lived here at one time. Double back on Tenth Street around the corner on Sixth Avenue and you will come upon Milligan Place, comprised of four secluded little houses facing a small inner court (set behind a wrought-iron fence) built in 1852, also as boardinghouses. The playwright and novelist Susan Glaspell lived here in the teens and the early 1920s with her husband, George Cram Cook, the founder of the Provincetown Players.

Exiting from Milligan Place, cross Sixth Avenue and head east on Tenth Street, a block with some of the wealthiest residences in New York, whose early-nineteenth-century architecture has been preserved almost intact. Notable residences on the south side of Tenth Street include 48, a little brick house built in 1829 in the Federal style (the mansard roof was added in 1871); 50, next door, was a stable built between 1863 and 1879, still with the original stable doors. It was owned successively by actor Maurice Evans, who performed Shakespeare on Broadway, Edward Albee, and Jerry Herman, author of *Hello Dolly*. Next door is 52, a Federal townhouse built in 1830 that was once the home of designer Isamu Noguchi and opera diva Concetta Scaravaglione. The nine-story brick apartment house at 44 Tenth Street was built in 1917 and is called the John Alden. Playwright Paul Foster is one of the current occupants. The "terrace" of connected townhouses in the Anglo-Italianate style from 20 to 38 was built in 1856 and is attributed to the same architect, James Renwick, Jr., who erected the Greek Revival townhouses that are the Village's pride and joy on Washington Place North east of Fifth Avenue. The townhouses are four and a half stories high and feature unifying balconies at the second floor with French doors opening onto them and fine ironwork, all original. Artists Louis Bouche and Guy Pène du Bois lived here. Architecturally distinctive examples of Gothic Revival style are the two brick townhouses built in 1854 for a distinguished importer named Clinton Gilbert (14) and Henry L. Pierson (16), an iron merchant. Mark Twain lived at 14 in 1900–01, and a plaque on the building refers to his short residency (apparently the housekeeping was too much for Mrs. Clemens or they were afraid of the ghosts). In recent years, the house was infamous for the horrible child abuse perpetrated by lawyer Joel Steinberg and Hedda Nussbaum on Lisa, the little girl who died at their hands from beatings and neglect.

On the corner of Fifth Avenue and Tenth Street is the Episcopal Church of the Ascension, designed by Richard Upjohn and built in the English Gothic Revival style in 1841. It features notable stained-glass windows executed in the 1880s by John LaFarge, who also painted the famous mural inside, *The Ascension of Our Lord*. President John Tyler was secretly married to Julia Gardiner (of Gardiner's Island, the large privately owned island at the eastern end of Long Island) at this church in 1844.

Cross Fifth Avenue and continue east on Tenth Street. This block features rarely seen Gothic Revival houses (4 and 18), Greek Revival townhouses with studios and Italianate architecture as well as two adjoining buildings of East Indian architecture with richly carved teakwood bay windows (7 and 9).

Turn left at the corner of East Tenth Street and University Place, turn left again at Eleventh Street and walk west. At 15 on the north side of this block is the Hotel Van Rensselaer (formerly the Hotel Alabama), built in 1902 in the Italian Renaissance manner of the Eclectic period. Sandwiched in between the Rensselaer and the massive 1905 Beaux Arts–style apartment building at the corner of Fifth Avenue is a small, two-story building at 11 East Eleventh Street that houses the Conservative Synagogue. Set well back from the street and practically obscured by trees and bushes, the synagogue, built as a stable before 1898, was resurfaced in the 1920s with stucco and diamond-shaped tile patterns at its parapet. Eleanor Roosevelt, a staunch Villager, maintained a residence at 20 East Eleventh Street between 1933 and 1942.

Turn right onto Fifth Avenue and stroll up to the last remaining stoop on Fifth mid-block between Eleventh and Twelfth Streets. This is the entrance to the famous Salmagundi Club, America's oldest club for artists. Its members have included Stanford White, Louis C. Tiffany, and John La Farge, all of whom worked on projects in Greenwich Village. This Italianate brownstone mansion was completed in 1853 and has been the artists' club since 1917.

Cross Fifth Avenue and walk back down to Eleventh Street, then turn right. The First Presbyterian Church between Eleventh and Twelfth Streets on Fifth Avenue is an early example of the Gothic Revival style, built in 1846. The design by Joseph Wells is after the Church of St. Saviour in Bath, England. The tower is adapted from the tower of Magdalene College, Oxford. The first Church Parish House on Eleventh Street was designed by McKim, Mead and White.

On the south side of West
Eleventh Street between Fifth and
Sixth Avenues, the uniformity of an
exceptionally long row of Greek
Revival residences is broken by 18,
a new building in the same style
whose front window is angled to
permit a fine view east and west.
The original building was accidentally blown up in the early seventies
by the radical group called the
Weathermen, who used it as a
bomb factory. Coauthor John
Gilman was sitting at his desk in
the First Presbyterian Church
House (actually on Twelfth Street)
when the explosion knocked him
out of his chair, sending him scur-
rying through the church's underground passageway until   he
emerged from the Parish House
doorway opposite the burning
building in time to see a stark-

*First Presbyterian Church, Fifth
Avenue*

naked woman streak down the steps, up the block, and around the
corner, where she disappeared. A few months before this devastating
explosion, which also blew up the west wall of the residence at 16
where Dustin Hoffman lived, John encountered another Hoffman—
Abbie—at the corner of Fifth Avenue and Twelfth Street. Knowing
he was recognized, he jokingly offered drugs or guns, laughing,
"Whichever turns you on." It's a lucky thing Abbie wasn't visiting the
Weathermen that day: Three of their members died. Dustin, who was
at home and was pretty shaken up, later sold his house and moved
uptown.

The rest of the block has beautifully maintained townhouses
from the Greek Revival period (1840–65) interspersed with handsome apartment buildings from the Eclectic period (1893–1915).
On the north side of the street at 63–69 is the Jacob M. Kaplan
Building, the south wing of the New School for Social Research (on
West Twelfth Street). It was designed in 1955 by Mayer, Whittlesey
and Glass and opened in 1960. On the south side of Eleventh
Street, almost to the corner of Sixth Avenue, is the Second Ceme-
tery of the Spanish and Portuguese Synagogue of the Congregation
of Shaearith Israel. Sliced into a tiny triangular plot by road-
building in the 1830s, it was actually established in 1805, and a
peek through the iron gate at the center reveals well-kept eighteenth-

century tombstones and a stone obelisk under a canopy of twisted fir trees.

Stop for a quick bite or a cup of cappuccino at the French Roast Cafe (open twenty-four hours) on the corner of Eleventh Street and Sixth Avenue; or you may want to cross the street to the northwest corner for a slice of Ray's Pizza—taxi drivers swear by it, and this really is the Original Ray's. Walk up Sixth Avenue to Twelfth Street and turn right, heading east again. The north side of this beautiful block boasts imposing apartment buildings; the south side features uniform rows of Greek Revival brick townhouses and several handsome Anglo-Italianate residences. The ultra-modern New School for Social Research at 66 West Twelfth Street is the exception. It was designed in 1930 by Joseph Urban, Florenz Ziegfeld's masterful scenic artist and set designer who also became an architect and industrial designer after leaving his native Vienna. The severe horizontal design of the building, with alternating bands of black- and light-colored brick, was acclaimed as epitomizing America's modern spirit. Its auditorium is an Art Deco masterpiece and can be viewed from the main lobby of the school, which is open to the public. The theater often sponsors films as well as concerts and readings. The fifth-floor dining room of the New School has a mural portraying revolution by the Mexican artist Jose Clemente Orozco; the third-floor conference room features murals depicting the speed and power of the industrial era by famed American artist Thomas Hart Benton. The New School, housed in the Urban building and the Jacob M. Kaplan building (constructed in 1960), was founded in 1919 by a group of liberals headed by Charles Beard, James Harvey Robinson, and Alvin Johnson, who were joined later by the economist Thorstein Veblen and educator John Dewey. This group of men, as well as Lucy Sprague Mitchell, invited distinguished refugee scholars from Europe to form the school's graduate faculty. The New School offers an accredited academic program in a variety of disciplines leading to undergraduate and graduate degrees.

The uniform row of six brick Greek Revival townhouses from 54 to 64 were built in 1843 and are excellent examples of the well-preserved and meticulously maintained nineteenth-century buildings in the Greenwich Village Historic District. The decorative detail employed in the fourteen-story apartment building at 59, designed by Emery Roth for S. Kaplan in 1931, immediately identifies it as an excellent example of Art Deco architecture. At 45 on the north side of the street, a tiny brick Greek Revival house sits on an oddly shaped lot that follows the approximate course of Minetta Brook. The narrow and charming brick houses at 41 and 43 were built in 1861 for a Wall Street banker and broker, Frederick P. James. The ten-story apartment building at 31–33, called the Ardea, featuring a wraparound stone balcony and ornamental wrought-iron railings, was completed in 1901 by J. B. Snook & Sons. Filmmaker and performer Naomi Levine, featured in several Andy Warhol films, lives and works in her apartment on the tenth floor. The Church House of the First Presbyterian Church at 12 West Twelfth Street was built in 1958 to complement not only the church but the surrounding neighborhood, and is sheathed in a beautiful dark-green terra cotta.

The next block, across Fifth Avenue, is commercial. Near University Place is an old art-film theater called Cinema Village, and mid-block are two restaurants directly across from one another. The Asti, on the north side of the street, is the famed Italian restaurant where the waiters sing opera; and the Gotham, on the south side, is one of the trendiest and most expensive of the new eateries.

At Twelfth Street and Fifth Avenue, turn left. The Forbes Magazine galleries are located on the ground floor of the Forbes Building (formerly Macmillan Publishers) at 62 Fifth Avenue between Twelfth and Thirteenth Streets. The unique collection, assembled by the remarkable Malcolm Forbes and perpetuated by his sons, contains eight of the golden mirrored glass panels designed by Jean Dupas for the Grand Salon of the Art Deco ocean liner *Normandie*, models of Forbes's five yachts, and over five hundred toy boats manufactured between the 1870s and the 1950s. A gallery beyond this nautical section contains twelve thousand toy soldiers presented in a series of dioramas. These feature the figurines of such makers as Britains, Heyde, Mignot, and Elastolin. A gallery called "Mortality of Immortality" presents "175 testimonials to moments of moment," ranging from

---

ARCHITECTURAL PERIODS AS FOUND
IN THE BUILDINGS IN THE GREENWICH
VILLAGE HISTORIC DISTRICT

Federal: 1790–1835

Greek Revial: 1828–1848

Gothic Revival: 1840–1865

Italianate: 1850–1865

French Second Empire: 1860–1875

Queen Anne: 1880–1893

Eclectic Period: 1893–1915

Art Deco/Art Moderne: 1925–1940

Reminiscence, Fifth Avenue between Thirteenth and Fourteenth Streets

the prize for the best pen of White Leghorn chickens at the Northamptonshire Egg Laying Trials to the urn that once held the ashes of Marion Hanbury Stewart, all of them examples of once-treasured objects purchased by the wry Forbes at auction, in pawnbrokers shops, or at flea markets. Presidential papers revealing the personalities and problems faced by America's presidents occupy one gallery, while another exhibit features over three hundred fantasies and objets de luxe made by master jeweler-goldsmith Peter Carl Fabergé. The cream of the exhibit are twelve of the fabled Easter Eggs made by the House of Fabergé for the last Czars of Russia. The Forbes Magazine galleries is free; the hours are 10 A.M. to 4 P.M., Tuesday through Saturday (Thursdays are reserved for group tours and the galleries are closed Sundays). Call 212-206–5548 for information.

For another tour of the past, albeit with a contemporary flair, walk up to 74 Fifth Avenue to Reminiscence (between Thirteenth and Fourteenth Streets), a trend-setting must-stop for out-of-towners, uptowners, and Villagers alike. Stewart Richer, the owner, stocks a full line of clothing for men and women, boys and girls, all manufactured after originals from the 1920s to the 1950s. Vintage hats, gloves, ties, and accessories such as sunglasses and jewelry are featured along with actual vintage clothing. There is also a book section and a shoe department.

At Thirteenth Street and Fifth Avenue is Kate's Art Supplies and Kate's Paperie, which supplies neighborhood artists and the Parsons School of Design on the corner. At 40 is the Rambusch Company's 1898 New York atelier, which is home to a stained-glass studio and an art metal shop that works in bronze, aluminum, iron, and stainless steel to produce grilles, railings, gates, and other elegant appointments for theaters, churches, and other public buildings. A mural and sculpture studio designs and creates statues, bas-reliefs, mosaics, and ceramics; a painting and decorating studio devises large environmental murals. The extensive lighting division of Rambusch has specialists in mood lighting, and craftspeople work on wall sconces, elaborate chandeliers, and intricate stage lighting. Harold Rambusch decorated New York's famed 5,880-seat Roxy Theater in 1927 as well as hundreds of movie dream-palaces around the country. His headquarters on Thirteenth Street is renowned the world over as the center of Renaissance artistry and craftsmanship.

The 13th Street Repertory, just down the block from Rambusch, is an unusual little neighborhood theater that has been showing Israel Horovitz's *Line* since 1968. The Japanese restaurant Taste of Tokyo, just next door, was a favorite hangout of John Lennon and Yoko Ono back in the sixties.

Cross Sixth Avenue and continue west on Thirteenth Street. The Markle Evangeline Residence for Young Ladies at 123 West Thirteenth Street is a residential hotel run by the Salvation Army. This seventeen-story Art Deco miniskyscraper was designed by Voorhees, Gmelin, and Walker, the architectural firm responsible for the 1923 Barkley–Vesey Building in lower Manhattan that was one of New York's first Art Deco skyscrapers, built as an equipment and administrative center for New York Telephone. The Bell Telephone Company, expanding its communications system with great rapidity in the 1920s and 1930s, employed Voorhees, Gmelin, and Walker to design telephone headquarters in cities across America, specifically in the Art Deco style.

The Village Community Church at 143 West Thirteenth Street (originally known as the 13th Street Presbyterian Church) has a handsome, hexa-style Greek Revival facade that was retained intact during a 1980s condo conversion of the church building. Built in 1846, it was reconstructed in 1855 and in 1903 after fires, and today the church facade with its white wooden columns helps to preserve the character of this beautiful Village block. On the south side of the street, long rows of Greek Revival brick townhouses bring the mid-nineteenth century to life. The City and Country School, consisting of three simple brick buildings dating from 1842, was remodeled in 1940 according to the designs of John C. B. Moore, the architect for Lucy Sprague Mitchell, who founded the City and Country School as well as the New School for Social Research. Villager Matthew Broderick is an honors graduate of this progressive school.

The northwest corner of Thirteenth Street and Seventh Avenue is occupied by the Metropolitan Duane Methodist Church built in the

"The Center" bathroom mural by Keith Haring

Gothic style in 1931. The unusual architecture of the Edward and Theresa O'Toole Medical Services Building on Seventh Avenue between Twelfth and Thirteenth Streets, featuring portholes as windows, is explained by its original tenant, the National Maritime Union of America, which erected it in 1963 from plans by Arthur A. Schiller and Albert Ledner. It is now a clinic and outpatient center for St. Vincent's Hospital. Headquartered here is St. Vincent's Alcoholic Services in conjunction with St. Vincent's Psychiatric Department. At 208 West Thirteenth Street is the Lesbian and Gay Community Services Center, which occupies a beautiful city-built school constructed in stages from 1869 to 1887. The Center houses the National Museum and Archive of Lesbian and Gay History as well as a theater, meeting rooms and halls, a charming interior garden, and a bathroom painted with highly graphic sexual images by East Village artist Keith Haring. The Center hosts walk-in peer counseling, a community health project, the Coalition for Lesbian and Gay Rights, the Stonewall Business Association, stress reduction programs, rap groups of every kind—Alcoholics Anonymous, Co-Dependents Anonymous, Sexual Compulsives Anonymous, Overeaters Anonymous, Rage-aholics Anonymous (a gay men's Al-Anon group), Survivors of Transsexuality Anonymous, and a lesbian switchboard. There are also regularly scheduled meetings and events for bisexual groups, Gay Veteran associations, elderly gays (SAGE), safe-sex workshops, ACT-UP forums, Men-of-All-Color meetings, dances, and socials.

The Great Building Crackup at 251 West Thirteenth Street at the intersection of Greenwich Avenue was originally the Jackson Square

The Lesbian and Gay Community Services Center, 208 West Thirteenth Street

branch of the New York Public Library, designed by the famous architect Richard Morris Hunt in 1887. A gift to the city by George W. Vanderbilt, it was purchased and altered in 1971 by Paul Rudolph for artist Robert Brown and his heiress wife, Rhett Delford Brown. Inside the now-recessed ground-floor space is a large plaque commenting on the relationship of architect and client. An excerpt:

> The Great Building Crackup is an actual collision . . . . Since this
> is an event and not a building in accepted nomenclature, it possesses
> a fluidity which is more easily understood if apprehended as a
> metaphor concerning molecular physics. It is not a record of what has

happened but a continually changing phenomenon functioning on a time scale which is not as recognizable to human sense perception.

Next door to the Great Building Crackup at 253 West Thirteenth Street is one of the many utilitarian structures built in the Art Deco style in 1930 for New York City's own subway system. This IND (Independent line) Electrical Substation is just across the street from Jackson Square.

Jackson Square, actually a triangle, bounded by Greenwich Avenue, Thirteenth Street, and Eighth Avenue, was acquired by the City of New York in 1826 and was restored to its original grandeur in 1990. Across Eighth Avenue to the west is New York City's historic Gansevoort meat market district. Abingdon Square is two blocks down the avenue.

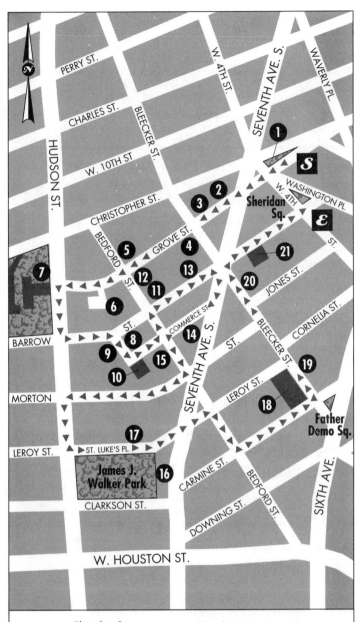

Map labels:

PERRY ST.
CHARLES ST.
W. 10TH ST
HUDSON ST.
BLEECKER ST.
CHRISTOPHER ST.
W. 4TH ST.
SEVENTH AVE. S.
WAVERLY PL.
WASHINGTON PL.
Sheridan Sq.
BEDFORD ST.
GROVE ST.
JONES ST.
CORNELIA ST.
BARROW
COMMERCE ST.
BLEECKER ST.
MORTON
LEROY ST.
Father Demo Sq.
LEROY ST.
ST. LUKE'S PL.
CARMINE ST.
James J. Walker Park
SIXTH AVE.
CLARKSON ST.
BEDFORD ST.
DOWNING ST.
W. HOUSTON ST.

Start: Sheridan Square
1 Christopher Park
2 Marie's Crisis (Thomas Paine)
3 Five Oaks
4 Grove (restaurant)
5 17 Grove Street
6 Grove Court
7 St. Luke's in the Fields (church and gardens)
8 The twin houses
9 Grange Hall
10 Cherry Lane Theater
11 Pamela Court
12 Chumley's
13 Bette Midler's sister's house
14 1920s Esso gas station
15 Edna St. Vincent Millay's house (the narrowest in the Village)
16 Keith Haring pool mural
17 Mayor Jimmy Walker's house
18 Our Lady of Pompeii
19 Bleecker Street Pastry & Cafe
20 Second Childhood
21 Greenwich House
End: Sheridan Square

Sheridan Square—West Village

START: *Sheridan Square at the intersection of Seventh Avenue South, Christopher Street, West Fourth Street, Grove Street, and Washington Place*

Sheridan Square, a drilling ground after Revolutionary times, is now occupied by the triangular-shaped Sheridan Square Viewing Garden, surmounted by an eye-high wrought-iron fence. The triangle park with the statue of General Philip Sheridan of Civil War fame at its tip is called Christopher Park. This leafy park also features a statuary group by George Segal of two standing men and two seated women, depicting in white-painted bronze gay and lesbian love. Christopher Park has a slight rise at its center that gives an overview of the square. On the east side of the park at 88 and 90 Grove Street are two Federal-style buildings constructed in 1827. Number 88 was remodeled in French Second Empire after the middle of the nineteenth century, and 90 was converted to create a two-story artist's studio in 1893. The triangular fourteen-story brick apartment building to the right of these historic structures was designed by Emery Roth in a simplified version of neo-Romanesque with modern Art Deco features such as well-scaled setbacks, decorative stone carvings of griffins and nude maidens, and a colorful mosaic lobby on Washington Place. The handsome building was erected in 1929 just before the Great Crash. The mid-nineteenth-century buildings on Christopher Street directly opposite Christopher Park house some of the Village's most famous bars, including the Lion's Head, the 55 Bar, and Stonewall. The building on the corner of Christopher and Seventh Avenue South, opposite the park, is entirely new, built according to the specifications mandated for buildings in the Greenwich Village Historic District. A legendary cabaret and club called the Duplex (originally across the square on Grove Street) occupies two stories with apartments above.

Exit Christopher Park on Grove Street and cross Seventh Avenue South, walking west on Grove. Thomas Paine, author of "Common Sense," the pamphlet that proclaimed American independence and helped ignite revolution, died on June 8, 1809, in a frame house on the site of 59, now occupied by Marie's Crisis, one of a group of clubs and cabarets on this short block of Grove Street between Seventh Avenue South and Bleecker Street. The "Crisis" in the bar's name commemorates the title of Tom Paine's series of pamphlets that called for the Colonies to revolt from Britain. In 1923, a bronze tablet was placed on the building by the Greenwich Village Historical Society. It reads:

Grove Street

The world is my country—all Mankind are my brethren.
I believe in one God and no more.
To do good is my religion.

Thomas Paine—Born 1737
Died—1809

On this site.

On the wall behind the back bar inside Marie's Crisis are two large sand-blasted, tinted-glass panels depicting the "Rights of Man," the American Revolution on the left and the Russian Revolution on the right with the words "Liberté, Egalité, Fraternité" in the center. These panels, in the WPA style, are said to be from a 1930s

Grove Court

Commerce Street

Commerce Street

luxury ocean liner. Up a short flight of stairs above the main room of the club is another testimonial to Thomas Paine and his revolutionary times, a six-by-eight-foot hand-carved wooden panel depicting Robespierre, Danton, and Thomas Paine himself. The employees and regulars at Marie's Crisis will be glad to tell you all about Thomas Paine and the other famous Villagers who used to hang out in this cozy, sing-along bar.

Arthur's, a renowned jazz club, Rose's Turn, a cabaret bar, and the Five Oaks, a fine restaurant and piano bar at 49 Grove Street, make this a very lively block indeed. Rose's Turn (the Duplex until it moved across Seventh Avenue) at 55 was originally an intimate cellar tea room run with gay abandon by Romany Marie, a restaurateur and arts patron whose place was frequented by artists and writers such as DeHirsh Margules and Sinclair Lewis. The atmospheric one-flight-down Five Oaks, which used to be a speakeasy, was the home base of Marie Blake, a legendary scat singer and stride pianist whose repertory on any given night might range from cozy interpretations of Cole Porter rendered with a throaty purr to a wake-'em-up "Rag Mop." *New York Times* writer Richard Lyons said in her obituary (December 8, 1993) that "Miss Blake had a following of hundreds, if not thousands, of people who believed that listening to a live musician at 3 A.M. in a smoke-filled cafe was a major part of what living in Manhattan was all about. Her banter and ad-libbed one-liners endeared her to two generations of club audiences." A featured entertainer at the Cafe Society in midtown Manhattan, appearing with the Duke Ellington and Count Basie bands and singing alongside Billie Holliday and other stars, she moved her act forty years ago to Marie's Crisis to entertain the troops in Sheridan Square. After nineteen years at Marie's Crisis, Marie Blake moved down the block to the Five Oaks, where she sang and played for another twenty-two years before pass-

ing away, drawing record crowds
to the end.

Across Bleecker Street on the
corner of Grove is Sybille's
Gallery (316 Bleecker), an interesting frame shop and boutique
whose proprietor, Steve Cooper,
grew up around the corner in an
apartment at 45 Grove Street.
This magnificent house built in
1830 for Samuel Whittemore,
an important manufacturer and
Greenwich Village real-estate
developer, was originally a free-
standing late Federal–period
mansion with its own cistern,
well, hothouse, and stables.
Over the years the house was

*Corner of Grove and Bleecker,
circa 1960*

used for a variety of purposes, including a makeshift hospital during
the Spanish-American War. Poet Hart Crane lived there at one time.
Steve Cooper, who still lives in the house, can tell stories of many
restless ghosts he's encountered there through the years. His sixteen-
foot vaulted bedroom is the exact spot where the assassination plot on
Abraham Lincoln was hatched by John Wilkes Booth and his cocon-
spirators.

Six fine row houses, representing the Greek Revival to Italianate
style and built in 1851 and 1852 (28 to 38 Grove Street), give this
block a pleasing, symmetrical appearance enhanced by the canopy of
trees at the curbs and the distinct lack of traffic, accounted for by the
twisting and winding streets to the west beyond Bedford Street. At
the Bedford Street corner at 17 Grove Street is a wood-frame house
that is one of the oldest in the Village, built in 1822 for William F.
Hyde, a window sash-maker. Mr. Hyde, who served as a Village Al-
derman, built the small shop in the back (around the corner on Bedford Street) for his business. Known as Twin Peaks, the building at
102 Bedford Street (next to the sash shop) was built in 1835 and remodeled as artists' studio apartments in 1930 by wealthy philan-
thropist Otto Kahn, who employed an architectural style borrowed
from Nuremberg, Germany.

The Village is renowned for hidden courtyards and Grove Court,
at the bend in the street between Bedford and Hudson, is one of the
most famous. Though inaccessible due to a wrought-iron gate that is
usually locked, Grove Court can be viewed from the street. Mixed Ale
Alley, as it was known when the buildings were constructed for local
working men between 1848 and 1854 (the name referred to the

drinking habits of its residents), became Grove Court in 1921. It comprises six connected three-story Greek Revival houses. The houses to the right of the court at 10 to 2-1/2, built from 1825 to 1834 with their front stoops and dormer windows intact, complete the picture of a street that looks much the same as it did over 150 years ago.

At Grove Street's end is the Church of Saint Luke in the Fields (487 Hudson Street), which began in 1821 as a chapel originally connected to Trinity Church. The Episcopal Congregation sponsors many vital neighborhood programs. The church, St. Luke's School (prekindergarten through eighth grade) behind the church, the buildings to the right and left of the church between Christopher and Barrow, and the buildings on Barrow around the corner (between Hudson and Greenwich Streets) comprise the St. Luke's compound, which originally included a burial ground and a garden. The Federal-style brick houses facing Hudson Street are all from about 1825. The famed St. Luke's gardens started with a tiny slip taken from England's famous Glastonbury thorn in 1842. The thorn actually survived until 1990, when the tree it had become was blown over in a freak windstorm.

The Barrow Street garden, the largest, was designed and planted by Mrs. Barbara Leighton in 1950. It has paths for strolling and benches for sitting and always seems in bloom. Villagers often sit reading papers in the afternoon while cats prowl through the underbrush. The Rectory Garden features a rose garden and a wildflower path. The South Lawn, with the ruin of the east wall of the old Parish Meeting House—which burned down in the late 1970s—as a picturesque backdrop, was designed as a place where people can sit on the grass and children can roam. The Biblical Garden is opposite the South Lawn and is planted with fig and apricot trees, pomegranate, rosemary, broom, and juniper (all mentioned in the Bible). The gate at the corner of Hudson and Barrow Streets is open on Sundays from 1 to 4 P.M. During the week the gardens may be approached through the school entrance to the right of the church though they close at dusk. Father Flye, who practiced his ministry and lived in this complex, had a famous correspondence with critic James Agee that was published in book form. The ghost of Clement Moore, St. Luke's first warden and the author of *Twas the Night Before Christmas*, is often seen at the upstairs window of the old Parish House. Writer Bret Harte also spent his boyhood years living in the Parish House.

Cross Hudson again and walk down to Barrow Street, turning left. The apartment complex at 72 Barrow is known as Green Gardens and was constructed in 1926. The charming inner courtyard, approached through an open passageway under a wrought-iron trellis, features the same multicolored terra-cotta panels that can be seen on the parapets of the building from the street. The "twin houses" separated by an open patio-garden on Commerce and Barrow Streets were originally built by a milkman named Peter Huyler in 1831–32, and then modified with the addition of French Second Empire mansard roofs in the early 1870s.

Jackie and Jay are the hosts of the Grange Hall at 50 Commerce Street, which retains the same 1940s ambience of its beloved predecessor, the famous old Blue Mill, owned for fifty years by the family of Alcino Neves. The Grange features fresh American-style food at moderate prices. Its restored wooden bar, over which hangs a picture of Franklin Delano Roosevelt, has a separate entrance on Barrow. The restaurant entrance is on Commerce Street. The wood paneling and off-lighting, comfortable, padded booths, parquet floor, two fluted columns (emulating Frank Lloyd Wright's Johnson Wax Building in Racine, Wisconsin), and a WPA-style mural by contemporary artist David Joel provide a warm ambience for the young Wall Street crowd that gathers here.

The Cherry Lane Theater on Commerce Street, constructed as a brewery in 1836, was one of the earliest off-Broadway experimental theaters founded by a group of playwrights led by Edna St. Vincent Millay in 1924. The Isaacs Henricks House (77 Bedford on the corner of Commerce) is acknowledged as the oldest building in the Village (1799), though some complain that its recent renovation makes it look like a replica.

Turn left on Bedford, walk one block to Barrow Street, and turn right again. At 58 Barrow Street, turn at the gate and walk through tiny Pamela Court if it isn't locked. At the far end of this hidden courtyard, in a building erected in 1831, is Chumley's, once a famous speakeasy with an upstairs casino and a frequent haunt of John Dos Passos, F. Scott Fitzgerald, Theodore Dreiser, and Edna St. Vincent Millay. Other frequent visitors included Ring Lardner, James Agee, J. D. Salinger, Lillian Hellman, Willa Cather, Edna Ferber, and William Burroughs. Chumley's, whose main entrance, though also unmarked, is at 86 Bedford Street, was the last of the rendezvous where the Provincetown theater group and young liberals who followed Max Eastman found a congenial atmosphere. Chumley's solid fare runs from lobster to hamburgers to pastas with porter, ale, beer of every kind, and a full liquor bar. The dimly lit interior is lined with the dustjackets of some of the books of its long-gone patrons.

Exit Chumley's through Pamela Court back to Barrow Street. A plaque placed at the corner of this block by the Bedford-Barrow-Commerce Block Association states that the street used to be called Reason Street, after Thomas Paine's tract, "The Age of Reason." People started calling it Raisin Street and residents voted to rename it Barrow in 1828 after the artist Thomas Barrow, who drew a print of

Trinity Church that was widely distributed at the time. The BBC Block Association, which sponsors the annual Ye Olde Village Fair, the proceeds from which directly benefit the community, also has a glass-enclosed bulletin board that contains neighborhood announcements and other interesting local information.

Walking up Barrow Street (between Bedford and Seventh Avenue South), you will see one of the most attractive streets in the Village, lined on both sides by houses ranging in style from the late Federal through the Italianate to Eclectic. The wrought-iron railings of the Greenwich House Music School at 44 and 46 contain clef musical symbols. The oldest buildings on the block, 34 and 36, built in 1828, are identical and 36 once belonged to Bette Midler. A passageway to the right of 34, with the address 34-1/2 and 36-1/2, leads to a small house in the garden at the rear. Across the street at 39 an ancient grapevine canopies the entranceway. Mark Van Doren, the poet and writer, lived at 43 in the mid-1920s.

Turn right on Seventh Avenue South, walk one block downtown, and turn right again onto Commerce Street. A quaint, abandoned 1920s Esso gas station sits on the southern corner of the block. A plaque at 11 Commerce Street declares it to be the Irving House—built in 1826 and formerly the home of Washington Irving, Jr.'s sister. If you feel the sudden urge to buy something or to discuss some pressing legal matter, stop in at 19 Commerce Street. The storefront, displaying Depression glass and 1940s advertising signs, is emblazoned "Robert P. Reiter—Attorney at Law—I Also Dabble in Antiques." Robert Reiter Esquire is usually seated at his desk just inside the door. The houses at 24, 26, and 28 are early even for the Village, dating from 1821, all in a plain Federal style.

At Bedford Street, turn left. Just across the street, at 75-1/2 Bedford, is the house popularly known as the narrowest in the city (less than 10 feet wide), built in 1873 with an unusual stepped gable reminiscent of the Dutch tradition. The poet Edna St. Vincent Millay lived here in 1923 and 1924, after winning the Pulitzer Prize for *Renascence*. The back of the house faces the street and its front door is reached through a passageway on Commerce Street, which leads to a large inner court and garden. Lionel Barrymore and Deems Taylor were other notables who at one time lived in this house.

Walk east on Bedford to 70. This Federal-style house built by a sailmaker named John Roome in 1807, though altered several times, has been meticulously restored. A plaque on the building proclaims John Roome "a crier of the courts and Terminor and Gaol delivery of the general session of the peace." At this corner, turn right onto Morton Street. At first heading south, Morton Street bends and widens mid-block, then proceeds directly west. This block, one of the Village's most varied, includes a distinguished house at 59 (constructed

Edna St. Vincent Millay's house,
Bedford Street

in 1828), selected in the 1930s by the Federal Arts Project as the outstanding example of late Federal style in New York City, and a fine Greek Revival house at 44 built in 1844 that served as a set for the TV series "Naked City." The four handsome Anglo-Italianate houses at 46, 48, 50, and 52 were built in 1852. The six-story apartment building at 55 with an Art Moderne facade and details added in the 1930s was the home of playwright Charles Ludlam.

At the corner of Morton and Hudson Streets is Village Atelier, an intimate restaurant serving American/French country food. Dominique is the hostess, and the owner, Craig Bero, has enlisted the inestimable talents of his mother, Charlotte, who bakes incredibly mouth-watering, old-fashioned pies and cakes. Craig Bero also owns and operates the sweet shop Bespeckled Trout and the restaurant Anglers and Writers, next to each other at the corner of Hudson and St. Luke's Place. Mrs. Bero's pies and cakes are sold at the shop, which specializes in old-fashioned penny candies, teas, jams, teapots, and other Old World dishware, while the elegant relaxed restaurant next door has become the place of choice for sumptuous teas and light meals for Villagers and visitors alike.

Turn left onto St. Luke's Place, which extends three-fourths of a block before turning into Leroy Street, which curves to the left. A beautiful row of fifteen Italianate townhouses faces the James J. Walker Park, which includes a baseball field, a bocce ball court, a children's playground, a handball court, a large outdoor swimming pool (actually part of the Carmine Recreation Center on Seventh Avenue South) with a mural by Keith Haring. The houses, all built between 1851 and 1854 from a master design for well-to-do merchants,

Carmine Pool with Keith Haring mural

have high stoops with pedimented round-arched doorways, long French windows, and bracketed roof cornices. One of the most desirable streets to live on in the Village, the open and airy feeling of St. Luke's Place is enhanced by dozens of tall Gingo trees, hardy "exotics" that are often the first to bloom in the spring and the last to shed their leaves in the fall. Distinguished occupants of these houses over the years have included James (Jimmy) Walker, mayor of New York from 1926 to 1933, whose father owned number 6 (two "lamps of honor" on the newel posts, symbols of a mayor's residence, are still there), Broadway actress Marion Winters, playwright Arthur Laurents (*West Side Story*), painters Paul Cadmus and Jared French (at 15), the sculptor Theodore Roszak (at 1), and Theodore Dreiser (16).

Cross Seventh Avenue South and turn right on Bedford Street, heading east to Carmine Street. Orbit and the Universal Grill, across from each other on Leroy at Bedford, are relatively new additions to Greenwich Village's ever-changing and ever-increasing roster of restaurants; Mary's at 42 Bedford is an older occupant, having once

St. Luke's Place

Bleecker Street was the center of vegetable pushcarts in the Village; today this is the last authentic Italian one, at Carmine Street.

been a speakeasy that became so popular it grew into a multi-level, multiroom Italian restaurant. At Carmine Street, turn left. This block has some of the best record shops in the city, from hard-to-find and out-of-print oldies to the latest grunge rock and reggae.

Where Carmine crosses Bleecker and joins Sixth Avenue, the wide intersection and park is known as Father Demo Square. Dominating the square is Our Lady of Pompeii, the church where St. Frances Cabrini often came to pray. When Mother Cabrini was canonized in July 1946 to become the first American saint, the mothers of Village veterans raised a shrine-altar to her in thanksgiving for the safe return of their boys. Pompeii, built on a site that was once a vaudeville house and later the black Roman Catholic Church of St. Benedict the Moor (the first black Catholic church north of the Mason–Dixon line), was completed in 1928 and is the only Catholic church in New York with a weekly mass, confession, and radio program in Italian. Every Christmas the church assembles an outdoor crèche and it also sponsors the annual Carmine Street Fair, which is held during the summer months.

Turn left on Bleecker for a stroll up the street that once was lined with outdoor markets and pushcarts. The Vegetable Garden is the last remaining vestige of the greengrocers, occupying an indoor market in a low, two-story building with Joe's Pizza Parlor on the corner (highly rated for a slice) and the A&S Smoke Shop at 237 Bleecker. Bleecker Street between Sixth and Seventh Avenues is a paradise for the casual food shopper. The Bleecker Street Pastry and Cafe at 245 is open every day for zuppa inglese, tartufo, pastiera di grano, egg bread Veneziana, panettone, cappuccino, and espresso. Donato Di-Saverio and his wife and children create an atmosphere in their sparkling cafe that is both relaxed and efficient. Rocco's Pastry Shop and Cafe, right next door at 243, displays pineapple upside-down cakes and zabaglione in their windows. Zito and Sons Bakery at 259 Bleecker Street has been selling fresh loaves of French, Italian, and whole wheat bread since 1924. Other food shops along this stretch of old Bleecker Street include Faicco's Sausage Shop (260) for home-

Bleecker Street Pastry Shop

made mortadella, sausages, bologna, salami, Italian olives, and other specialties; Murray's Cheese Shop on the corner of Bleecker and Cornelia Streets; Greenwich Village Fish Company at 265; and Ottomanelli's Butcher Shop at 281, where you can stock up on pheasant, venison, wild boar, rabbit, and lamb.

The tiny storefront Neighborhood Church is the unexpected occupant of a two-story Federal-style brick building (c. 1833) at 269 Bleecker Street. The church offers daily prayer meetings and Bible study and its motto, "You shall know the truth and the truth shall make you free," is proudly displayed in the front window.

Second Childhood at 283 Bleecker Street is world-renowned and a must-stop for anyone interested in tin wind-up toys from the 1920s

Bleecker Street

Barrow Street restaurant One If by Land,
Two If by Sea is a converted stable

and 1930s, lead soldier sets, or bisque handpainted Donald Duck and Mickey Mouse toothbrush holders. Proprietor Grover Van Dexter loves to show customers his favorites, which are metal toy cars and train sets or anything Charlie McCarthy or Little Orphan Annie.

A sharp right off Bleecker onto Seventh Avenue South and another right off Seventh Avenue South onto Barrow Street will bring you to the steps of Greenwich House (27 Barrow), which was erected in 1917 as a community center. There are presently eight different sites in and around Greenwich Village connected to this center, offer-

Nineteen thirties hand-painted "Made in Japan" bisque Mickey Mouse toothbrush holder, with pal Pluto, at Second Childhood on Bleecker Street

ing an array of social programs, mental health services, and cultural opportunities, including a halfway house for recovering alcoholics on the Bowery. Greenwich House was the first settlement house in the country to open a nursery school; the Senior Center offers breakfasts and lunch to the elderly as well as counseling; theater and musical events are performed in the hall; Village youngsters play in the gym; and the annual Greenwich Village Antique Show is headquartered here. Drop in for a visit and afterward walk to West Fourth Street, where you will find yourself back where you started your tour, at the Sheridan Square Viewing Garden.

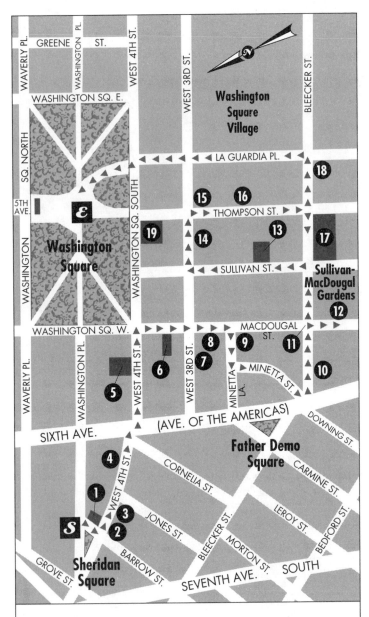

Start: Sheridan Square
1 Ridiculous Theatrical Company
2 The Silversmith at 184 3/4 –
 the Village's smallest store
3 The Slaughtered Lamb Pub
4 The Pink Pussy Cat
5 "Peace Church" — Washington
 Square United Methodist
6 Provincetown Playhouse
7 Bleecker Bob's Record Shop
8 Reggio Cafe
9 Minetta Tavern
10 Little Red Schoolhouse

11 Cafe corner
12 Bob Dylan's old digs
13 Greenwich Village Children's
 Aid Society
14 #2 Fire Engine Company
15 Thompson Street newsstand
16 Stella Dallas Vintage
 Clothing
17 The Mill's Hotel #1
18 Village Corner
19 Judson Memorial Church
 and Campanile
End: Washington Square

Positively Fourth Street—In the Footsteps of Freewheelin' Bob Dylan

START: *Ludlam Lane, east end of Sheridan Square Viewing Garden*

*T*he home base of the Ridiculous Theatrical Company, founded in the sixties by Charles Ludlam and continuing today under Everett Quinton's inspired leadership, occupied the basements of two buildings. Part of the Charles Ludlam Theater, across from the Sheridan Square Viewing Garden, the theatrical company was at 2 Sheridan Square, in a wedge-shaped building dating from 1834 with an entrance on West Fourth Street. The other part of the theatrical company was at 1 Sheridan Square, in a warehouse building, now converted to lofts, constructed in 1903 with an entrance on Washington Place. The Ludlam Theater was at 1 Sheridan Square too, on Ludlam Lane (named for the founder), which is actually the first short block of Barrow Street (between Washington Place and West Fourth Street). A zany ridiculous production might encourage you to have a drink at Boxer's, 190 West Fourth, a busy Village bar-restaurant with a huge, horseshoe-shaped bar. This attractive, spacious place used to be the popular Jimmy Day's.

The massive seventeen-story apartment building across from Boxer's was constructed in 1958 on the site of the original Circle-in-the-Square Theater, which presented revivals of O'Neill's plays as well as a revival of Tennessee Williams's *Summer and Smoke* with Geraldine Page. One of the Village's great and legendary pubs, Louie's Tavern, and a tea room called Pandora's Box, became memories at the same time the theater was demolished.

West Fourth Street between Barrow and Sixth Avenue is a great shopping, eating, looking, and walking block with two one-block-long streets (Jones and Cornelia) that intersect. At 185 is an 1899 stable that was remodeled into a garage in 1919 and then into a studio in 1937. Numbers 175 to 179 were built in 1833 and retain their classic Federal style with outstanding Federal dormer windows at 177 and 179. To the left of these buildings is tiny Chez Claude (187 West

Claude on West Fourth Street in front of his tiny patisserie, Chez Claude

Fourth), which has three or four tables at which to sip cappuccino and eat delicious Belgian pastries and genuine French croissants and brioches fresh-baked by Claude himself each day.

Pink Pussy Cat Boutique, West Fourth Street

The Silversmith at 184-3/4 is the Village's smallest store, where Ruth Kuzub sells, makes, and repairs fourteen-carat and sterling-silver jewelry, evenings only. The Slaughtered Lamb Pub (182 West Fourth), with a Werewolf Lounge at the corner of Jones and West Fourth Street, is on the "eerie" pub crawl of Sheridan Square (the other two are Jekyll and Hyde at 91 Seventh Avenue South and Jack the Ripper Pub at 228 West Fourth Street), where you can have your pick of over two hundred beers and ales, and enter into a Dickensian/Arthur Conan Doyle fantasy. The cozy Bagel Restaurant (170) has a one-table platform just under its open-flame window hearth. It's a good place for organic eggs, char-broiled hamburgers, bagels, and coffee, as well as for watching furtive customers parading in and out of the Pink Pussy Cat (167 West Fourth Street), purveyors of scanty underwear and sex toys. Occupying the 1825 building on the corner of West Fourth Street and Sixth Avenue is a Gap clothing store, which displaced O'Henry's, a third-generation-run Victorian restaurant, now just a Village memory. Cornelia Street runs off to the right; the Karavis (Greek fast food) occupies a corner restaurant that used to be the Humpty Dumpty owned by Adele Speare, who served a special known as the Big Three (a hamburger, a piece of pie, and a cup of coffee) for ninety-five cents. Mrs. Speare also owned Mother Hubbard's Restaurant on Sheridan Square, which, according to a 1961 restaurant guide, sold large take-home homemade apple pies for $1.25 and $1.65 for sour cherry.

Cross Sixth Avenue to the Washington Square Restaurant at 150 West Fourth Street, now a Greek diner in one of the last wood-frame houses in the Village. The early-nineteenth-century silhouette of the building that once housed the world-famous Mad Hatter Tea Room can be clearly viewed from the Sixth Avenue side. Midway up West Fourth Street, between Sixth Avenue and MacDougal Street, is the Washington Square United Methodist Church, nicknamed the Peace Church in the sixties for giving aid and council to draft resisters, supporting Native American rights, and openly welcoming gays and lesbians. Mathew Simpson, the church's first bishop, who delivered the sermon at Abraham Lincoln's funeral, said the church and its members should offer an "ark of safety and refuge" for the people of New York. The Romanesque Revival–style church was built of marble in 1860, and it has supported ministries of social justice, peace, and healing as well as providing housing for women and supporting workers' rights throughout the nineteenth century. Today it is known as a "jazz" church with a worship experience on Sunday mornings unlike any you've ever attended. The church still provides a homeless shelter as well as an active theater company and continues its leadership in disarmament and nonviolent ministries.

At the corner of Washington Square West and West Fourth Street, pause and look, before going down MacDougal Street, out over the eight acres of Greenwich Village's historic Washington Square Park and the fountain in the center where Bob Dylan sang his first folk songs in the sixties. On the west side of MacDougal Street between West Fourth Street and West Third Street, in the middle of the block, is the Provincetown Playhouse, site of the original productions of Eugene O'Neill's first one-act plays. The theater has since presented many extraordinary theatrical productions, including Edward Albee's *The Zoo Story* on a double bill with Samuel Beckett's *Krapp's Last Tape*, David Mamet's *Edmond*, and Charles Busch's *Lesbian Vampires of Sodom*. The Provincetown Playhouse was preceded on this block by a group called the Liberal Club. The club founded the Washington Square Players, presenting noncommercial works by intellectual rebels and poets like Louis Untermeyer, Vachel Lindsay, *Masses* editors Floyd Dell and Max Eastman, and author Sherwood Anderson. George Cram Cook was the life spirit of the Provincetown Players and founded the Provincetown Playhouse after a summer spent producing one-act plays on Cape Cod. Susan Glaspell, Cram's wife, wrote *The Inheritors* for the MacDougal Street theater, and innovative productions of O'Neill's *Bound East for Cardiff*, *Ile*, *The Long Voyage Home*, *The Hairy Ape*, and *Emperor Jones* followed, forever changing the face of American theater.

La Lanterna, a few doors down from the Provincetown Playhouse, is a cafe popular

Charles Manson T-shirt at Bleecker Bob's

with NYU students; the rear tables face out over a pleasant garden. At the corner of Third Street, turn right and cross over to Bleecker Bob's Record Shop, which also has an amazing T-shirt emporium in the back, stocked with such ghoul classics as cultist Charlie Manson; or you can buy an "E Is for Empty" Dan Quayle shirt or ones featuring the Butthole Surfers, the Dead Kennedys, or other off-beat rock 'n' roll groups. You can also get your favorite T's with punk rock, folk rock, glitter rock, avant-pop, post-funk, soul, hip-hop, or disco logos. Bleecker Bob, a

Tourists reading a map at Caffe Reggio on MacDougal Street

Village character himself, and his associates John DeSalvo, Chris Wiedner, and Louie My, will sell you records, tapes, and CDs of the latest music, including the best in grind-core, indie-grunge, heavy metal, progressive rock, ska, jazz funk, acid-jazz, new wave, hardcore, and hip-hop. Bleecker Bob's shop is on the sight of the Night Owl, where the Lovin' Spoonful, the Mamas and the Papas, and other sixties groups performed.

Outside of Bleecker Bob's, look down West Third Street to the el-

Nedal Chater, Mamoun's son, at Mamoun's Falafel, MacDougal Street

egant grand-piano canopy of the famed Blue Note Jazz Club, which features jazz-great headliners like Maynard Ferguson or the Ramsey Lewis Quartet or Nancy Wilson. Also on this block, across from the Blue Note, is the Kettle of Fish, an atmospheric bar and music scene. The inevitable, a McDonald's, is located on the corner with a spacious second-floor dining area affording an excellent view of the bustling street activity at West Third and Sixth Avenue. This Greenwich Village McDonald's attracts a new breed of

Village characters—"rappers," uptown downtowners who stand around and rap on Third Street, hoping to be discovered by a talent scout. Head back to MacDougal Street and turn right. The first landmark is the historic Reggio Cafe, next to famous Mamoun's Falafel and the Comedy Cellar. Bob Dylan's first New York performance was at the Cafe Wha? on the corner of MacDougal and Minetta Lane, where today you can dance to live rock 'n' roll, rhythm and blues, and Motown music from the sixties and seventies.

The Minetta Tavern, across the lane, began in the 1920s as a speakeasy called the Black Rabbit. The back dining room of this excellent restaurant is encircled by a unique mural showing the history of Greenwich Village. You can count on an authentic Italian meal here; the chefs make your pasta-to-order fresh out of an antique pasta machine right on the premises.

Take a right off MacDougal Street down Minetta Lane, which provides a quiet contrast to the circuslike, touristy hubbub, and enter another world peopled with the ghosts of the "Minettes," the long-gone, early residents of what was once New York's worst slums. Many houses in Minetta Lane and Minetta Street (twisting off to the west) were part of the under-

Cafe Wha?

In the dining room at Minetta Tavern

A local pauses in front of the old Fat Black Pussy Cat on Minetta Street

ground railroad that harbored runaway slaves. In the 1920s, Minetta Lane and Minetta Street were filled with speakeasies. The Fat Black Pussycat, its painted sign still visible on the brick at 13 Minetta Street, was a popular club in the fifties and sixties. Frank Serpico, the undercover cop who blew the whistle on his corrupt buddies and who was immortalized in the film *Serpico* with Al Pacino, lived at 7 Minetta Street. The curve in Minetta Street follows the old Minetta Creek, still flowing underground, across Sixth Avenue west over to Downey Street.

Turn right onto Bleecker Street, heading east. At 196 Bleecker Street is the Little Red Schoolhouse, which has been educating prekindergartners through eighth-grade children at this location since 1932. It was founded in 1921 by the education pioneer Elisabeth Irwin, an associate of Eleanor Roosevelt, and teaches students to associate education with accomplishment and challenge, not anxiety and pressure. The upper division of the Little Red Schoolhouse, the Elisabeth Irwin High School at 40 Charlton Street, has graduated Angela Davis and Mary Travers of Peter, Paul and Mary, among other notables. The Porto Rico Importing Company at 201 Bleecker Street has been selling coffees and teas (and coffeepots and teapots) since 1907. Peter, a third-generation proprietor who now has branches of the original store in the East Village at 40 St. Marks Place and in SoHo at 107 Thompson Street, roasts his own blend on Bleecker and you can smell the coffee aroma a block away.

The four corners of Bleecker and MacDougal Street are all occupied by cafes. The Borgia, on the northeast corner, has been there the longest; it features a wonderfully dim mural of an Italian landscape, and little marble tables and wire stools. The cookies, cakes, and cappuccino are a treat and the view out of the floor-to-ceiling windows is fantastic. The Figaro, on the southeast corner, is the newest incarnation of a cafe of the same name that closed down in the 1970s. In the sixties, the Village Figaro, modeled after the original one in Paris, was the place to sip cappuccino while wearing an all-black outfit and reading a copy of James Joyce's *Finnegan's Wake*, Proust's *Remembrance of Things Past*, or some thick Dostoevsky novel. Sally Kirkland would have been your waitress in those days at the Figaro; and Howard Smith, later the "Scenes" columnist for the *Village Voice*, was also a waiter for a while. Kitty-corner from the Figaro in the sixties, and for decades before that, was the San Remo Bar, a popular hangout for the likes of Maxwell Bodenheim, Edward Albee, and other glitterati. On the site of the Remo now is Carpo's Cafe, a new and popular coffee-eaterie. The restaurant across the street attempting to look like a cafe is a Greek diner, on the site of an old Italian mortuary that also closed its doors in the late 1960s.

Continue truckin' on down MacDougal Street to the Caffe Dante & Gelateria, at 81 MacDougal. If you sit down here at one of the immaculate little tables, you will be directly in front of the two houses Bob Dylan bought and combined (92–94 MacDougal Street) after becoming a folk-rock recording star. Caffe Dante opened in 1915 and has been owned for the past twenty-two years by Mario Flotta, who will tell you that the best coffeehouses in all of Italy are in his native Napoli. Nattily dressed Mario (the best tailors come from Napoli too) serves extraordinarily unusual Italian desserts, offers a fine selection of gelatos and sorbets, and claims to make the best cappuccino in the Village.

Walk back up MacDougal to Bleecker and turn right, passing by the front of the Figaro. To view the block-long communal garden behind Bob Dylan's old house, you can go to the back bar in Figaro, or you can go to the back dining area of the Pizza Box (mid-block between MacDougal and Sullivan Streets). The Pizza Box is the best bet, offering a better view and mouth-watering slices. In 1923, the Hearth and Home Corporation transformed a slum neighborhood (a square block bounded by Bleecker, Sullivan, Houston, and MacDougal) into a residential enclave for middle-income professionals. Each house has its own low-walled garden opening onto a tree-filled central mall with communal seating and play areas. This unusual and bucolic spot is called the Sullivan-MacDougal Gardens, and it is now regarded as choice Village residential real estate.

At Bleecker and Sullivan, look south at the Sullivan Street Playhouse, home of the *Fantasticks*, the longest running off-Broadway show in history. The

MacDougal and Bleecker Streets

playhouse was founded by producer Lee Paton, now known as performance artist Lee Nagrin, who lives and works on Bleecker Street. Turn left on Sullivan Street and walk up to the Lion's Den (214 Sullivan between Bleecker and West Third Street), which used to be called Sing Sing, one of the earliest karaoke bars. Today, the Irish manager, Sean, presents straight-up rock 'n' roll bands, funk

and reggae bands, West Coast grunge bands, and even transvestite glamrock bands like Satyr and the Sex Dolls. Groups like the Road Vultures, Finster Baby, the Moodbreakers, and Pillbox perform loudly every hour on the half-hour from 8:30 P.M. often until 3 A.M. The acoustics are not subtle at the Den, which has a cement floor, a long bar with stools, a raised platform with tables and chairs, and a vast "standing floor" for "packin' 'em in." All in all a fun place, and there's a pool table for a quick game between acts. Across the street, for the younger crowd, is the Greenwich Village Children's Aid Society in a handsome new building, at 209. Architecturally notable on this block are the three nineteenth-century buildings at 220, 222, and 224, which were combined as an apartment complex in the early 1930s. The Art Deco, WPA-style decorations on the stuccoed front and the wrought-iron gates are worth careful investigation. Just down the block at 240 is the smallest bar in New York—the Samurai Sushi Bar and Pub. Across the street is a famous old Village saloon Googies, which continues to be a popular hangout for NYU students and the hip swinging singles set.

Turn right on West Third Street and head east toward Thompson Street. You'll be passing the site of the legendary Cafe Bizarre, where coauthor John Gilman served lighted sparkler sundaes to the Velvet Underground just before they hit paydirt with Andy Warhol. Mid-block, the No. 2 Fire Engine Company stays alert in a completely restored, meticulously maintained, Victorian-era firehouse decorated with painted stone Medusa heads and soaring eagles. The Thompson Street newsstand, on the corner of Thompson and West Third, became a pop-culture site when it appeared as the background for a famous James Dean photograph.

Turn right and stroll down Thompson Street toward Bleecker for a tour of one of Greenwich Village's noted restaurant rows. You can take your pick from the Grand Ticino, since 1919, to Rincon de Espana to Mexican Village, to Livorno, to Portobello, or to Ponte Vecchio. They are all reasonable and serve good food and wine in pleasant dining areas. Aside from the rock clubs and coffee cafes, these restaurants are the chief attraction in this old Village neighborhood south of Washington Square Park. Notable shops on the block include the Chess Shop at 230, which sells elaborate to simple chess sets and provides tables for players inside, the Village Bath and Candle Shop, Stella Dallas Vintage Clothing, and Nostalgia-Jazz for rare record albums, celebrity photos, and posters. To satisfy your obsession with superheroes, such as Captain Marvel or Batman, or to pick up an original edition of R. Crumb comics, priced at about $65, go around the corner to Village Comics, on the second floor at 163 Bleecker Street. Video games, bubble gum, comics, posters, you name it, it's all here—and you can stock up on your comic book Baggies and boards as well. For even more superheroes, try the Science Fiction Shop at 168 Thompson between Bleecker and Houston.

Across the street from Village Comics is the old Village Gate, Art D'Lugoff's famed entertainment center, which was located in an 1896 building occupying the entire block on Bleecker between Sullivan and Thompson Streets. Designed by Ernest Flagg, it was known as the Mills Hotel No. 1, where impoverished "gentlemen" could find short-term lodging, that is, a place to flop. There were fifteen hundred tiny rooms in the hotel, each with a window, some looking into interior courts, and each room cost twenty cents a night. In the film classic *Gold Diggers of 1933*, a gold-digging Aline MacMahon refuses a check given to her by Warren Williams after he had passed out drunk on her sofa with the quip "This is not enough for a night's lodging. What d'ya think this is, the Mills Hotel?" It is now an apartment dwelling called the Atrium.

The two blocks between Sullivan and La Guardia are the Via Veneto of the rock clubs. There's a different group every night of the week at the Back Fence (155 Bleecker Street) with poetry readings on Sundays (at 3:30 P.M.). Guns 'n Grunge, Tramps Like Us, Voodoo Child (the only authentic Jimi Hendrix show!), Johnny Youth and the Verdict, and Phil's Psychedelic Rock Show are the acts you can catch at the Rock 'n' Roll Cafe. Kenny's Castaways, the Bitter End, the Red Lion, and the Peculier Pub are also on the strip, offering live entertainment every night until the wee hours. Pick a band at one of the clubs and catch a set or some hip-hop poetry and jazz. Afterward, head over to the Village Corner (Bleecker and La Guardia) for one of their hamburgers or a basket of southern-fried chicken and a pint of beer. This high-ceilinged old tavern is a comfortable place to relax while you figure out if the group you saw will make it big like other performers who played the Bleecker Street strip, such as Jimi Hendrix, Janis Joplin, Jim Morrison, Blondie, the Talking Heads, Patti Smith, Eric Anderson, Joan Baez, Peter, Paul, and Mary, Buddy Holly, the Velvet Underground, Lou Christie, Phil Ochs, Tom Paxton, Tim Hardin, Janis Ian, Simon and Garfunkel, Credence Clearwater Revival, Steppenwolf, Frank Zappa and the Mothers of Invention, Kinky Friedman and the Texas Jew Boys, Zal Yanofsky, John Sebastian and the Lovin' Spoonful, the Mamas and the Papas, Gayle Garnett, the Village People, Madonna, Buster Poindexter and the New York Dolls, and of course that freewheelin' soul, folk-rock legend Bobby Dylan. If at this point you feel "just like a rolling stone," don't worry: The Dylan tour is almost over.

To get your bearings, turn left on LaGuardia Place and walk two blocks north to Washington Square Park. You'll pass the Elmer Bobst Library on your right and the NYU Loeb Student Center on the left, across from the park. One major landmark on the south side of the square at Sullivan Street is the Judson Memorial Church and campanile, built in 1896 with funds donated by the Astor family and John D. Rockefeller. The aligned American Baptist and United Church of Christ Judson congregation has always had a mission for the poor and disenfranchised. In 1956, Howard Moody introduced an activist era at the church, taking stands on controversial issues such as the Vietnam war, abortion rights, decriminalization of prostitution, and lesbian and gay rights. An avant-garde musical theater company directed by the Reverend Al Carmines achieved success in the 1960s and 1970s. Today, the Judson Dance Theater, the Judson Gallery, and other innovative Judson projects proceed unabashedly under the leadership of Peter Laarman, a forty-six-year-old labor and community organizer who became senior minister at Judson in 1994. The church was designed by Stanford White of McKim, Mead and White, in the Italian Renaissance Eclectic style, with stained-glass windows by John La Farge and a marble chancel decorated by Herbert Adams after a design by Augustus Saint-Gaudens. Washington Arch, at the Fifth Avenue entrance to Washington Square, was also designed by Stanford White. Giovanni Turini's monument to Garibaldi was erected in 1888 by the Italian immigrants of Little Italy on the eastern side of the square; on the western side is

Judson Church

Chess players in Washington Square Park

J.O.A. Ward's bronze bust of Alexander Lyman Holley, developer of the Bessemer process for manufacturing steel. Now it's time to just sit down on a park bench in Washington Square for a well-earned rest where you just might see a young Dylan look-alike, with guitar, howling "It Ain't Me Babe!"

Washington Arch and Washington Square

The Washington Square Arch was originally a white-painted plaster-of-Paris and wooden lathing structure erected for the Washington Inauguration Centennial celebrated on April 30, 1889. This original arch, standing one-half block north on Fifth Avenue from the present arch, had a single sixteen-foot-high blue wooden statue of George Washington at the top. The seventy-one-foot-high and fifty-one-foot-wide arch was lit at night by several hundred of Thomas Edison's new incandescent lights, which had just been invented, causing visitors to gasp in awe and amazement. The New York City Committee on Art, spurred on by the popularity of the temporary wooden arch, asked architect Stanford White to create a permanent structure in white marble, using $180,000 raised by private fund-raisers. White's beautiful arch was completed in 1892 and the formal proceedings and dedication took place three years later on May 4, 1895. Washington in War, *a carved statue of Washington in his full general's regalia, was sculpted by Hermon Atkins MacNeil and put in place on the eastern side of the arch in 1916. In 1918 another statue,* Washington in Peace, *showing America's first President in civilian garb, was created by A. Stirling Calder, the father of famed mobile artist Alexander Calder. Legend has it that Charles Atlas posed for the Calder statue that was placed on the west side of the arch. Etched in marble on the south side on the top expanse of the arch are the words " 'Let us raise a standard to which the honest can repair. The event is in the hand of God.'—Washington."*

When ground was broken for the permanent arch in 1890, a discovery of human skeletons was made. Digging at first five feet and then ten feet below the surface, well-to-do residents were shocked when they learned that the area in which they lived was a burial ground, the south side having been a kind of Potter's Field and the northern section a more formalized German graveyard. Headstones dated 1803, 1804, and earlier were unearthed. Some accounts had it that American Indians were buried there as well; and some remains were found wrapped in yellow shrouds, indicating they were victims of Yellow Fever. Superstitious people today feel the park to be haunted by those that were buried, since not all of the skeletal remains were removed. This is the reason many Village residents will not walk through the park late at night, particularly on All Hallow's Eve.

Washington Square Arch

Still, the nine-and-a-half-acre Washington Square Park is a haven for local families who come with their children, folksingers, soap-box orators, rappers, tourists, Frisbee throwers, dogs, poets, and chess players. The square also serves as the campus for New York University, its forty-five-thousand-plus students, and the faculty, many of whom reside in apartment and dormitory buildings near or surrounding the park.

"Let us raise a standard to which the wise and the honest can repair. The event is in the hand of God."
—George Washington, quoted atop
the south side of the
Washington Square Arch

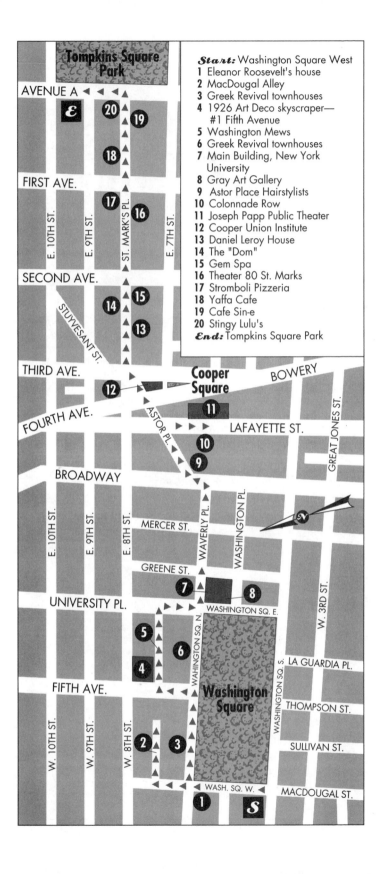

Start: Washington Square West
1 Eleanor Roosevelt's house
2 MacDougal Alley
3 Greek Revival townhouses
4 1926 Art Deco skyscraper—#1 Fifth Avenue
5 Washington Mews
6 Greek Revival townhouses
7 Main Building, New York University
8 Gray Art Gallery
9 Astor Place Hairstylists
10 Colonnade Row
11 Joseph Papp Public Theater
12 Cooper Union Institute
13 Daniel Leroy House
14 The "Dom"
15 Gem Spa
16 Theater 80 St. Marks
17 Stromboli Pizzeria
18 Yaffa Cafe
19 Cafe Sin-e
20 Stingy Lulu's
End: Tompkins Square Park

Crosstown Walk—Washington Square to Tompkins Square

START: *Washington Square Park, northwest corner*

*T*he sixteen-story neo-Gothic brick apartment house at 29 Washington Square West has a bronze plaque to the left of the entranceway that reads:

> Eleanor Roosevelt, October 11, 1884–November 7, 1962, Humanitarian, Reformer, Stateswoman, made this her Greenwich Village home from 1942 until 1949.

Franklin Delano Roosevelt and his wife, Eleanor, leased the apartment until his fourth-term reelection in 1944 changed their retirement plans. When he died in office April 12, 1945, on the eve of the Allied victory in World War II, Mrs. Roosevelt went to Washington Square alone with their famous black Scottish terrier, Fala. They became a familiar sight strolling together in the evenings in the park.

The Washington Square Hotel, originally the Hotel Earle, at 103 Waverly Place, was constructed in 1902 (the three-story annex facing MacDougal was erected in 1916). This conveniently located hotel has 160 guest rooms ranging in price from $65 (single standard) to $75 (single deluxe) to "deluxe quads" at $136. A restaurant on the corner, called CIII, serves the needs of the hotel guests and is open to the public as well.

Half a block up MacDougal toward Eighth Street is MacDougal Alley, which extends east two-thirds of a block, ending abruptly at the back of a massive apartment building fronting on Fifth Avenue. MacDougal Alley is a private street with iron gates blocking traffic and an iron sidewalk gate open from 8 A.M. to 6 P.M. on weekdays and from 9 A.M. to 2 P.M. on Saturdays (locked Sundays and holidays). MacDougal Alley was created in 1833 by landowners as a private court for stables behind the grand townhouses facing Washington Square and the residences facing Eighth Street. The stables were first converted to garages and later into residences facing the uneven cobblestoned street. A three-story stable built in 1854 at 21 was remodeled in 1920 by Raymond Hood. The striking curved brick corners at 10

Eleanor Roosevelt

and 10-1/2 face an inner patio behind 24 Washington Square North; in the sixties producer Richard Barr had a salon for new playwrights there. Mrs. Harry Payne Whitney converted the stable at 19 into a residence and studio in 1934. Numbers 15-1/2 and 17-1/2 were combined for the first

Eleanor Roosevelt's apartment building on Washington Square West

Whitney Museum, now the New York Studio School on Eighth Street.

The simple brick Tenth Church of Christ Scientist facing the alley on MacDougal was remodeled in 1966. The church reading room is open to the public. Return to Washington Square North and turn left. The brick and granite "Richmond Hill" apartment building on the corner at 27–28 was built in 1898 on a site that had been the permanent home of the Young Women's Christian Association in 1868. Architects Robert Gwathmey and Everett Shinn lived here in the 1940s. Theatrical occupants have included Uta Hagen, Herbert Berghof, Leticia Ferrer, James and Patsy Broderick, their son Matthew Broderick, Rochelle Oliver, Tony Award winner James Patterson and his son John Patterson. Uta Hagen, Rochelle Oliver, and Patsy Broderick still maintain their apartments there. Matthew, who grew up here, visits his artist mom Patsy, but now has his own space elsewhere.

The imposing Greek Revival townhouses on Washington Square Park were erected for wealthy merchants and bankers between 1835 and 1837. The exception is the Federal-style mansion at 20, which in 1829 was the first building constructed on the block. The brick building at Fifth Avenue (14 Washington Square North) was constructed by Emery Roth and Sons in 1952 on a scale comparable to the mansions it replaced, one of which, a handsome Greek Revival house at 18 Washington Square North, was the home of Elizabeth Walsh, Henry James's maternal grandmother. As a child he visited frequently, and the house was the inspiration for his famed novel *Washington Square*.

Turn left up Fifth Avenue, pausing in front of 2 Fifth Avenue, the undistinguished twenty-story high-rise apartment building that you viewed at the end of MacDougal Alley, now the home of ex-mayor Edward Koch. Across Fifth Avenue is 1 Fifth Avenue, originally a hotel when it was built as a miniature Art Deco skyscraper in 1926. In the 1960s it was purchased by NYU and converted into an apartment building with some housing for NYU students. A recent occupant of one of the Deco penthouses was noted photographer Robert Mapplethorp. Washington Mews, like MacDougal Alley, was a lane for the stables behind the townhouses on Washington Square North and for a complex of buildings facing Eighth Street. The row of two-story buildings on Washington Mews offers light and air and a wonderful sense of another time. In 1939, to blend in with the rest of the Mews, garden apartments were constructed (from 3 to 10) out of stucco and glass blocks. There is no traffic on the Mews, but the east sidewalk gates are locked at 7 P.M., so get there before sundown. Deutches Haus (42 Washington Mews), at the corner of University Place, offers language courses and lectures with frequent showings of German films. La Maison Française, NYU's Institute of French Studies, is just across the lane.

Turn right on University Place and walk to the northeast corner of Washington Square Park. The uniformly designed Greek Revival townhouses on Washington Square North between Fifth Avenue and University Place that face the open space of Washington Square Park are an outstanding example of community planning; all were erected in 1832–33. With the exception of 3, which was completely remodeled in the Queen Anne style in 1884, the houses are considered a prototype of the Greek Revival style in America, and these buildings still retain most of their original features. Such features include white Doric columns, stone newel posts, marble staircases and walkways, handsome balustrades, and original iron railings and gates. The iron

Washington Mews

fence around the entire row includes the Greek lyre, Greek fret, and acanthus-leaf motifs.

Originally called the University of the City of New York, New York University was chartered in 1831 and classes began in

Eighth Street between University and Fifth Avenue

1832. The university's main building across from Washington Square was built in the early twentieth century on the site of a Gothic tower that was demolished in 1894. A portion of the tower is on display at Gould Plaza on West Fourth Street. World-famous personages who worked and taught in "The Tower" include Samuel F. B. Morse, who demonstrated the first telegraph there, John Draper, who shot the first daguerreotype, Samuel Colt, who perfected his six-shooter, Walt Whitman, who taught poetry, and Winslow Homer, who painted all day and studied all night. The Gray Art Gallery, which opened in 1977, is in the main building at 33 Washington Place. It houses NYU's permanent art collection, which features work from the 1940s to the present with special exhibitions mostly comprised of the work of current photographers and artists. Recent exhibits have included the photographs of Peter Hujar and the early advertising work of Andy Warhol.

Head east over Waverly, crossing Green Street, Mercer Street, and Broadway, where Waverly begins. Turn left up Broadway to Astor Place, then turn right. The Astor Place Hairstylists at 2 Astor Place will cut your hair and dye it purple, green, or pink for your walk into

Washington Square North

the East Village. No reservations are necessary. A simple haircut—be it a German "Bund" or an English "Mersey"—takes only ten or fifteen minutes and costs ten or fifteen dollars. There are dozens of haircutters standing by their chairs just waiting to give you the latest hairstyle. For wines and spirits, there is no better bargain place for Villagers, both East and West, than Astor Place Wines and Spirits on the corner of Astor Place and Lafayette Street. Down Lafayette on the west side of the street at 428–34 are the august remains of La Grange Terrace, known as Colonnade Row, which was built in 1846 and attributed to A. J. Davis. The distinguished personages who lived here in the past include the Delano family (ancestors of Franklin Delano Roosevelt), Peter Cooper, the businessman-philanthropist, and editor William Cullen Bryant. Five of the original houses on Colonnade Row, named after Lafayette's French chateau, were demolished.

Across the street at 425 Lafayette is the Joseph Papp Public Theater, named after the founder of the New York Shakespeare Festival who died in 1991. The five playing spaces and one cinema at the Public Theater are contained in an Italianate building constructed in 1854 at the bequest of John Jacob Astor, then the richest man in America, who lived at Broadway and Prince Street and died in 1848. The largest library in the country, the Astor, was a showplace for the City of New York, containing 350,000 volumes and counting among its borrowers Washington Irving, William Makepeace Thackeray, and Charles Dickens. In 1895, it combined with Tilden Trust to form the New York Public Library, and in 1911 it moved uptown to Forty-second Street and Fifth Avenue. The Astor Library became the home of the Hebrew Sheltering and Immigrant Aid Society for several decades, but was almost demolished. It was saved from the wrecker's ball with a symbolic check of one dollar from theatrical entrepreneur Joseph Papp, who engineered a deal with the city to run the building as a nonprofit theater. Broadway productions of *Hair* and *A Chorus Line*, originally produced at the Public, enabled the theater to financially produce new and experimental work and to continue to present the Shakespeare Festival in Central Park every summer. After the Astor Library closed, books were disseminated in the neighborhood and used bookstores sprang up everywhere. Today only the enormous emporium of the Strand bookstore on Broadway, at Thirteenth Street, remains. Writer Fran Lebovitz calls the Strand her favorite used bookstore, and it is a haunt for many other bibliophiles.

In 1967, Bernard Rosenthal's cube sculpture the *Alamo* started swiveling in the center island of Cooper Square. The Astor Place subway station (Lexington Avenue-IRT local) has a cast-iron and glass replica of the Paris Métro entryway. The restored stop below features some of New York's best terra-cotta ornamentation, which

Andy Warhol's Exploding Plastic Inevitable at the Dom on St. Marks Place, a film of the Velvet Underground projected above the group and Nico performing

can be viewed without passing through the turnstiles; the terra-cotta beavers are the most artful of these and are worth a look.

The building on the south side of Astor Place, facing Cooper Square, is the Cooper Union Institute of Science and Art, where Abraham Lincoln, among other Presidential candidates, made his "Might Makes Right" speech. The latest architectural methods of the day were employed in the construction of the building in 1857; rolled, wrought-iron beams supporting the floors was one innovation, a precursor of building methods used for skyscrapers of the twentieth century. The great vaulted hall at Cooper Union has been the setting for speeches from presidents and labor leaders to lectures by Victoria Woodhull, Emma Goldman, H. L. Mencken, William Jennings Bryan, Susan B. Anthony, and Mark Twain.

Eighth Street becomes St. Marks Place at Third Avenue. The block between Third and Second is the busiest in this neighborhood filled with shops, bars, and restaurants and teeming with street peddlers and strollers. Coming from the west, this block of St. Marks Place is the gateway to the East Village. Looking up above the passing parade, you'll see the block is comprised of four- and five-story brick buildings erected from 1870 to 1890 during a great wave of German immigration. Number 12 St. Marks is elaborately decorated in molded terra cotta and the inscription "Deutsch Amerikanische-Schutzen-Gesellschaft—1888" tells us it was once the German American Shooting Club. At 20 the city landmark plaque reads:

Daniel Leroy House—This mansion was once part of the row that lined the entire blockfront. With its arched Federal-Baroque doorway, grand proportions and original wrought-iron handrailings at the stoop, it is now a rare survivor of the type which because of its great cost was never common. The row, one of the few ever built in this style

in New York, was constructed in 1832 by Thomas E. Davis, a specu-
lative builder. #20 was purchased by Dan Leroy, brother-in-law of
Hamilton Fish and son-in-law of Nicholas Fish, whose nearby home
at #21 Stuyvesant Street is also a landmark.

Hamilton Fish and the Germans have departed, and St. Marks is
now thronged with Poles, Greeks, Indians, Ukrainians, Russians,
Puerto Ricans, Italians, African Americans, and a youth culture mix
of people from all over the world seeking freedom of expression and
inexpensive rents. The dollar can be stretched much farther in the
shops and restaurants of the East Village than in other New York
neighborhoods. On the north side of the street, the combined row of
buildings painted a deep blue is a community center that offers
twelve-step recovery programs for visitors and residents alike. This
used to be known as the Dom, where Andy Warhol's Exploding Plastic Inevitable in the sixties attracted worldwide fame. Later it became
the Electric Circus disco. Dojo (24 St. Marks Place), a popular and
inexpensive restaurant with an outdoor dining area right on the
street, had the following message (on a recent visit) written on the
men's room wall: "Wake up rent slave! Your freedom is an illusion."

On the corner of St. Marks and Second Avenue, the Gem Spa
evokes feelings of nostalgia even in youthful visitors. This newspaper-
magazine, candy, ice-cream, and tobacco shop has always been rated
highest for its eggcreams, and the current Indian proprietors carry on
the tradition; for $1.10, they'll mix the right ingredients for a vanilla
or chocolate eggcream and serve it to you in a glass. Sip it through a
straw while perusing magazines.

Second Avenue and St. Marks Place

Around the corner on the west side of Second Avenue (between St. Marks and Ninth Street) is the Otten-dorfer branch of the New York Public Library, de-signed by German-born William Schickel for the ar-chitectural firm of Richard Morris Hunt in 1884 in a combined neo-Italianate and Queen Anne style fea-turing extraordinary molded terra-cotta busts and decora-tives. It was built in conjunc-tion with the dispensary next door, thus serving both the physical and intellectual needs of the German immi-

The late Howard Otway with screen star Myrna Loy at hand-in-cement ceremonies at Theater 80 St. Marks

grants in the neighborhood. Both the clinic and the library still serve the community.

Return to St. Marks Place and cross Second Avenue, which has some of the best, and cheapest, Polish and Ukrainian restaurants in the East Village. The B & H Dairy Restaurant at 127 Second Avenue is a tiny vegetarian place with small tables and a counter; their borscht and challah bread are tops and their potato pancakes and daily specials, including pea soup, are consistently good. If it's meat you're after, the Second Avenue Kosher Deli (156 Second Avenue) at Tenth Street has the best pastrami sandwiches and excellent knishes.

Continue on down St. Marks Place. The block between Second Avenue and First Avenue is residential and startlingly peaceful after the boisterous, spilling-out-all-over quality of the previous block. Cafe Or-lin at 41 is a good spot for coffee, drinks, or a light repast. What was once the First German Methodist Episcopal Church at 48 is now Igle-sia Metodista Unida Todas Las Naciones. Fine French food can be found at 65 at Bistro Jules. Revival films have been giving East Vil-lagers an education since 1971, when Howard Otway's Theater 80 St. Marks opened. During the festive opening celebrations that year, and in the following years, Joan Crawford, Myrna Loy, Jane Russell, Gloria Swanson, Kitty Carlisle, Hildegarde, Lillian Roth, Joan Blondell, Ruby Keeler, Fifi Dorsey, Winifred Shaw, Alan Jones, and Dom De Luise all impressed their hands or feet into cement on the sidewalk in front of the theater. Theater 80 St. Marks, the Grauman's of the East Village, closed in 1994 upon the death of its founder. Otway's son Larry now leases the theater to acting companies. For a fast bite,

Stromboli Pizzeria, on the northwest corner of St. Marks and First Avenue, is recommended. North on First Avenue are two of the East Village's hottest hotbeds of experimental theater and performance art: P.S. 122, on the corner of First Avenue and Ninth Street, is the headquarters of the innovative downtown performance art scene and presents such East Village headliners as Jeff Weiss, Penny Arcade, Karen Finley, Meredith Monk, Lee Nagrin, Bill Irwin, and Quentin Crisp. On the west side of the avenue, between Ninth and Tenth Streets, Theater for the New City presents dozens of new plays every year by aspiring and established playwrights, a center of activity for hundreds of creative theater people in the East Village. Street theater and street festivals that incorporate the ethnic diversity of this neighborhood are a specialty of T.N.C. First Avenue has its fair share of Polish, Jewish, Ukrainian, and other ethnic restaurants. In addition, the bakeries and butchers and other specialty shops that supply the restaurants are all here to sell you a pound of potato salad, homemade bologna, stuffed cabbage, and pieroggi to take home. Polish spreads in the restaurants include przekaski hors d'oeuvres Koreczki, Canapes Kanapeczki, Prsystawka, salatka cwiklowa, kasza gryczana, zrazy wolowe zawijane, zupa and gruszki w czekoladzie (chocolate-covered pears).

Continuing east on St. Marks Place, Villagers often stop at the Yaffa Cafe (97 St. Marks Place) for a late supper and to sit in the back garden for noodles or a vegetable plate. Eastside tenement life can be viewed from Yaffa's garden. The Cafe Moydor at 101 has tables on the street for lunch or dinner; exotic Middle Eastern music and belly dancing are featured most evenings. Also at 101 is the East Village Books and Records. Live music events and poetry readings can also be heard across the street at Cafe Sin-e (Gaelic for "That's It"), located in the St. Marks Flats at 122. Sivish at 115 sells the latest designer clothes with an East Village panache, and St. Marks Thrift Shop at 119 sells quite a selection of funky vintage clothing. Stingy Lulu's at 129 St. Marks Place is almost at the end of the block, just across Avenue A from Tompkins Square Park. Stingy Lulu's has 1950s chromium tables topped with boomerang-

Justin Vogel of Atomic Passion,
East Ninth Street

Atomic Passion

imprinted Formica, comfortable leatherette Art Deco booths, and a Formica counter with stools. There's a full bar behind the counter and they'll mix you up an ice-cold strawberry daquiri or margarita or a delicious ice-cream soda or chocolate sundae. Vintage 1940s and 1950s ice-cream and Coca-Cola signs decorate the walls and there is a photo gallery of old roadside diners from across America. Hamburgers, pastas, and salads are good and the records on the 1950s Seeburg jukebox represent the decades from the fifties through the nineties. In good weather you can sit outdoors at Stingy Lulu's, enjoy a cool drink, have a sandwich and a cup of coffee, and watch the parade of weirdly dressed, oddball skinheads across the street in front of Alcatraz, a wild, rowdy bar popular with the motorcycle crowd. The riots in Tompkins Square Park in 1988 over the rights of the homeless to camp out there prompted a complete city-park renovation and relandscaping as well as a midnight closing. The park is well maintained and patrolled, and Avenue A, with interesting shops and good restaurants, its sidewalks overflowing day and night with idiosyncratic East Villagers, is deemed to be safe. This is certainly a fun-filled and exciting area, reminiscent, many claim, of the old days in the West Village. To get back to the start of this walk in Washington Square or to other locations in the West Village, walk up to Ninth Street and turn left, heading west. The crosstown bus, an option, stops right on the corner. Buster (the coauthor's mascot Boston terrier, to whom this book is dedicated and who has lived on Christopher Street all of his life), huffing and puffing after this west-to-east walk, prefers to jump into a yellow cab to get him back to the West Village.

*Tompkins Square Park—
Battleground for the
East Village*

Tompkins Square Park was named after the popular New York Governor Daniel Tompkins, who went on to become the Vice President of the United States, serving under James Monroe. A battleground in the Revolution, these ten acres of land were later set aside to become a park in 1834. Governor Tompkins, who is interred in a vault at St. Mark's-in-the-Bowery on Tenth Street and Second Avenue, died in 1825 at the age of fifty-one, too soon to see a park named in his honor.

The riot in August 1988, when the police clubbed East Village residents and homeless people who were living in makeshift shelters in the park, was not the first time such violent outbreaks occurred here. Hunger riots in 1857 were sparked when loaves of bread supplied by a baker were thrown at groups of local German immigrants who were protesting the lack of employment opportunities. A similar but more violent riot happened in 1874 when a rally that had an official permit was arbitrarily canceled. Many citizens, angered by persistent financial

Tompkins Square Park

hardships, fought with mounted police who billy-clubbed them from on high. The founding of the American Federation of Labor, in 1886, was inspired by this incident. Samuel Gompers, who had participated in the clash, became the first president of the AFL. This organization also fostered subsequent labor movements in the early decades of the twentieth century.

Many who were around or at the scene of the Battle of 1988 objected to the idea of renaming what was once the "Lower East Side" to the "East Village." They said "East Village" was a term invented by greedy real-estate agents in the late 1950s who placed apartment ads in The New York Times *under "East Village" or "Village East" listings. Nevertheless, "East Village" took hold and is still the designation on maps and in geographic references. It was Robert Moses in 1954 who eyed the East Village area as ripe for "improvement" and "urban redevelopment," displacing many original residents and unsettling the ethnic mix by tearing down existing tenement buildings and replacing them with high-rise coops; and ultimately charging expensive rents after promising affordable rents to the community.*

Eventually the homeless, who used to sleep in the park and cook over open fires, were chased out by the city government. New paved pathways were put in to accommodate police cars, and high, wrought-iron fences to protect trees along with bright jailyard lights to discourage crime were installed. A police curfew was established at midnight in order to keep out vagrants and to prevent drug dealers from practicing their trade. Many residents complained of previous conditions in Tompkins Square Park, pointing out that they could not sit there without being harassed or accosted by "undesirables." The park has beautiful old shade trees, which make it a refuge for many during the heat of summer. While "improvements" may seem bland and the park may be overly controlled, it is now deemed safe for strollers, tourists, and children.

Labor Day in Tompkins Square Park usually finds hundreds of men in full drag, one more startling and outrageous than the other, participating in an annual event called Wigstock. This "Glen or Glenda" syndrome causes a lot of confusion since that dame that looks like Dolly Parton may actually be a real girl underneath all the hair, makeup, and uplift bra. In 1994 Wigstock was held in the West Village, and "the bewigged" paraded down Christopher Street and along the waterfront.

Nineteen eighties Yuppies have replaced yesteryear's Yippies in the East Village, and aspiring Madonna-lookalikes mix here with business types who work in offices uptown or in banks in the fi-

RuPaul (right) and escort at Wigstock,
Tompkins Square Park

nancial district. Many dissolute, long-haired young men or
women, all wearing face rings, fantasize about an imminent return to the sixties. A young woman in Tompkins Square recently
said she came to the East Village to "get away from all that crap
out there in suburbia." She added that she had tried crack but it
was "nothing." In the East Village, she dyed her mouse-brown
hair platinum and also dyed the roots black, just for a laugh.
Dressed entirely in black, this eighteen-year-old beauty sported the
standard tiny metal nose rings, dead-white makeup, and black
lipstick and had outlined her blue eyes with India-black charcoal.
"Man, I gotta get outa here soon. Maybe I should go back to Jersey.
Of course there is always Hollywood; but what if the ground opens
up? You could get swallowed up." In a flash she was gone, but not
before attracting a lot of stares. "Who knows, she could be some-
body someday," an onlooker commented, "like Cyndi Lauper."

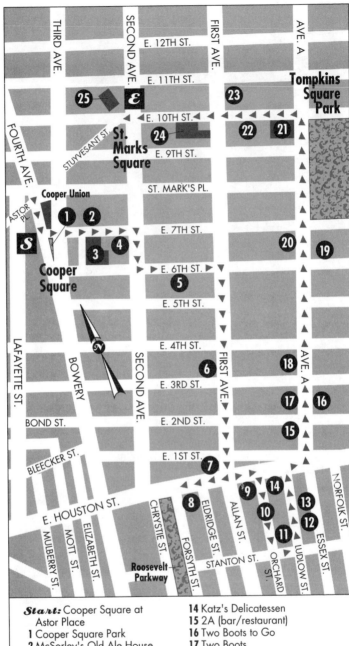

Start: Cooper Square at Astor Place
1 Cooper Square Park
2 McSorley's Old Ale House
3 St. George's Ukrainian Church
4 Kiev Ukrainian Restaurant
5 Little India
6 Little Rickie's
7 Peretz Square
8 Yonah Schimmel
9 Pit Bull Center
10 Orchard Street
11 Ludlow Street Cafe
12 Pink Pony Cafe
13 Max. Fish Bar

14 Katz's Delicatessen
15 2A (bar/restaurant)
16 Two Boots to Go
17 Two Boots
18 Ageloff Towers
19 Wonder Bar
20 Pyramid Club
21 St. Nicholas Carpatho-Russian Orthodox Greek Catholic Church
22 Tenth Street Baths
23 De Robertis Pasticceria
24 Theater for the New City
25 St. Marks Church-in-the-Bowery
End: St. Marks Square

The East Village and the Lower East Side

START: *The* Alamo *cube sculpture on Astor Place at Cooper Square*

*T*he Old Bowery Road was renamed Fourth Avenue above Cooper Square to give the impression of a classier address in the old days; Lafayette Street, East Eighth Street, and Astor Place all intersect at Cooper Square. Walk south to the triangular Cooper Square Park at East Seventh Street and the Bowery. This tiny park has a statue of Peter Cooper by Augustus St. Gaudens and faces the Great Hall of the Cooper Union Institute, built in 1859. Politically oriented forums in this historic building included an address from Abraham Lincoln in 1860 that is credited with winning him the Presidential nomination. Across the street to the west is the headquarters of the world-famous music publisher Carl Fischer. A few doors down are the editorial and production headquarters of the *Village Voice*, New York's "alternative" weekly newspaper.

Head east and cross Third Avenue at Seventh Street. "Honest Abe" and other notables after him including Franklin Roosevelt and John Kennedy headed down Seventh Street to slake their thirst with a pint after speeches at the Cooper Union at McSorley's Old Ale House (15 East Seventh Street). This famed old landmark tavern, completely intact with dark wood paneling, beveled mirrors, and tile floors covered with sawdust, has been serving ales and beers and liverwurst and onion sandwiches (in the old days they were free) since 1854. Right next door at 11 East Seventh Street is the Surma Ukrainian Shop, which has been supplying "old country" knick-

Young couple out for an East Village walk

knacks to the Slavic community of the East Village since 1918. At Surma you can buy pysanky (egg decorating) kits for Easter egg dying. An old-country legend has it that chains of pysanky will keep the "evil monster" from enveloping the earth. The proprietor, Myron Surmach, will tell you other middle-European tales and sell you a Slavic newspaper or travel book or a peasant blouse with hand-embroidered lace similar to the ones worn by Maria Ouspenskaya and other peasant women in the movie *Wolfman* or by Maria Montez

McSorley's Old Ale House, East Seventh Street (window detail)

in *Gypsy Wildcat*. If you look hard enough, you will be able to find the magical wolfbane used to ward off evil spirits and werewolves in olden times, or you might meet a Dracula look-alike out for a stroll.

St. George's Ukrainian Church, across the street on Taras Shevchenko Place, hosts an annual Ukrainian street festival with ethnic dancing and specialty foods. This church was erected in 1976 after the original structure was razed.

Continue east to Second Avenue and turn right. Kiev Ukrainian Restaurant is on the corner; across the avenue midway between Seventh and Sixth Streets is the Middle Collegiate Church, which is Protestant Dutch. At Sixth Street turn left (east again). You're now in "Little India," an extraordinary brownstone tenement block lined with over a dozen Indian and Bangladeshi restaurants. Juxtaposed in the middle of the block (on the north side), a stolid old synagogue incongruously faces the colorful and exotic line of Eastern immigrant eateries that offer

East Sixth Street—the East Village Indian restaurant block

samosa, gobi pakora, murug kaliji, shami kebob, and papadum all afternoon and late into the night. Prices at Passage to India, Rose of India, the Taj, Mughul-e-Azam, Raga, Calcutta, Kismoth, Sonali, Taj Mahal, Nishan, Mitali, Anarbagh, Rose of Bengal, Prince

Little Rickie, First Avenue and East Third Street

of India, Gandhi, and Windows of India, so close together that one imagines a back corridor supplying them all from one central kitchen, are reasonable, ranging from $4.50 for chicken vindaloo to $11.25 for lobster shag (spiced lobster curry cooked with spinach). Vegetarian dinners and lunches are on all the menus and many of the places serve cocktails and wine. The Dowel Indian Grocery (around the corner at 91 First Avenue) sells all kinds of Indian spices, chutneys, fish, halal, meat, and fresh vegetables to the restaurants and for take-home.

Specialty Indian supplies and utensils can be bought at Spice of India down First Avenue at Fifth Street. Continue down First Avenue to 49-1/2, where the phantasmagorical shop Little Rickie is located on the corner of Third Street. The outside of Little Rickie is matched by the inside, an environmental collage that explodes with treasures ranging from painted-plaster Elvis busts juxtaposed alongside statues of Jesus Christ and the Virgin Mary. Like the New Deal dimestores in the 1930s, the 1940s, and the "nifty fifties," Little Rickie's mix of mostly new, un-boutiquey whatnots and some good vintage items are displayed with humor and pizzazz by proprietor Phillip Retzky and his able associates. The place glitters and glows with unique T-shirts, jewelry, buttons, religious icons, tricky impulse items, pink flamingo decals, cowboy neckerchiefs, and a selection of popular culture travel and cookbooks. Have your picture taken by the automatic picture-machine, and have a rollicking good time in the East Village.

Walk down First Avenue to First Street and Houston Street. This is Peretz Square and the boundary (Houston Street) between the East Village and the Lower East Side. The large, densely populated neighborhood east of Allen Street (Avenue A below Houston Street) is a world of its own, dating from the earliest immigration waves in the nineteenth century. Before leaving on a short sidetrip into this historic neighborhood (just one block down and one block back), walk west on Houston to Yonah Schimmel at 137 E. Houston (at Eldridge), an East Village and Lower East Side landmark since 1928. Looking exactly like some forgotten diner or an automat to be found at the Smithsonian Institution, Yonah Schimmel is precisely as it was when it originated. Bagels, potato knishes, potato latkes, chocolate cheese knishes, apple strudel, cheese blintzes, and potato blintzes are all made fresh on the premises and cost from 70¢ to $1.50 (liver knish). A beet borscht drink is 85¢. A dozen rugalech is a good takeout bet, and try their legendary homemade yogurt.

Head back east on Houston (still on the south side). Stop in at the J.B.J. Discount Pet Shop at 151 E. Houston. This is the neighborhood's pit bull center and comes highly recommended by Buster, the Christopher Street dog. The owners don't sell pit bulls, only pets like snakes, lizards, fish, and rodents, but they discourse at length on pit bull lore and legend and carry a full line of pit bull books and breeding-tip pamphlets about the most popular breed of dog in the East Village. The highlight on the block of Houston between Allen and Orchard Streets is Russ and Daughters specialty foods, which include fresh halvah, smoked eel pickles from the barrel, lox, schmaltz herring, gefilte fish, and Beluga caviar (2 kilos, $1,750; 14 ounces, $398; 7 ounces, $199; or 1.75 ounces, $59.95). The third-generation proprietor is justly proud of his immaculate store, which also sells cheese and special salads as well as tinned fish, nuts and candies, and dried-fruit baskets.

Turn right, south, off Houston onto Orchard Street, America's original shopping mall. Bargain prices abound for everything in little shops that line both sides of the street and extend south for several blocks, all the way to Grand Street. On Sundays, this historic Jewish marketplace is free of traffic and the shopkeepers bring their wares outside; Saturdays, because of the Jewish Sabbath, most of the stores are closed. Women's, children's and men's clothing stores are most in evidence, and fabrics, bedding, shoes, and other personal and household goods can be purchased for 20 to 60 percent less than what you would pay uptown (or in a suburban shopping mall). The old open-market tradition of "hondling," or bargaining, is still acceptable on Orchard Street and rewards adept shoppers good at feigning disinterest in something they want. Cash is a valuable negotiating tool on Orchard as well. Eastern-European Jewish immigrants peopled this area in the 1880s, living in the tenements with many selling from their pushcarts. Now, though many Jewish merchants remain, some of the shops are run by more recent émigrés who stock exotic wares from Africa, Russia, South America, even Paris and Florence.

Turn left at the corner onto Stanton Street. Another neighborhood entirely, this short block is home to no less than two carnicerías and three bodegas, catering to the predominant Latino population living in the nineteenth-century tenements. On the corner, at 103 Stanton Street (corner Ludlow), is the upscale Amy Downs, milliner extraordinaire for chic, one-of-a-kind *chapeaux*.

Turn up Ludlow Street at this point, but be sure to pause and look south over the Lower East Side, still vital and teeming with a new generation of tenement-dwellers. On another trip, you might try investigating this historic district starting with the *Jewish Daily Forward* at 175 East Broadway; Congregation Anshe Slonim at 172–176 Norfolk Street (the oldest synagogue in New York, 1849); the Eldridge Street Synagogue (at 12 Eldridge Street between Canal and Division Streets, 1887), with a combination Romanesque, Gothic, and Moorish facade and a brilliant rose cathedral window; and the Lower East Side Tenement Museum at 97 Orchard Street (between Delancey and Broome, 212-431-0233), devoted to promoting tolerance and historical perspective through the presentation of immigrant experiences on the Lower East Side.

Ludlow Street, between Stanton and Houston, is the West Fourth Street of the Lower East Side, with an authentic feel that recalls "the way it was." Try out this otherworldliness first at the Ludlow Street Cafe (165 Ludlow), low-ceilinged and comfortably relaxed with a 12 P.M. to 6 P.M. happy hour every day. The eclectic menu features several south-of-the-border specialties including yapingachos, which is an Equadorian breakfast of fried eggs on lettuce with spicy peanut sauce served with black beans and salsa. Brunch and dinner menus feature huevos rancheros and Arizona burritos, chef's salad, fruit and granola, and classic eggs Benedict. Evenings at the Ludlow Street

Natasha in chapeau *on the Lower East Side at Amy Downs*

Cafe, see new music performed on the tiny stage. A small performance space next door called Nada recently achieved notoriety with a long-running hit featuring one hundred different Hamlets, all "ham-actors" from the Lower East Side or East Village. Across the street at 176 and 178 Ludlow are two very lively establishments, the Pink Pony Cafe (176) and Max. Fish Bar, the latter on the block for thirty years. The eclectic decor and live music till the wee hours is a mecca for residents like Warhol poet–film actor Taylor Mead as well as for uptown slummers looking for a good time. The Pink Pony next door is a relatively new, very laidback coffee and juice bar with plenty of space, lounging chairs,

Patron at Max Fish is an East Village transvestite

and with art magazines and poetry journals for sale. Occasionally, there are poetry readings, theater pieces, and independent movie showings. Max. Fish Bar has "far-out" art shows once a month.

At 205 East Houston (corner of Ludlow Street), Katz's Delicatessen should be visited even if you're not hungry. Katz's is a large, high-ceilinged, L-shaped restaurant with steam tables along one wall and tables and chairs in the center. You take your ticket and yell out an order (hot corned beef, hot pastrami, hot brisket of beef, cold

Ludlow Street bar scene by John Terhorst

rolled beef, roast beef, tongue, salami, bologna, liverwurst, garlic wurst, chopped liver, or real sliced turkey), on rye with Russian dressing or hold the sauerkraut. Down the line you get your ticket punched for potato salad made with sour cream, french fries, cole slaw, Heinz baked beans, and other delicacies; Dr. Brown's Cel-Ray tonic drink is a good pick-me-up. You can also buy a bottle of beer, and hot tea is served in a glass. There are pickles, pickled tomatoes, and homemade Katz's mustard on all the tables, and hanging from the ceiling is a famous slogan Katz's coined during World War II, "Send a Salami to Your Boy in the Army." High-grade Katz's provisions, including salamis and other meats, can be purchased for delivery anywhere in the world. Take home a jar of Katz's deli-mustard.

Leaving Katz's, turn right, continuing east on Houston to the corner of Essex Street. The Bank is a popular disco for dancing to the latest DJ music; before that it was Jasper John's home and art vault, and before that, of course, this solid, turn-of-the-century stone building was a place to keep your money. Turn left and cross Houston to Avenue A, walking north. The 2A at 25 Avenue A is run by Laura Flauto. Two-A means that it's at the corner of Avenue A and Second Street, and the upstairs dining room has a view of this East Village intersection from wraparound windows. The bar on the main floor is fun; there's a terrific bottle and tap beer selection and a good wine menu. House wine by the glass is $2.75, a bottle of Beaubassin Cuvée Blanc is $10, Rolling Rock by the glass is $1.50 and by the pint $2.50. The delicious menu, prepared by an excellent chef, includes appetizers and salads like spinach and cheese raviolis; baked gorgonzola bread; little neck clams on the half shell; fresh mozzarella, tomato, and pesto salad; burgers or sandwiches served with salad and fries; entrees of focaccia, penne, fettucine, linguine bolognese, half-roasted chicken, aged shell steak, or steak au poivre. The prices range from $5.95 for sandwiches to $13.95 for entrees. The kitchen here is open until midnight and there is a burger bar menu as well.

In recent years, Avenue A has become famous for two pizza restaurants: Two Boots, one a sit-down and one a takeout, directly across from each other between Second and Third Streets. The takeout place, Two Boots to Go, has a small, sit-down room on the side for munching a slice or two and there is a red-painted bench outside. The primary Mexican colors inside highlight one of the best bulletin boards in the East Village. The thin-crusted pizza is prepared with a cornmeal base and is served, along with bottled health sodas, by a friendly staff who keep the latest taped music loud and pounding. Two Boots (37 Avenue A), across the street, with Naugahyde-padded booths and Formica-topped tables, faces a large enclosed courtyard in the back, beautifully maintained in its original 1930s condition. Din-

East village mural

ners at Two Boots range from Crawfish Etouffee at $10.95 to seafood pasta jambalaya at $11.95 to *perciatelli melanzana* (eggplant and tomatoes) at $7.95. Appetizers include Cajun garlic bread, Creole popcorn, wild mushroom *aglio e olio* on sage polenta, and the chef, Drew Scannelli, offers a children's menu and home-baked desserts. Of course, you can order a whole pie here with almost anything on it from crawfish to artichoke hearts to black olives. Another Two Boots to Go-Go at 74 Bleecker Street opened to meet the demand for a slice of this good pizza in NoHo (north of Houston) at Broadway.

Two large connected apartment buildings, erected in the late 1920s, occupy Avenue A between Third and Fourth Streets. The outside is decorated with Art Deco motifs and features two fantastic separate Egyptian Deco-style lobbies, one on East Third Street and one on East Fourth Street. Built for local residents who wanted to emulate their more affluent relatives living in modern skyscraper-type buildings on the Upper West Side, the Ageloff Towers is an anomaly amid the low-lying nineteenth-century brick tenements in the neighborhood. The Limbo at 47 Avenue A is a New Age coffee shop painted in soft pastels that features 1950s Formica-topped, chrome-legged kitchen tables in a variety of colors. Coffee is served in multihued Fiesta-ware cups; and the walls are lined with changing photo exhibits.

Performance pieces are done here and poetry is read on special nights. Check the bulletin board, which is bursting with local news information about apartment shares, performance announcements, and emergency cash-flow sales. In the next block at 51 Avenue A, Medina Natural Foods, run by Siyad Sharaf, offers a beautifully selected array of fresh, often out-of-season vegetables and other exotic delicacies.

Benny's Burritos is at the busy corner of Sixth Street and Avenue A, decorated (as is

Junk art on Avenue B

Avenue A and Sixth Street—Sidewalks

their original restaurant on Greenwich Avenue) with funky 1950s lamps with outrageous shades and paint-by-number framed oils of bullfights. The dining room and takeout counter are always packed with East Village locals. Kitty-corner across the avenue is Sidewalks, a bar-restaurant with outdoor tables popular with bikers, who line their motorcycles up on Sixth Street, and with locals, who tie up their pit bulls to the iron railings outside. Just down a few doors on Sixth Street is the "Wonder Bread" exterior of the Wonder Bar, named after the Paris nightclub depicted in the 1934 Warner Brothers movie *Wonder Bar*, which featured Al Jolson as the impresario, Dolores del Rio and Ricardo Cortez as the Spanish dancers (with choreography by Busby Berkeley), and an all-star musical cast. The Wonder Bar is a popular hangout for gays and lesbians with special events and movie nights drawing big crowds.

Don't miss the famed Pyramid Club at 101 Avenue A between Sixth and Seventh Streets, its black-painted entranceway thronged with an assortment of East Village characters with rings in their ears, lips, noses, and eyebrows, dressed in stormtrooper boots, ripped, sagging black jeans, and leather studded jackets. Many also sport extreme Day-Glo Mohawk hairstyles. Musical and performance pieces usually start at 10 P.M. at the Pyramid, with special late shows on Friday and Saturday nights. Performers like Satyr and the Sex Dolls entertain, and Psychotic Eve, Transvestite Bingo, Petting Zoo, and tarot readings are attractions here. Tompkins Square Park is on your right as you stroll up Avenue A toward Tenth Street. On the west side the avenue is lined with stores and bars, restaurants and pizza joints. During the day it is a pleasant walk in or out of the tree-shaded park. Alphabets at 115 Avenue A and the little narrow shop next to it carry

all the latest boutique items and upscale tchotchkes and home accessories like lamps and writing desk appointments. Postcards and T-
shirts prevail in the Little Shop. At the north end of Tompkins
Square Park, which was completely relandscaped after the 1988 riots
(now there is a midnight curfew), a row of nineteenth-century townhouses, many unaltered and all well-maintained, bring to mind the
Greek Revival townhouses on Washington Square North in the West
Village. The restoration of these townhouses has helped inspire a
preservation movement throughout the East Village.

The Lower East Side's "Little Russia" is on Tenth Street between
Avenue A and First Avenue. On the southwest corner is St. Nicholas
Carpatho-Russian Orthodox Greek Catholic Church. The Boy's
Club of New York occupies the building on the northwest corner.
Further west on the block is Boris Weeks's Tenth Street Baths and
Health Club at 268 East Tenth Street. Since 1892, the Russian and
Turkish Tenth Street Baths has offered refreshment for city dwellers
and visitors alike. Monday, Tuesday, Friday, and Saturday are coed,
Thursday and Sunday are for men only, and Wednesday is "Ladies
Day"; the baths are open from 9 A.M. to 10 P.M. In addition to a red-
wood sauna and Swedish showers, Chinese and Japanese massage
rooms (for salt and oil massages), whirlpools, an exercise room, suntan machines, a juice bar and restaurant, a sundeck and lounge areas,
black mud packs, and cable television as well as locker rooms with
beds, the Tenth Street Baths offers Russian and Turkish steamrooms
where you can get a "platza" you'll never forget; fresh oakleaf
"brooms" provide a "silk-rub" or a soapwash. And if you like, Russian boys will stimulate you by thrashing your back and buttocks with
twig-branches. For an invigorating finale to all this, you can jump
into the completely retiled, ice-cold (45–50 degrees) pool. One day
admission is $16, a thirty-minute massage is $24 (one hour with two
therapists is $78), a fifteen-minute platza is $20, and suntan machines are $3.50 for ten minutes up to $10 for thirty minutes. The
Bath's brochure recommends a "sit and shvitz" in the steamroom
and states that it is a "straight place," presumably meaning that there
is no overt cruising among the patrons. Celebrity visitors include
John F. Kennedy, Jr., Hollywood television actor Paul Leiber, and
East Village writer and performer Jeff Weiss. Check out the two weird
curio shops on the north side of Tenth Street, just before you hit First
Avenue, side by side at 249 West Tenth Street. This might be just the
place to find that perfect tchotchke as a souvenir of your visit to "Little Russia" in the East Village. If you're lucky enough to run into resident Ricardo Martinez, the director and composer, he will fill you in
with more stories about this interesting block.

This walk continues west on Tenth Street across First Avenue up
to Second Avenue. But before proceeding on this last leg of the jour-

ney, visit a block that seems to have been lifted out of Little Italy and planted in the East Village. On the east side of First Avenue between Tenth and Eleventh Streets, the Lanza Restaurant has been a local landmark since 1907. The elaborate stained-glass window in front hints at the old-world atmosphere inside, where the original decor, including dark wood paneling, old-time murals, and light sconces, has been preserved and restored. Lanza offers a classic Italian prix fixe dinner from 4 P.M. to 6:30 P.M. for only $14.50 per person; their late-night "Pasta Dinner," served from 9 P.M., comes complete with appetizers, Lanza's ricotta cheesecake, and cappuccino for $10.95.

De Robertis Pasticceria, a few doors north of Lanza's, is another East Village landmark, since 1904. Two steps below street level, this beautiful Italian bakery and cafe preserves its original brightly lit decor and the cappuccinos are served in little glasses with 1920s metal holders. The big, chocolate-covered Italian doughnuts are a specialty, and De Robertis's cheesecake is legendary. Veniero's at 342 East Eleventh Street, just across First Avenue and around the corner, is another venerable Italian pastry shop and coffee cafe owned by the same family for one hundred years. Cheesecake, cookies, cannoli-kits, bake-'n-serve sfogliatella, and other Italian delicacies can be mail-ordered.

Head back to Tenth Street and walk west past Theater for the New City's spectacular air-brushed mural featuring pop-culture superstar icons such as Jimi Hendrix and Marilyn Monroe. TNC's building, actually fronting First Avenue, was originally a New Deal market constructed in the WPA-style during the Depression. In the 1930s, residents could get fresh vegetables, fruit, and other staples trucked in daily from farms outside the city. Today, Theater for the New City offers daring, experimental performances in their permanent home. During the summer, the creative director of Theater for

East Tenth Street mural, Theater for the New City

St. Mark's steeple

Petrus Stuyvesant, St. Mark's Church-in-the-Bowery

the New City, Crystal Field, produces a politically oriented, anti-establishment street theater performed in parks in all the five boroughs of New York City, always saving Washington Square Park as their last stop. Call 212-254-1109 for information. The brownstone tenement buildings on the north side of Tenth Street, at 213, 215, and 217, are decorated with terra-cotta gargoyles, Medusa-head pediments, crouching satyrs, and lions and reclining angels. The same arresting mythological figures festoon the building at 206, across the street.

Cross Second Avenue to St. Marks Square (a triangle), in front of historic St. Mark's in the Bowery, the second-oldest church in Manhattan (after old Trinity), built of fieldstone between 1795 and 1799, on the site of a garden chapel belonging to Peter Stuyvesant, the fourth director of New Netherland of Curaçao and the Dutch West Indies. "Peg Leg Pete," as he came to be known (for his wooden appendage), bought land in 1651 and created Stuyvesant Street, which runs west from Second Avenue to Third Avenue (then the Bowery Road). The uniform facades of 25 to 35 Stuyvesant Street, stretching around to 128–114 East Tenth Street, earned the "Renwick Triangle" (as it is called after James Renwick, who is regarded as the builder) historic landmark status. They were built in the Italianate style in the 1860s. The church itself, with a portico added in the 1840s and a new steeple after a fire in the 1980s, stands atop the interred remains of Peter Stuyvesant, and his bronze bust can be found in the East Graveyard. The West Graveyard, heavily shaded under ancient trees, is covered with meticulously placed New York City cobblestones. St. Mark's Church is a neighborhood creative and cultural center, and it has always been in the vanguard with poetry readings and theater productions as well as musical and dance events. Theater Genesis was headquartered here in the sixties, home base of playwright Sam Shepard and performance artist Patti Smith, who quit their jobs as busboy and waitress at the Village Gate to put on shows from 1964 through 1969. Handsome Gary Cooper lookalike Sam wanted to be a rock star but instead became a Pulitzer Prize–winning playwright cum movie-star instead.

Sam Shepard

From cobblestoned St. Marks Square, you can wander across the Avenue to the Second Avenue Deli, which is another landmark and tradition in the East Village. Pastrami sandwiches, chicken soup, and gefilte fish have been served up here for almost half a century. A new place on the southwest corner of Second Avenue and Tenth Street (159 Second Avenue), across from St. Marks Square called Rectangles (authentic Yemenite and Israeli cuisine), serves an Israeli lunch special until 5 P.M. consisting of shakshuka with an Israeli salad, mlawach, kibbeh, couscous, stuffed cabbage, and broiled filet of Nile perch. The prices are reasonable and the drinks include Turkish and Yemenite coffee, malt beer, Kaliber, and Middle Eastern pastries. If you are starved, you can eat up a storm at one of these East Village emporiums and contemplate this zigzag walkathon!

Allen Ginsberg, East Village poet-laureate and fixture

My Sister Eileen—The Story of Two Girls Who Lived at 14 Gay Street

The saga of My Sister Eileen *began at 14 Gay Street (located on one of the shortest blocks in the city, which connects Christopher Street to Waverly Place), where a writer named Ruth McKenney had a basement apartment with her sister Eileen, an aspiring actress. The original* My Sister Eileen *stories were first published at regular intervals in the influential* New Yorker *magazine. These were so popular that by 1938 a book version of the work was published. On December 26, 1940,* My Sister Eileen *opened on Broadway as a comedy starring Shirley Booth as Ruth McKenney and JoAnn Sayers as Eileen. A movie version of the play was made in 1942, starring Rosalind Russell as older sister Ruth and Janet Blair as Eileen. Brian Aherne played the romantic male lead. The movie was remade in 1955 in technicolor starring Betty Garrett and Janet Leigh with Jack Lemmon. On February 26, 1953, Rosalind Russell repeated her movie role as Ruth in* Wonderful Town, *the Broadway musical version of the story with music by Leonard Bernstein, lyrics by Betty Comden and Adolph Green, and directed by George Abbott. It was then that all hell broke loose. The opening night of this brilliant show at the Winter Garden roused the audience and critics alike to a fever pitch of excitement and thunderous applause that had not occurred on the Great White Way since the original* Guys and Dolls *blew into town.*

Gay Street—the basement apartment in the first white house was the residence of Ruth McKenney and her beloved sister Eileen

*Rosalind Russell, 1942. She played Ruth in
the movie* My Sister Eileen, *and played
Ruth again in 1953 in* Wonderful Town,
the Broadway musical.

*The story of two sisters from Ohio living in 1935 in a New
York apartment where the walls shook from blasts from a subway
tunnel under construction, and their zany adventures with
neighbors, Village crazies, artists, and a group of Brazilian
naval cadets, will always be an image of life in the Village for as
long as there is a Greenwich Village. The opening song from
Wonderful Town, entitled "Christopher Street," extolls the lives
of the "interesting people" who live there—poets, actors, writers,
artists, all searching for self-expression in the cradle of Bohemia.
Wonderful Town was made into a television special, again starring Rosalind Russell, in 1958. A tragic ending of the real story
occurred just four days prior to the opening of the original
Broadway play: Ruth McKenney's kid sister, Eileen, and her new
husband, the novelist Nathanael West, both died in a car crash
in California.*

*Among the "interesting people" who still live on Christopher
Street is glamorous Helen Rogers, who moved onto the block in
1941. Helen played the role of Ruth in Chicago and other cities
in the national touring company of* My Sister Eileen. *She remembers meeting author Ruth McKenney and found her charming and also "interesting."*

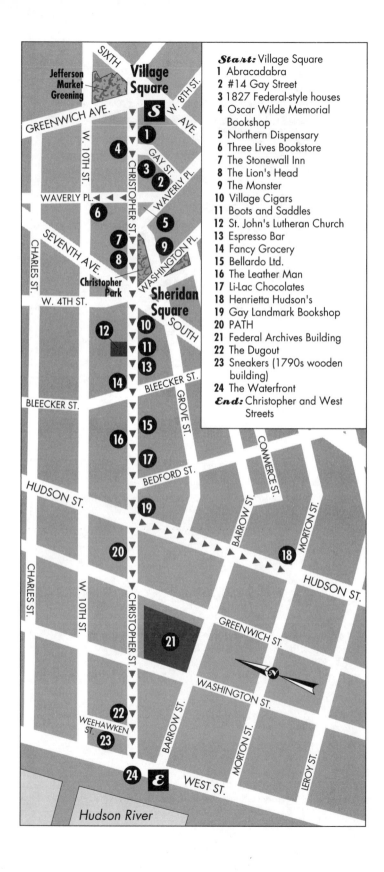

Start: Village Square
1 Abracadabra
2 #14 Gay Street
3 1827 Federal-style houses
4 Oscar Wilde Memorial Bookshop
5 Northern Dispensary
6 Three Lives Bookstore
7 The Stonewall Inn
8 The Lion's Head
9 The Monster
10 Village Cigars
11 Boots and Saddles
12 St. John's Lutheran Church
13 Espresso Bar
14 Fancy Grocery
15 Bellardo Ltd.
16 The Leather Man
17 Li-Lac Chocolates
18 Henrietta Hudson's
19 Gay Landmark Bookshop
20 PATH
21 Federal Archives Building
22 The Dugout
23 Sneakers (1790s wooden building)
24 The Waterfront
End: Christopher and West Streets

Such Interesting People Live on Christopher Street—Highlighting the Gayest Street in Town

Standing like a stone wall, Christopher
Street divides us more North from South
Running West to end

With the river continuous Christopher Street
To me the wind ascends across it
One way, surviving its latex rebellion

—John Reid Currie,
Christopher Street resident
and New York poet

*I*n 1664, the English ended Dutch rule on the island of Manhattan, and by 1696 three small villages, at Greenwich and Eighth Avenues, Vandam and Charlton Streets, and at the foot of Christopher Street (and Greenwich Avenue), were named Greenwich Village. In 1733, one of the first English settlers, a retired British Navy ádmiral named Peter Warren, bought a farm of three hundred acres, building a manor house on the block now formed by West Fourth, Bleecker, Charles, and Perry Streets. Warren returned to England to die, leaving his wife and three daughters in the care of a valued trustee. Sometime before 1811, the lane that formed the southern border of Peter Warren's farm was named after his trustee, a Mr. Christopher. Before the English, and—earlier—the Dutch, Christopher Street was an old Sapokanican Indian trail.

In the twentieth century—1960 to be exact—Elizabeth Taylor won an Academy Award for Best Actress for her role in *Butterfield 8*. In one scene she is seen jumping out of a cab and entering the sixteen-story brick apartment building (constructed in 1931) on the corner of Greenwich Avenue and Christopher Street. In the movie, Miss Taylor plays an expensive call girl visiting her mother, played by Mildred Dunnock, in her apartment at 1 Christopher Street. Queen of the movies Elizabeth Taylor seems to have helped give the street royal status; nine years after she made the movie, several drag queens, some made up to look like their idol, clashed with the police at the Stonewall Inn, a gay bar on Christopher Street. Several nights of protest followed the first violent night (Friday, June 27, 1969), tweedy uptowners and others joining in the fray that came to be known as the Stonewall Riots. Christopher Street has since become the symbol of the transformation of the oppression of gays and lesbians into pride and action. Each year, New York City's gay and lesbian community commemorates the Stonewall Rebellion with a rally, march, festival, and dance. On Saturday, June 25, 1994, the cele-bration of the twenty-fifth anniversary of Stonewall began with a candlelight vigil on Christopher Street,

The Stonewall Inn on Christopher Street

honoring the heroes of the riots. The following day, the International March on the United Nations to Affirm the Human Rights of Lesbian and Gay People became the biggest human rights parade in history, drawing 1.5 million people from around the world.

START: *Christopher Street at Greenwich Avenue*

A RUBY-RED SLIPPERS "EASE ON DOWN THE ROAD" TO OZ WALK (NO WAY IS THIS KANSAS, FOLKS!)

Take your own gay, straight, or "whatever" walk! Christopher Street is a fun-time, rainbow-colored thoroughfare of dreams and it has always been known for its avant-garde specialty shops, bars, and restaurants. In the 1950s and 1960s, the street-level clothing shop Village Square (entrance on Greenwich Avenue), which sells outsize plaid and patterned "grunge" shirts, emblem-emblazoned caps, combat and worker boots, roomy pants, field vests, and carry-all backpacks, used to be called Casual Aire, regularly fitting its all-male customers just a size too tight, in the fashion of the time. The first gay watering hole you will find on the block is Pieces Bar at 8 Christo-pher Street, a glittery, light-show, disco-style environment with a de-cidedly seventies beat. Pieces features Karaoke singalongs, Monday night beer blasts, and drag acts. Gay-owned and -operated, the bar cultivates a decidedly outdated and unhip gay style, that is, square-shaved at the neck, perfect gel-stiff hairdos, and white shirts open to the waist along with black rayon pants, black loafers, and, the finish-ing touch, a gold chain necklace. Pancake makeup for men is back in style at Pieces. One of the most interesting stores on the block is Abracadabra, at 10 Christopher Street, which zaps passersby with a hideous window display of gruesome rubber head masks and mon-ster costumes, including *Friday the 13th* "Freddy" heads, John Wayne Gacy clown heads, bloody hatchet heads, skeleton faces, red devil masks, ghouls, goblins, big prop snakes, giant rats, and the like. Abracadabra sets the pace for Christopher Street in the 1990s by hosting events like the first "Rally for Friends of Pee Wee Herman" and the annual April Fool's Day Parade, which began in 1994.

Abracadabra life-size wooden Indian (a Sapokanican on the old trail) on Christopher Street

Abracadabra's windows extend around the corner onto Gay Street (between Christopher and Waverly), which is one of the oldest, and shortest, streets in the Village. Originally home to the servants of the well-to-do folk on Washington Square, Gay Street was later inhabited with tinkers, carpenters, bricklayers, and other working-class people. The little Federal row houses on the west side of the street are almost as picturesque as the row of Greek Revivals on the east side. The house at 12 Gay Street was owned in the 1950s by Frank Parris, creator of Howdy Doody, and before that, in the Roaring Twenties, Mayor Jimmy Walker maintained the building for his mistress, Betty Compson, dividing his time between there and his official residence on St. Luke's Place, where he lived with his wife. This house is reported to be haunted by several ghosts. The house at 14 Gay Street was built in 1828 for a plough manufacturer named Curtis Hitchcock and was occupied in the 1930s for a time by Ruth McKenney and her younger sister, Eileen. Ruth wrote a well-known, popular account of their lives in Greenwich Village called *My Sister Eileen.*

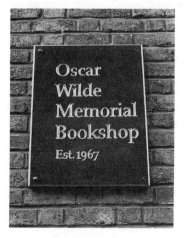

The high, sloping gambrel roofs and Flemish bond brickwork at 18 and 20 Christopher Street bring the past alive for time travelers. These unaltered two-and-a-half-story Federal buildings from 1827 have had quaint wooden shopfronts added, and today at Rumbul's

Coffee and Dessert Shop, you can sit in back and look down into the
courtyard garden where Ruth McKenney derived some of her inspiration for *My Sister Eileen*. Sharing the sense of history, and keeping
Village ghost stories circulating, are proprietors you will meet in the
shops At Home and Matt McGee. At 15, the small, intimate, and in-
formative Oscar Wilde Memorial Bookshop has been selling gay literature and guides, magazines, T-shirts, and gay-power–gay-pride
buttons since 1967. Three Lives bookstore is just one block north (at
Waverly and Tenth).

Heading west toward the Hudson River, cross Waverly Place. To
the left is the Northern Dispensary, situated in a triangular island and
surrounded by four streets, two of them Waverly Place (which splits
around the building), Grove Street, and Christopher Street (which is
called Stonewall Place between Waverly and Seventh Avenue). The
handsome Northern Dispensary was erected in 1831 as a clinic and
health-care provider for neighborhood poor. One of its most frequent
visitors was Edgar Allan Poe, who lived nearby. Later, the building
became a dental clinic servicing Greenwich Village. At 45 Christopher you can stock up on gay theme greeting cards at Greetings! Several doors to the west, at 53 Christopher Street, is the site of the 1969
Battle of Stonewall. The Stonewall Inn, a Village mecca, has a steady
flow of regulars and tourists all week—and don't forget to check the
brass plaque on the front of the building. Live jazz is performed regularly at the old 55 Bar, which serves stiff highballs and has a great
jazz jukebox as well. The Lion's Head at 59 Christopher has been
around since the sixties, and over the years has become an unofficial
headquarters for legions of writers and performers, many of whose
book jackets decorate the walls of this engaging, low-ceilinged cellar
bar and restaurant owned by 100 percent Irish-American Mike Reardon. Pete Hamill, Jimmy Breslin, Norman Mailer, Mike McAlary,
Vincent Patrick (*Pope of Greenwich Village* and *Family Business*),
Lanford Wilson, Rod Steiger (who lives across the street), and others
all wrestle with their muses (or method-acting problems), sitting on
stools under the carved lionhead above the bar, or in the dining room
while eating hamburgers and gobbling up french fries or other Lion's
Head specialties. Actress Jessica Lange is an alumna of the Lion's
Head, having been a waitress there before she had her first starring
role in the remake of *King Kong*.

The Duplex, at 61 Christopher, includes a street-level and sec-
ond-story bar as well as a full cabaret arena. The building, com-
manding a prominent view of Sheridan Square, was constructed in
the 1980s under Greenwich Village Historic District guidelines on
the site of a previous building from 1922, which was demolished after its long-term occupant, the Village Voice, moved to a new location
on Thirteenth Street. The Voice is now ensconced in offices on

George Segal sculpture, Christopher Park

Cooper Square. Rick Panson is the proprietor of the legendary Duplex Cabaret and Piano Bar and, in addition to presenting a constant parade of entertainers, he sells bumper stickers, compact mirrors, key tags, zipper pulls, bolo slides, tie tacks, money clips, charms, necklaces, T-shirts, belt buckles, and boxer shorts with the club's logo imprinted on everything in his souvenir shop. Regular performers include Michael Henderson and pianist Jay Bradley.

Cross over into Christopher Park for a look at George Segal's ghostlike statues of a lesbian couple sitting on a bench and a gay male couple standing and seemingly conversing. Toward the narrow end of the park is the aged bronze statue of Civil War general Philip Sheridan, after whom the square is named. Across the park at 80 Grove Street, the Monster pulsates with energy every night of the week, with a downstairs dance floor featuring disco music, two bars, a cabaret, and a singing piano player who is usually wearing a feathered *chapeau*. There's something gay here for everybody and the five-dollar Friday and Saturday night cover doesn't deter lines from forming up the block at that flash-point eleven o'clock hour. The real-life brethren of the white-bronze statues are constantly clicking away with

Christopher Street at Sheridan Square (main thoroughfare, Seventh Avenue South)

*Looking east on Bleecker
from Christopher Street*

*Fancy Grocery Store at
Christopher and Bleecker,
84 Christopher Street
(with awnings) on right*

their Kodaks, so be sure to bring your own camera along; and then cross Seventh Avenue to pause in front of another world-famous tourist mecca—tiny Village Cigars, formerly known as United Cigars. Here tourists bend over to examine a tiny cracked triangular mosaic embedded in the sidewalk, whose inscription reads: "Property of the Hess Estate Which Has Never Been Dedicated for Public Purpose." No one knows what it means, but everybody and his brother has some harebrained explanation for this sidewalk anachronism.

There's a bar, an espresso cafe, several shops, two grocery stores, a billiard parlor, and a church on the short but busy stretch of Christopher Street between Seventh Avenue South and Bleecker. There's an upbeat airiness on this crowded block, an aura of excitement and of subversive subculture sensuality. Many here wear tight shorts, no bras, leather pants, and torn jeans. Outrageous, skimpy sex outfits on dummies displayed in the windows of World Clothing (75 Christopher Street) can be purchased for the next Gay Pride Day parade or for an any-day Christopher Street walk; glad rags at this shop are the latest from Sauvage, Diesel, Male Power, Dolce & Gabbana, Gianni Versace, House of Field, and Cabana Joe. Fat Cat Billiards, in the basement next door, attracts a mix of fun-loving, gay macho and straight macho players, most of them Gen-X'ers. Boots and Saddles, a cowboy-chaps type of bar whose customers sometimes jokingly call it

"Bras and Girdles," hails back to post-Prohibition days before legislation outlawed a drinking establishment on the same block with a house of worship. From the 1920s through the 1960s, the place was known as George Herdt's, a hangout for Village down-and-out types and confirmed alcoholics, and was known for its tasty tap ales and porter. Local residents still drop in to hear the great CDs on the truck-shaped jukebox and to reminisce about the good old days when the place packed them in on weekdays and nights and not just on weekends and special holidays. A framed songsheet of Gene Autry's signature song, "Take Me Back to My Boots and Saddle," is the theme of this funky corral bar complete with an inside hitching post.

Street and sidewalk traffic come to a halt when the cast of *Tony and Tina's Wedding* marches up the steps of St. John's Lutheran Church for a mock Archie Bunker–type "wedding" ceremony that has been playing to appreciative and participatory crowds for over eight years. After the wedding, the actors parade across Sheridan Square in full makeup and red tulle bridesmaid getups for a champagne toast and a sit-down baked ziti dinner complete with cake at Gus' Place at 149 Waverly Place. Gus' Place is run by Gus Theodoro, who opens the French windows of his restaurant and bar in good weather, providing a perfect setting to enjoy a Mediterranean dinner and a glass of wine. Gus used to work at a legendary Village Italian restaurant called Emilio's on Sixth Avenue (now a McKay's Drugstore), which, like his own place, had a congenial bar, excellent food, and an informal, relaxed atmosphere. The *Tony and Tina* theater actors march by Sheridan Square often, dragging their entire audience with them, joining the crowds on Christopher Street; and they also don't mind including everybody else in their wedding "event."

An ideal spot for watching the real passing parade on Christopher Street is the Espresso Bar at 82 Christopher, an attractive new place that serves cake and cappuccino. To the left of the Espresso Bar, also at 82 Christopher Street, is the trendy My Optics, where you can get cool shades to guard against high-noon and sunset glare. Drop in and ask owner Tim Fabozzi's advice—he'll recommend what glasses suit your particular face, from wire-rims and tortoise-shell frames to 1920s round frames and aviator-style frames. Tim runs three other My Optics at 42 St. Marks Place, 247 Third Avenue, and 96 Seventh Avenue.

Reminders of an earlier day on the block are the two houses at 84 and 86, which both preserve features of the Federal and Greek Revival styles. Painter Vincent Canadé lived at 86 in the 1930s. In the 1960s, actress Sally Kirkland practiced the Stanislavski method in her rear apartment at 84. Visitors to Sally's salon included Shelley Winters,

Robert De Niro, Bob Dylan, Keir Dullea, and Rip Torn, some of whom rehearsed scenes to present to Lee Strasberg at the Actor's Studio. Zal Yanofsky, a member of the Lovin' Spoonful, lived on the second-floor rear at 84 with his Canadian actress girlfriend Jackie Burrows. And the film actress Lisa Pelikan, who appeared in *Julia* and other films, lived in the second-floor front before going to Hollywood. The four-unit apartment buildings on the north side of the street, 85, 87, 89, and 91, surmounted by an arched pediment above a projecting cornice at 89 that reads "Gessner—1872," help keep an old-time atmosphere on the block and shelter St. John's Church (1821) on the right and the tiny building to its left, one of the oldest in the Village. Erected sometime between 1802 and 1808, this two-story structure at the corner of Christopher and Bleecker Streets has always had a grocery store at street level, first owned by one William Patterson. Today it is run by Hercules Dimitrious, a neighborhood fixture since 1969, supplying locals and tourists with rare imported and domestic beers and ales and other edibles and thirst quenchers. Actress Glenn Close, in rehearsal for her role as the psychotic stalker in *Fatal Attraction*, accidentally left her script at Hercules's store while practicing her obsessive look on Villagers. After he returned it, a picture of Close and Hercules appeared in the *New York Post*, which is proudly displayed in the window alongside all the neon beer signs. Hercules, who likes to sing and play his guitar in the store, leaves fresh fruits, vegetables, and nuts to the two Korean all-night stores, one at Christopher and Bleecker, and one at Christopher and Bedford. Both stores maintain year-round outdoor flower and fruit stands. Before continuing down Christopher Street, drift into the Loft, a spacious, all-white-and-mirrored store at 89, where you can gather up all the latest gay literature and special club invites. Try on an axe-wielding Joan Crawford T-shirt that reads "Don't Fuck with Me, Fellas—This Ain't My First Time in the Boardroom," or a jewel-studded Carmen Miranda T-shirt. Or choose from a selection of tropical cruise-wear, from skimpy bathing trunks and satin jockstraps to brand-new rayon Hawaiian shirts and gay umbrellas. The Loft is considered a "must visit" for those planning their wardrobe for summer Fire Island vacations or winter sojourns to the Cayman Islands.

Across Bleecker Street is a sixteen-story yellow-and-white brick apartment building unmistakably Art Deco in design that features wide horizontal band courses between the windows and contrasting shallow verticals rising to the top. This handsome building was constructed in the Depression year 1931. Across Christopher at 92 and 94, two well-proportioned Italianate-style buildings retain the original ornamental cast-iron window railings. The stores at street level were in the original plans for these buildings. Number 98 is a six-story apartment house constructed in 1856 with progressively smaller floors at each level. It is generally regarded as the first apartment house in the Village. If you need a Victorian-style glass paperweight, an ornate clock, an exquisite goblet, or a decorative mirrored picture frame with a picture of Errol Flynn in it, Paul Bellardo or his manager, Thomas Parker, of Bellardo, Ltd., at 100 Christopher Street, are on hand to help you make a selection. Hand-blown glass objects, beautiful and individually made American crafts, Tiffany reproductions of lamps, and signed original jewelry are also sold here. Bellardo's dazzling seasonal window displays are award winners, and the store attracts visitors and celebrities from all over the world. Ruby Keeler, Alice Faye, Kim Novak, and Kaye Ballard (Paul's cousin) have all shopped here at one time or another, and Liz Taylor bought a set of lavender goblets from Bellardo when she was appearing on Broadway in *The Little Foxes*.

There is plenty to choose from in the clothing emporia on this shopper's block, from the Village Army and Navy at the corner of Christopher and Bleecker, which offers all the latest in jeans and sweats, socks, and Jockey or Calvin Klein underwear, boots, sneakers, and jackets, to Streetwise (113 Christopher), which carries Scotch-plaid mini-skirts for men, gay Ken dolls (with skirts), dogtag necklaces, special "cleanup" towels, leather jackets, rainbow-colored socks, handcuffs, bathing suits, red AIDS ribbon-jewelry, New Age–Rainbow Coalition crystals, stomper work boots, fancy cigarette lighters, "Bitch" and "Slut" T-shirts, and baseball caps with "Gay Pride" and other insignia. The Leather Man, at 111 Christopher Street, will completely cover you in plain or studded black leather, from undergarments to stormtrooper

boots, zippered face masks, and Lash LaRue–style whips for about three thousand dollars (for a total leather ensemble). Chrome-studded leather belts and other spiky accessories can be bought at this emporium of sadomasochism that has been on the block supplying customers with dog collars and other accoutrements for over thirty years. When you leave, you will be ready to play out your favorite fantasy at the Lure, the Spike,

Thomas Parker (left) and Paul Bellardo in front of their shop

or the Eagle. Don't Panic at 98 has a gay and lesbian

mail-order catalog and stocks a significant selection of T-shirts sporting such slogans as "It's OK! To Be Gay!," "We Grease to Please," and "I Can't Even Think Straight!" They also carry a special line of very good T-shirts called "Queertoons," which satirize the Sunday funnies with a gay slant, gay-specific and Rainbow Coalition jewelry, gay coffee mugs, and other gay paraphernalia.

Stick, Stone and Bone, at 111 Christopher, is an excellent artifact store featuring Native American jewelry and assessories. McNulty's Tea and Coffee Co., at 109, has been a

The Leather Man on Christopher Street

Village landmark since 1895 and features gourmet coffees of the world from Tanzanian Kilimanjaro and Yemen Mocha Mattari to Sumatra Mandehling and Hawaiian Kona as well as flavored, decaffeinated, and special house-blend coffees. McNulty's owner, David Wong, also proudly offers black, oolong, green, and his own special tea blends from China as well as herbal and decaffeinated teas. Li-Lac Chocolates at 120 Christopher has been a Christopher Street tradition since 1923, when the doors of this candy store opened. Li-Lac makes chocolate daily on the premises and uses only the finest ingredients. Dark chocolate–covered marshmallow bars or raspberry jelly bars are a real taste treat and excellent for a quick-energy pickup. Though they haven't produced a chocolate Washington Square Arch yet, Li-Lac specializes in hand-molded solid chocolate replicas of the Empire State Building in milk, dark, or white chocolate ($28.50) and a Statue of Liberty ($17.50). At Thanksgiving they make gigantic chocolate turkey sculptures, and at Christmas it is a large-size Santa that fills the small shop window here. Li-Lac has a handy shipping form for sending these home-style chocolates to friends or loved ones back home. The Candle Shop at 118 Christopher sells the widest and wildest variety of sculpted wax candles in the neighborhood, including hand-dipped candles and all types of special holders, candle chandeliers, and candle globes.

The Lucille Lortel Theater at 121 Christopher Street was converted from a movie house (which itself was converted from two three-story brick houses and a rear stable built in 1868) in the 1930s when it became an off-Broadway house called the Theater de

Lys. The stars appearing here during its twenty-five-year history include Dame Sybil Thorndike, Richard Burton, Kim Stanley, and Alfred Ryder. Kurt Weill's *Threepenny Opera* premiered here and ran for eight years with Weill's wife, Lotte Lenya, in the lead role. Bernadette Peters got her start off-Broadway (after originating off-off Broadway at the Caffe Cino in the same musical) in *Dames at Sea* at the Theater de Lys. Larry Kramer's *The Destiny of Me*, about the author's struggles with AIDS politics and his own gay identity, had a successful run here, as did drag star Charles Busch in *The Red Scare*.

The perennial happy-hour scene (till 4 A.M.) on Christopher Street is enlivened by two bars, one across the street from the other. Ty's is an old standby that draws a crowd who like to wear lumberjack workboots, plaid shirts, and worn jeans. Ty's (at 114 Christopher) has special Tony, Grammy, and Academy Award television parties and other special events. The Hanger at 115 Christopher is a new gay bar that includes heavy cruising, sleaze performances, and skin flicks, and features a go-go man performing at ten-thirty every Friday night. The Hangar attracts a muscle-toned light leather crowd and their professional admirers; both bars are perfect for just sitting in the window to watch the goings-on on Christopher Street while sipping a Bloody Mary or a bone-dry martini. You can order a Virgin Mary or a pineapple tutti-frutti—pineapple juice, cranberry juice, club soda, an orange wedge, and a maraschino cherry with a mini paper umbrella on the side—if you are off the sauce. The latter nonalcoholic drink is also called a Shirley Temple or a Davy Crockett, and the bartenders here will not flinch or mince when you order one of these concoctions.

You don't have to buy a gay sex magazine, a porn video, or a dildo to take a peek at the giant exploding, pink neon penis inside the front door of the Gay Landmark Bookshop on the corner of Christopher and Hudson Streets. Across Hudson Street the terrain changes; St. Luke's School and playground are on the south side of Christopher Street between Hudson and Greenwich Streets. The three-story Federal brick at 133 Christopher on the north side of the street is unusual for its width, the result of an 1850s alteration that incorporated what was once an alley. The original building dates from 1819. In the middle of this block is the Hudson Terminal powerhouse, the Christopher Street entrance to the Port Authority Trans-Hudson (PATH) Tubes that takes commuters to Hoboken, Jersey City, and points south and west in New Jersey as far as Penn Station in Newark. The largest building in the Village is a massive and monumental red-brick eleven-story Romanesque Revival structure bounded by Christopher, Barrow, and Washington, with an entrance at 666 Greenwich Street; it is a converted luxury apartment complex with 479 units. Its previous incarnation was as a repository for federal

Lamp mecca at Uplift Lighting on Hudson Street (just north of Christopher)

archives and at one time part of it was a Village post office. The 1899 building provides 54,000 square feet of low-rent space to community groups, including Senior Action in a Gay Environment (SAGE), and houses a gay theater company called Wings and an art gallery called White Columns. A D'Agostino supermarket occupies part of the ground floor of the building at Greenwich Street and Barrow.

The imposing red-brick St. Veronica's Roman Catholic Church at 153 Christopher Street (constructed in 1900) originally served the spiritual needs of the many longshoremen who worked on the Hudson River docks. Today, it offers infrequent masses and is host to a variety of twelve-step programs for Villagers and visitors alike in its spacious basement hall called the Meeting Place. The presence of Two Potato on the corner of Greenwich and Christopher is another leftover from pre-Prohibition days before legislation outlawed taverns on the same block as churches. Two Potato has a blaring rap, disco, and soul jukebox, male strippers on Wednesdays and Sundays, and a midnight drag show on Saturdays. At 159 Christopher, at the corner of Washington Street, Caffe Passione serves elegantly prepared food and delicious coffee in a corner spot once occupied by an eccentric, picturesque coffee shop called the Silver Dollar that catered to a mix of drag queens, transsexuals, hustlers and their johns, as well as neighborhood people. Photography exhibitions also help to give the Caffe Passione a lot more class than its looney-tunes predecessor. Kitty-corner across Washington Street and Christopher, another location brings back fond memories to old-time Villagers such as novelist Marguerite Young. On this site, before the Mitchell-Lama housing (known as West Village Houses) was constructed in the late 1960s, the Market Diner, in an authentic railroad dining car, served cornbread, eggs, beef hash, ten-cent coffee, and glasses of buttermilk to neighborhood regulars up and down Washington Street. Cheap meals like lamb shank and American meatloaf were served with mounds of fresh mashed potatoes, canned creamed corn, peas, or string beans, not to mention piles of fresh white bread.

The next gay hot spot on Christopher is the Dugout at 185 Christopher (on the corner of Weehawken Street), which often has live rock and country bands and two-step dancing. Special Dugout events include Saturday underwear parties—check your pants after midnight for a free shot of whiskey—a "Hump Day" revue, nonstop sports events on cable TV, and a Sunday brunch followed by a disco beerblast. The Dugout clientele, including bike boys, muscle men, and other tough-looking guys and goons, spill out onto Christopher and Weehawken Streets in the spring, summer, and fall for an all-weekend party bash. Weehawken Street (named after a town on the New Jersey side of the Hudson River) is the shortest block in all of New York and in the middle of the block is a building that is regarded as the oldest wood-frame structure in the Village, dating from about 1790. Occupying this historic building is Sneakers, a gay neighborhood hangout, entered at 392 West Street around the corner. Pairs of sneakers hang from the ceiling, which not only gives the bar its name but is also meant to discourage the S&M crowd.

The Neutral Zone, at 162 Christopher Street, is a social center for lesbian, bisexual, and transgender youth of fourteen to twenty-one years of age and their friends. Open late with a fruit-juice and soda bar, lounge areas, billiard-ball tables, and live entertainment, the Neutral Zone won't let you join in the fun if you're over twenty-five. Their focused outreach program, headquartered at Our Lady of Pompeii

West Street between Christopher and West Tenth Street

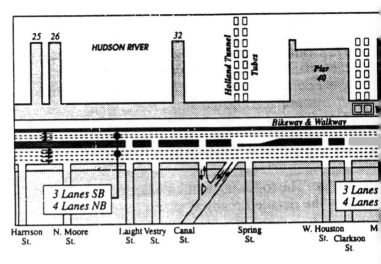

Church at 37 Carmine Street, embraces social-service providers who have established themselves in the gay community and who have historically assisted the often-elusive, "at-risk" population drawn from the Christopher Street/West Street crossroads. The Neutral Zone, dedicated to empowering youth and promoting personal responsibility, is a substance-free, violence-free haven for young people who need relief from the mean streets. It is sponsored by the Greenwich Village Youth Council.

The Bailey House occupies a building at the corner of Christopher and West Streets, which was once the upscale Christopher Street Hotel. Bailey House is now a residence for AIDS-afflicted men and women. The adventurous often trek one block south of Christopher on West Street (at Barrow) to the old Keller Bar in search of a "men-of-all-color" gay bar experience. The Keller is noted for its black disco, soul, and rap stereo jukebox, which is always played at top volume.

"The West Coast of Greenwich Village" is a name sometimes ascribed to the historic Hudson River waterfront, its great crumbling seawalls and the decaying platforms of its once-mighty piers a sad reminder of the bustling port it was in the past. Large liners and foreign naval vessels from Russia and Scandinavia were set to docks here. Greenwich Village's latest battle is between those who want to create a waterfront park, preserving access, views, and sunlight for Village residents, and the ever-greedy real-estate developers and politicians who want to build luxury, high-rise buildings that would limit access and block the river views and sea breezes. The Bedford-Barrow-Commerce Block Association, the Christopher Street Block and Merchants Association, and the West Village Committee, among

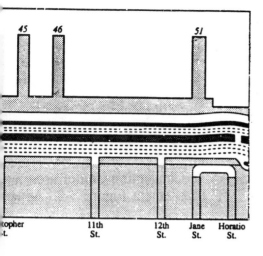

Proposed reconstruction project for Hudson River waterfront, courtesy of the Federation to Preserve the Greenwich Village Waterfront and Great Port

other civic and community groups, have all joined forces with the Federation to Preserve the Greenwich Village Waterfront and Great Port to wage this ongoing fight. Time alone will tell which faction will win this real-estate-developers vs. the natural-rights-of-the-citizens battle.

During the annual Gay Pride Day parade and the Christopher Street carnival, which are held on the Saturday closest to the June 26 anniversary of the Stonewall Riots, traffic is closed on Christo-

pher Street and West Street in this area, and the piers are opened up for disco parties and fireworks displays commemorating gay liberation. Thousands attend each year and there are many gay-information booths set up by gay bars, restaurants, and coalition groups from Asbury Park, New Jersey; New Hope, Pennsylvania; and other gay resort locations in the tri-state region. This is a day that celebrates what Greenwich Village is all about—the freedom to be what and who you are, without discrimination.

Carmen Miranda chapeau at the Gay Pride Parade on Christopher Street

The Battle of Stonewall

The Stonewall Inn, located at 51 Christopher Street, first opened its doors in the Depression year of 1930, having been converted from two hundred-year-old stables. Utilized for several decades as a hall for private parties, business banquets, and wedding celebrations, in the decade of the sixties it became a tawdry gay bar frequented by preppie types and drag queens alike. A call-boy service sometimes operated on the second floor. On the evening of June 28, 1969, it became the improbable site of the Battle of Stonewall during a police raid of the place.

Robert Bryan, a men's fashion magazine editor, was there that night and remembers policemen being driven back by angry drag queens tired of being intimidated and oppressed by John Law. A prominent "soldier" in the melee was Black Marsha (a.k.a. Marsha P. Johnson or Malcolm Michaels), a black drag queen and panhandling Christopher Street personality for over twenty years who, later, on July 6, 1992, was fished out of the Hudson River, having been murdered and thrown in by hoodlums.

Bryan vividly recalls the police grabbing people from behind and hitting them with clubs during the fray. He himself kicked an officer in the rear end. Before long, drag queens and others surrounded the police, trapping them inside the building. Rioters threw stones they picked up in Christopher Park, hurling them at the windows of the bar. Some threw in garbage cans and trash bins. Another group tried to set fire to the Stonewall. Today Bryan expresses amazement that the police never fired a shot at anyone. He was chased down the street by a policeman, but got away while others were rounded up and led into a paddy wagon.

On the second night of Stonewall, Bryan returned to the scene to see a lineup of what he describes as "trash queens" who formed a chorus line on one end of Christopher Street opposite the Stonewall, kicking their legs "like the Rockettes" and singing:

> *We're the Stonewall girls.*
> *We wear our hair in curls.*
> *We don't wear underwear. . . .*

Riot-squad police in helmets on the other side of the street confronted the chorus line, and with a loudspeaker called for the "Rockettes" and boys in bell-bottom trousers to disperse. A crowd of Stonewall-ites marched toward the police line, stopped, and

Black Marsha, the hero of the Battle of Stonewall and the saint of Christopher Street

both groups stared at each other in a tense confrontation. Eventually, things subsided with none of the violence of the night before, although Bryan remembers firecrackers being thrown onto the street from a rooftop.

Nothing appeared in the daily New York papers about this gay Bunker Hill–like riot, though the Village Voice did write about it the next week. Bryan says that at the time many gays were angered by the Village Voice, known as a liberal paper, which used terms such as "queens" and "queers." What was oddest to Bryan was that many of the preppie-type gays who usually hung out at Julius on Tenth Street, dressed in black-and-orange Princeton ties, khaki chino pants, blue blazers, white socks, and penny loafers, tended to side with the police during the battle. "The Stonewall was definitely not macho-gay, but these queens certainly could not be called 'fairies' that night," Bryan recalls. Police harassment of gay bars was nothing new in the Village, but on this particular night the "queers," "fairies," "faggots," "drags," and "dykes" fought back, smashing bottles and making a ruckus, turning the Stonewall into a battleground for freedom. In the sixties many had come to the Village, as they had in previous decades, to escape the oppression they felt everywhere else. Standing and watching the scene, many Villagers at the time felt it was just another gay bar raid. Today the Battle of Stonewall, which was led by the late Black Marsha, the drag queen patron "Saint of Christopher Street," is symbolic of the quest for gay freedom and gay identity that celebrated its twenty-fifth anniversary in 1994. The fiftieth anniversary, in the year 2019, promises to be a real bash.

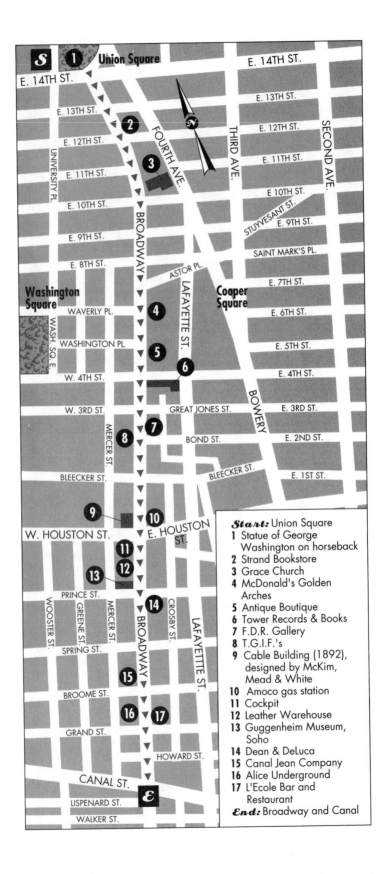

Start: Union Square
1 Statue of George Washington on horseback
2 Strand Bookstore
3 Grace Church
4 McDonald's Golden Arches
5 Antique Boutique
6 Tower Records & Books
7 F.D.R. Gallery
8 T.G.I.F.'s
9 Cable Building (1892), designed by McKim, Mead & White
10 Amoco gas station
11 Cockpit
12 Leather Warehouse
13 Guggenheim Museum, Soho
14 Dean & DeLuca
15 Canal Jean Company
16 Alice Underground
17 L'Ecole Bar and Restaurant
End: Broadway and Canal

Broadway—The Ultimate Shopping Mall—from Union Square to Canal

Before Upper Broadway was cut through the East and West Village, through a neighborhood now largely composed of cast-iron, stone, and brick industrial loft buildings erected at the turn of the century, the Bowery, set out in 1629, was the main north-south route of travel and commerce in the area. In recent years, the section of Broadway between Eighth Street and Houston was informally called NoHo (north of Houston). The stretch of Broadway south of Houston to Canal forms the eastern border of the historic SoHo Cast Iron District, which gained landmark status in 1971 from the New York City Landmarks Preservation Commission. Union Square, outside the Village, bounded on the east by Fourth Avenue, Broadway on the west, and Seventeenth and Fourteenth Streets, was originally developed to connect Broadway to the Bowery, a plan that never happened. The square, now a grassy, stepped-up park, was originally laid out in 1831. Union Square has always been noted for the commercial enterprises surrounding it. The Fourteenth Street area around the square was the center of live theater in the late nineteenth century and early 1900s, where star actors like matinee idol James O'Neill, father of playwright Eugene O'Neill, performed in plays like *The Count of Monte Cristo*, a part he eventually felt trapped in. (His discontent is the subject of O'Neill's masterful family drama, *Long Day's Journey into Night*.) Vaudeville houses featured George M. Cohen, Nora Bayes, Harry Lauter, and others in the 1890s. During this period, the square established itself as an arena for citizens' protests and daily heated arguments over political ideologies of one kind or another, which earned it the sobriquet "Soap Box Square." In the Depression era, from 1933, the worst year after the Crash for unemployment, through 1938, there were weekly demonstrations organized by Socialist and Communist groups, and many Village artists and radicals living on the edge joined in the fray. Twelve labor and political groups had offices on the square in the Great Depression, and often violent clashes ensued there. S.-Klein-on-the-Square, on Fourth Avenue, was a famous discount bargain-hunter's department store until it was demolished in 1984 in favor of the Zeckendorf high-rise apartment towers. May's Department Store occupied a block-long site on Fourteenth Street, south of the square, until it closed in the 1980s. Hearn's and Ohrbach's also had mercantile emporia on the square. Luchow's Restaurant was an old-style favorite place to dine on Fourteenth Street for decades before moving uptown to Broadway, where it eventually closed. The buildings of Union Square that were declared historic landmarks by the late 1980s include the Century, Union, and Everett buildings as well as the Guardian Life Insurance and the Bank of Metropolis buildings. There are several very trendy "in"-spot restaurants, bars, and coffee shops to the west of the square on the corner of Sixteenth Street. On Wednesdays, Fridays, and Saturdays, the square hosts probably the best outdoor farmer's market in the city. Fresh produce, cut flowers, homemade breads, and home-style jams, preserves, pickles, and relishes are brought in from New Jersey, Pennsylvania, and upstate New York farms. The farmers are interesting to talk with, and you can even take home a freshly killed pheasant or wild turkey for Thanksgiving or Christmas. All spring, summer, fall, and winter the festive Union Square Greenmarket draws crowds from all over the Village and other neighborhoods, with some vendors serving hot apple cider, fresh doughnuts, and Pennsylvania Dutch pretzels.

START: *Union Square at Fourteenth Street and Broadway*

Ultimately, Union Square leads us to the south, to what is sometimes referred to as Lower Broadway but which now more often than not is just called Broadway. Uptown Broadway is famous for its legitimate theaters, department stores, and the neon world of Times Square. The eastside subway stop is on Union Square and this is our starting point as we head from the square across Fourteenth Street and down Broadway into the Village and SoHo districts.

The Strand bookstore at 828 Broadway is a book browser's paradise, chock-full of used books, antiquarian books, and brand-new bestsellers mixed in with outsized art and coffee-table pop-culture books sold outside and inside. This is a floor-to-ceiling setup and there is also a full basement where books are categorized and distributed to their appropriate shelf areas, book stalls, and tables. It's easy to find what you are looking for at the Strand. An information desk tells you where you want to go and helps you find what you are seeking. The Strand will also search for that book you have been unable to find anywhere else. At the northwest corner of Broadway and Thirteenth Street is Forbidden Planet, the very best place to find old comics and reprints of comic and cartoon-related magazines and books, with a very extensive selection and a full basement. You will find sci-fi, horror, detective, mystery, and adventure, and meet favorite characters (in print) such as Captain America, Captain Marvel, Wonder Woman, Hawkman, Batman. Mickey Mouse, Donald Duck, Woody Woodpecker, Bugs Bunny, as well as "Zap" characters and those creatures found in Weirdo comics. Window displays often feature collectibles and arrangements that are meant to bemuse and amuse. A well-thought-out funky place.

As you head south down Broadway, the street of a million dreams, past Eleventh Street are rows of oddity import/export antique shops featuring curios, statuary, furnishings, giant vases, mirrors, and paintings on view in window displays. On Tenth Street and Broadway is one of New York's most distinguished landmarks, Grace Church. This magnificent Gothic structure was built in 1846 and in the mid-nineteenth century became the fashionable church of New York society. Designed by James Renwick, Jr., later the architect for St. Patrick's Cathedral on Fifth Avenue, the church is considered the finest example of Gothic Revival in the United States. It has been designated a landmark by the New York City Landmarks Preservation Commission and is a Department of the Interior National Historic Landmark as well. Of note in the churchyard fronting Broadway is a large, ancient urn said to be as old as Christianity.

Cross Ninth Street and the busy intersection of Eighth Street, famous for its souvenir shops, shoe emporiums, and fast-food eateries. You will encounter some of the same types of commercial enterprises as you "bugaloo down Broadway." The stretch of Broadway just below Eighth Street juxtaposes the Wiz next to a Deco-style McDonald's (on Broadway at Waverly Place), a Foot Locker, a Kay-Bee (noted for toys and stuffed teddy bears), with a number of outfitters selling urban-guerilla sports outfits created more for in-fashion rap streetwear or disco-strutting than for jogging or sports. At this point you have entered the ultimate outdoor-indoor shopping mall and, as some have called it, a shopaholic's delight. If you are a compulsive buyer, bring along plenty of cash and/or credit cards; but please, watch your wallet or handbag and do not wear a gold chain around your neck on this trip. It is also advisable to wear comfortable shoes, sneakers, or loafers as opposed to platform or spiked heels. Take time to look up at the decorative cast-iron and Medusa-head pedimentia of the nineteenth-century buildings that were originally small manufacturing lofts or sewing factories. The floor-to-ceiling windows allowed more light for workers in the days before Edison. If you look straight ahead downtown, you will see the Woolworth Building, New York's first skyscraper, constructed in 1913, and if you turn and look uptown, you can spot the great Art Deco Chrysler Building (built in 1930), which for several decades prior to the construction of the Empire State Building was New York City's and the world's tallest skyscraper. Now all have been dwarfed by the boxy, squared-off twin towers of the World Trade Center at the tip of Manhattan, the second tallest building in the U.S., after the Sears Tower in Chicago.

Some of the former office buildings on the west side of Broadway proceeding downtown are now owned by New York University, sprawling west to Washington Square and south to Houston. A very fine bookstore is Shakespeare & Co. Booksellers at 716 Broadway, where you will find a good selection of literary and academic books as well as current bestsellers in an intimate, friendly ambience.

If you are hungry and in need of a pit stop, try Bayamo on the east side of Broadway (704), several doors north of Fourth Street. Bayamo is a Cuban-Chinese restaurant and bar with a tropical-theme interior. Pina coladas and lemon-lime or strawberry daquiris are the fancy drinks at the bar. Try a Scorpion or a Bahama Mama to cool yourself down. Miami-style Cuban cooking includes various combinations of shrimp, chicken, or pork with yellow rice, black beans, and plantains. One customer describes the bill of fare at this atmospheric joint as "Chino-Latino-Cubano" with a bit of "Texano and Mehicano" thrown in for good measure.

The Antique Boutique is "the Largest and Best Vintage Clothing Store in the World," according to a sign outside. The big store at 712 Broadway (at Washington Place) is generously stocked with vintage and "new-old" Hawaiian shirts, baseball jackets, formal-wear tuxedo jackets for men, and crinoline and net pale-pink and baby-blue 1950s prom dresses for the girls, proof that "everything old is new again." The place for buying CDs, tapes, and videos is block-long Tower Records (692 Broadway at Fourth Street). Get the latest in rock, folk, jazz, dance-band, vintage 1920s through the 1980s. Andy's Chee-Pees Antique Clothing at 691 Broadway is another very reasonably priced outlet for the retro look, including 1940s Jantzen reindeer sweaters, geometric-patterned 1950s Ricky Nelson sweaters, old leather flyer's jackets, used dungarees, 1920s flapper dresses, embroidered Chinese silk robes, zoot suits, blue-suede Elvis shoes, and broad 1940s ties or skinny 1950s ties. Andy's has another, smaller store at 16 West Eighth Street (between Fifth Avenue and MacDougal).

The parking lot next door to Tower Records on Broadway between Fourth Street and Third Street is an open-air flea market on Saturdays and Sundays in good weather, where oldies-but-goldies, antiques, pop-culture oddities, and everything else under the sun (including the kitchen sink) is brought out to sell at good prices by dealers and pickers who turn over the "merch" and don't mind bargaining. Winter, summer, autumn, and spring they're there, but if it rains or snows, pickings will be slim. Pamela's Cafe across the street at 683 Broadway (corner of Third Street) is a nice luncheonette with outdoor tables in good weather. Cappuccino, espresso, and good chow can be found at Pamela's; Pamela herself reports that she has "been around for a good while." If you are in the mood to look at art, there is the F.D.R. Gallery at 670 Broadway. On a good day you might get to go to an opening, where you can usually find free drinks and snacks. Across the avenue is the restored facade of the Broadway Central Hotel, which was constructed in 1870. In 1973, the central part of the building collapsed after a gas explosion but was rebuilt (with an entrance on Bleecker Street) as an apartment complex. T.G.I. Friday's (at Broadway and Bond Street) is a swinging singles and family-style hangout. You can get just about everything here in this big, old-time bar/restaurant. From nachos to the perennial buffalo wings to Cajun fried chicken to Caesar salad to char-broiled one-half-pound hamburgers—an American hodgepodge mix-and-mess menu. Friday's also has a special kiddies' menu.

A more intimate restaurant is V-G's at 643 Broadway (at Bleecker Street). Don't phone for reservations, just come in. No one answers telephones here. For over ten years, the sparkling, unassuming V-G restaurant has been serving fresh, home-style cooking, and also features a small bar. A whole fresh turkey is cooked each day (no compressed turkey roll here) as well as roast chicken, beef stews, vegetarian combo plates, beef barbeque, sandwiches (the tuna-melt is excellent), and burgers (but not the frozen-patty variety). V-G's is a good place to go after or before a flick at the Angelika Film Center on Houston Street (just around the corner) with a date or friend. The bar is friendly and you can order a Bloody Mary at the bar with or without vodka. Hours are from 8 A.M. to 2 A.M. weekdays, and on Fridays and Saturdays until 4 A.M.

As you walk toward Houston Street, check the distinguished Cable Building at 611 Broadway, and be sure to take in the architectural detail on this fine building. The Cable Building was built in 1892 and designed by McKim, Mead and White. It houses office space and small businesses including a gym, a hair salon, and the Angelika Film Center, which contains six cinemas showing new American, foreign, and experimental films (entrance is on Mercer at Houston, around the corner). To the east, across the street from the Cable Building, is the amazing Amoco gas station, a beacon of jazzy, flashing electric light that resembles the glitzy nighttime glow of the Times Square light show on Broadway, forty blocks uptown. Here, you can fill up your car, enter a huge car-wash machine for a thorough cleaning, and park. If you drove in from New Jersey or Long Island, this is a good place to park the buggy (for twenty-four hours or longer) while you shop Broadway or visit other neighborhoods in the Village. This gas station complex seems like a circus (which it is when the cabbies start screaming and yelling), so join the parade and yell louder! This is an integral part of the New York scene.

Across Houston Street at 595 Broadway (between Houston and Prince) is the Cockpit, a store described as "an aviation experience." The small Cockpit chain has stores in Beverly Hills and Seattle. Here is the finest in reproduction leather jackets made to the exact specifications as those worn by military units of the Army, Navy, and Air Force during World War II. The Cockpit is almost a military museum; its walls and ceilings are filled with wartime memorabilia like original hand-painted jackets, canteens, flags, insignia, and the like. An actual airplane fuselage has its side panels painted with Nose Art, and you will find books on Air Force and aviation themes here. Special commemorative T-shirts and sweatshirts of "Remember Pearl Harbor," "D-Day," or "V.E. Day" or "V.J. Day" are available as are goggles, watches, insignia patches, Zippo cigarette lighters, and other military bric-a-brac. The Air Force jackets are not cheap, but there are after-Christmas or summertime sales to clear out last year's line. "Clothing Made from Heroes and Legends," at the Cockpit (595 Broadway—11 A.M. to 7 P.M., Sundays 12:30 P.M. to 6 P.M.), with its line of Avirex Ltd. clothing, is definitely worth a look.

The Leather Warehouse (589 Broadway) is just a few doors down from the Cockpit, and on the same side of the street. This warehouse-sized store has everything in leather including lightweight bike jackets, motorcycle jackets covered in chromium studs, handbags, carry-all bags, vests, pants, and all the trimmings. This store is a leather fetishist's dream come true, but don't look for sex toys or leather underwear here. After all, this block has seven buildings housing forty-five art galleries, fifteen at 560 Broadway alone, and it is known the world over for art, not leather. The New Museum of Contemporary Art, established in 1973 at 583 Broadway, with its giant "Silence=Death" neon, is open Wednesday, Thursday, and Friday from 12 M. to 6 P.M., Saturday from 12 M. to 8 P.M. This gallery-exhibition space has several mixed-media shows yearly, often featuring artists such as Keith Haring, Jeff Koons, and John Cage. Just down the block is the Museum for African Art at 593 Broadway. The Guggenheim Museum SoHo, designed by Arata Isozaki and located in a nineteenth-century brick building at 575 Broadway (at Prince), is one of the newest additions to Gallery Row. The SoHo Guggenheim, which is the downtown branch of the uptown Guggenheim (designed by Frank Lloyd Wright) at 1071 Fifth Avenue at Eighty-eighth Street, offers a special two-day ten-dollar pass that allows you to visit both museums. Single admission to the SoHo Guggenheim is five dollars and is free for children under twelve (if accompanied by an adult). SoHo Guggenheim is open Sunday, Monday, and Wednesday from 11 A.M. to 6 P.M., Thursday and Saturday from 11 A.M. to 10 P.M. It's closed New Year's, Christmas, and Thanksgiving. One of the SoHo museum's first shows in 1993 was "Four Rooms and a House Ball: Pop and the Everyday Object," a presentation of approximately thirty works drawn from the Guggenheim's holdings featuring artists Jim Dine, Jasper Johns, Roy Lichtenstein, Claes Oldenburg and Coosje van Bruggen, Robert Rauschenberg, James Rosenquist, George Segal, and Andy Warhol. The SoHo Guggenheim Shop (street level, corner of Prince and

Broadway) is a great attraction with its Roy Lichtenstein T-shirts, Claes Oldenburg "hamburger" pillows, pop-art calendars, jewelry, oddball arty furniture reproductions, and other art repro souvenirs. You can also buy postcards of Guggenheim artworks to send to the folks back home, and there is an extensive art book selection as well. The N and R subway stop is right here at Prince and Broadway.

On the opposite corner from the SoHo Guggenheim Shop is the famous Dean & DeLuca gourmet grocery store (560 Broadway) with its incredible array of artfully displayed vegetables and fruit, a full bakery, and every other kind of fancy produce and products like Kona coffee, home-style jams, hams, ready-to-take-home-to-eat dishes, plus all the best in kitchenware for the preparation and serving of your own at-home exquisite meal.

At the front of the store are stand-up tables (or you can sit on a stool with your shopping bags and look out the window), where you can drink a cup of coffee with a croissant, pastry, roll, or fancy sandwich. This food emporium is designed as a feast for the connoisseur's eyes, and you can't leave the place without buying something, be it Gorgonzola, Bundnerfleisch, a tin of Russian caviar, or a bunch of giant radishes from New Zealand. Across Broadway at 565 is the Nature Company, which offers another kind of environment to customers. Here you can buy anything you might need for an outing in the woods, including the appropriate outerwear, bird-watching telescopes, and other field-study equipment. Walking down Broadway toward Canal Street, you will encounter any number of stores that will attract the inveterate shopper, novice, or window shopper. Here are some of the most interesting:

Retail Shoe Outlet, 537 Broadway, guarantees to find whatever you are looking for in footwear at low prices.

The Broadway Panhandler, 520 Broadway, sells everything in pots, pans, cookware, bakeware, cutlery, and utensils, including a good selection of coffee pots, whistling tea kettles, and large coffee urns.

K. Trimming Company, 519 Broadway, helps you find antique or rare buttons you need for a set; they also sell new buttons, buckles, sewing notions and trim, needles, thread, yarn, and anything else you need for sewing.

SoHo Lighting, 513 Broadway, fills the bill in lighting needs including electronic appliances, lamps, and every variety of light bulb for almost any type of fixture. The world of lighting has come a long way from Edison and Mazda; and it is all to be found here at fair prices.

Canal Jean Company, 501 Broadway, is a famous major outlet-type store featuring, at rock-bottom prices, everything in outerwear including Lee, Wrangler, Levi, and other name-brand jeans, antique coats and jackets, scarves, gloves, Army T-shirts, field jackets, urban-guerrilla wear, sports outfits, and Army and Texas boots. A great store, and most items are, as one clerk put it, "real cheap."

Shopper's Paradise, 503 Broadway, specializes in low-cost towels, pillowcases, sheets, linens, curtains, and bedspreads.

The Soho Mill Outlet and the Broadway M F R S Supply Corporation are a row of shops at 488, 490, and 492 Broadway that sell fabrics, cottons, rayon, silk, for all uses, be it the making of dresses or pillowcases and drapes.

SoHo Futon, 491 Broadway at Broome, offers futons in any size at below-market cost.

Inter-Coastal Textiles, 480 Broadway, is another fabric shop in what is known as the Fabric District.

A special and unique store is Alice Underground, 481 Broadway, between Broome and Grand, filled with original retro clothing, including World War II uniforms, high school football or basketball jackets in wool or satin, western shirts, 1950s rock 'n' roll shirts and jackets, antique socks with original labels, Deco scarves, "geographic" kerchiefs with "Florida" or "Atlantic City" printed across them. Everything in rags may be found at this funky, fun place, be it a crushed-velvet 1920s gown, floral-patterned 1940s draperies, or a chenille bedspread with images of cowboys, broncos, boots, or steers on them.

A. Feisigs & Sons Paper Boxes Corporation, at 472 Broadway, has an impressive old-style neon sign. Here, you can assemble the best in creative packaging, and you can buy attractive boxes for storage or for use as a gift package.

Additional textile shops down the street are Clairex at 473 Broadway; Danco at 475 Broadway; the Broadway Linen Center (wholesale/retail) at 470 Broadway; Mark J. Fischer, at 466 and 468 Broadway (at Grand Street).

New York City's premier downtown outdoor market, featuring antiques, collectibles, and memorabilia, is held every Saturday and Sunday, from 9 A.M. to 5 P.M., in the empty parking lots at Broadway and Grand Street. Weather permitting, this market is bustling every weekend morning and is usually busier during the spring and fall.

One of the best places to dine in all of Manhattan is L'Ecole Bar and Restaurant at 462 Broadway at the corner of Grand Street. You may dine at this adjunct of the French Culinary Institute at modest cost and sample the very best in French cuisine, be it venison stew with chestnuts, mushrooms and berries, or a duck confit and lamb shank with white beans. The dining area is a large room in shades of tan, beige, and cocoa, and the atmosphere is intimate and friendly.

Another very enjoyable spot for dining and drinking is Amsterdam's Grand Bar & Rotisserie at 454 Broadway. The owner, Tony Neile, has kept the place busy at lunch- and dinnertime for over ten years. The fare is American, with offerings such as grilled pork loin sandwich, Amsterdam burger, spaghetti, and fried calamari. Prices are modest and the food rates high. A long bar attracts SoHo artists, and the large, loftlike space has an old-fashioned, Bohemian atmosphere. The art on the walls is by local artists and is for sale. Each month there is a new art exhibition where free champagne is offered. Amsterdam's is unpretentious, friendly, and has the feel of an old-time bar. A great place to hang out, eat, and be merry with the arty crowd.

Other outlet stores on Broadway include Dukane Upholstery Fabrics at 451 Broadway, Hymo Textile Corporation at 444 Broadway, and Broadway Sneakers at 430 Broadway (at Howard Street), a huge athletic shoe and sneaker outlet.

Once you hit Canal Street, turn left into humming Chinatown to sample the Orient's culinary delights. In the last two decades, New York's Chinatown, the largest settlement of Chinese outside China, has grown by leaps and bounds, now encompassing an area from Lafayette Street on the west, Grand Street on the north, the Bowery (and beyond) to Thomas Paine Street and Chatham Square (and beyond). The best streets in Chinatown for dozens of restaurants are Mulberry, Mott, and Elizabeth. There's an excellent Chinese coffee shop on Bayard Street, between Mott and Elizabeth, that boasts the best almond cookies in the world, the strongest coffee, and the rudest customers and waiters. Or you can turn left, cross Lafayette, Centre Street, Baxter Street, and turn left again on Mulberry Street into Little Italy with its cappuccino emporia, fancy food stores, and restaurants.

If you want to continue your shop-till-you-drop tour, or connect with the Sixth Avenue bus line or the Seventh Avenue IRT subway, turn right onto Canal Street at Broadway and stroll west. You can always get the most goods for the least amount of money at stores such as Pearl Paint, Canal Hardware, Canal Audio, and several wonderful, filled-to-the-brim industrial and novelty plastics stores. Canal Street is a mecca for office supplies, nuts and bolts for almost any machine on earth, typewriters, adding machines, computers, lightbulbs, shoes, plumbing supplies, file cabinets, bookshelves, electronic equipment including home telephone answering machines, television sets, CD players and tape player sets, and just about anything else, including military paraphernalia, that you will need for your home or apartment. All of this is set in a wondrous, zany, outdoor/indoor street-bazaar atmosphere that is a bargain hunter's dream of junk, what-nots, and gewgaws. Canal Street shopping, like shopping on Broadway, is a daytime affair with most stores ready to close before dark.

Previous page: A-2 horsehide-leather "Flying Tigers" United States Air Force bomber's jacket from Avirex Ltd., the Cockpit

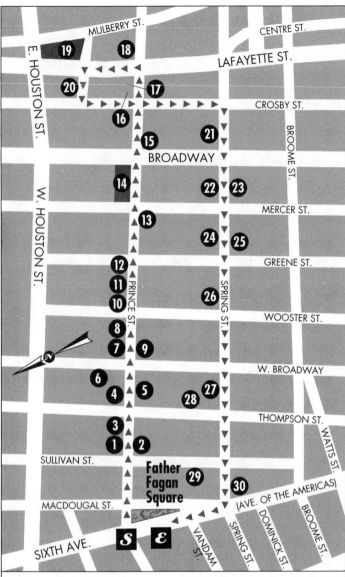

MULBERRY ST.   CENTRE ST.
E. HOUSTON ST.   LAFAYETTE ST.
19   **18**
20   **17**   CROSBY ST.
16
15   **21**   BROOME ST.
BROADWAY
14   **22**   **23**
MERCER ST.
13   **24**   **25**
12   GREENE ST.
11
10   **26**   SPRING ST.   WOOSTER ST.
8
7   **9**   W. BROADWAY
N
6
4   **5**   **28**   **27**
THOMPSON ST.   WATTS ST.
3
1   **2**
SULLIVAN ST.   **Father Fagan Square**   **29**
30   (AVE. OF THE AMERICAS)
MACDOUGAL ST.   VANDAM ST.   SPRING ST.   DOMINICK ST.   BROOME ST.
W. HOUSTON ST.   PRINCE ST.   SPRING ST.
SIXTH AVE.   **S** **E**

Start: Father Fagan Square
1 Mood Indigo
2 Ward-Nasse Gallery
3 Franciscan Friars offices
4 Caffe Borgia II
5 Vesuvio Bakery
6 Rizzoli's Bookstore
7 19th-century "vault cover" (glass sidewalk)
8 Louis K. Meisel Gallery
9 Harriet Love
10 Leslie-Lohman Gay Art Foundation
11 Dean & DeLuca (cafe)
12 Replay
13 Fanelli's Cafe
14 Guggenheim Museum, Soho

15 Dean & DeLuca (gourmet foods)
16 Paula Rubenstein (antiques)
17 Second-Hand Rose
18 Lost City Arts
19 Puck Building
20 Keith Haring's Pop Shop
21 New York Open Center
22 New Republic Clothing
23 Illustration House
24 Spring Street Market
25 Peter Roberts Antiques
26 E. Buk Antiques
27 Spring Street Books and Magazines
28 Palma
29 Melampo Imported Foods
30 Soho Fish and Chips
End: Father Fagan Square

Sidetrip to SoHo

I'd rather walk through the iron-front streets of Soho than up on Park
Avenue between the Bauhaus skyscrapers.
— E. L. Doctorow, *The New York Times*, April 10, 1994

For over a hundred years, the area south of Greenwich Village, now known as SoHo, was the hub of Manhattan's light manufacturing, an area of industrial buildings, cobblestoned streets, and scattered brownstones and tenements. By the late 1950s, the manufacturers were going out of business or moving out of the city. In 1959, a government commission declared the area "a slum," so empty of business were its once jam-packed buildings and bustling streets. Artists had been living and working in large lofts in the area since the 1940s, and by the late 1960s, when these often-illegal spaces were legally offered to artists who could prove that they were legit artists, several thousand applied. The A.I.R. (Artist in Residence) loft was born and it spurred a real-estate boom unabated to this day. In 1971, the twenty-six-square-block area known as SoHo (South of Houston), bounded by Sixth Avenue on the west, Broadway on the east, Houston on the north, and Canal Street on the south, containing over five hundred nineteenth-century cast-iron buildings, was given landmark status by the New York City Landmarks Preservation Commission. The SoHo Cast Iron District became a prime location for luxurious, spacious living. Uptown galleries began moving into the neighborhood, expanding their floor and exhibition space several times over and offering more adventurous and accessible art. The district attracted such hordes of art-loving crowds that eventually other companies opened large and attractive street-level outlets, and trendy restaurants and cafes soon followed.

This out-of-the-Village, side-trip walking tour crosses the "Valley of SoHo," over Prince Street, past West Broadway (SoHo's center) and Broadway, out of SoHo briefly to Lafayette Street, then back again, across Spring west to Sixth Avenue. In between, and all around, the streets of SoHo are teeming with galleries, museums, performance spaces, shops, and restaurants. Choose a side trip of your own and walk down a cobblestoned street to see what SoHo wonders you will find.

START: *Father Fagan Square, Prince Street and Sixth Avenue*

Father Fagan Square is a triangle like so many of the "squares" in the Village, with several benches and a pleasant canopy of trees. The uptown Sixth Avenue bus stop is here and the Spring Street subway station is just a block south. MacDougal Street enters the square from the north and one of the dozens of fine (and expensive) restaurants in SoHo, Restaurant Provence, is just up the block. For simpler fare, try Souen, a natural food restaurant across the street at 210 Sixth Avenue. A bowl of miso soup or a beansprout salad might be enough to start you off on your walking tour. Take a look at the succulent garden in the window of the building on the northeast corner of Prince Street. Green all year round, the astounding hanging plants growing in the window of this private house are for viewing only. Heading east on Prince and crossing Sullivan Street, look left (north) and right (south) to see the nineteenth-century brick tenement buildings in the area, actually the far western outposts of Little Italy. Setting the SoHo tone is the clubby Cub Room (131 Sullivan) and Raoul's Restaurant (180 Prince)—ask to sit at Raoul's famed celebrity booth in the back.

Mood Indigo, at 181 Prince Street, owned and operated by Diane Petipas, is one of the SoHo pioneer shops selling twentieth-century artifacts. Diane's selection of Bakelite jewelry and knickknacks is unequaled and her display of colorful Fiesta and Russell Wright dishware is astonishing in its variety. Decalcomania glassware, "streamliner" chrome toasters from the 1940s and 1950s, cocktail shakers and trays, and 1939–40 New York World's Fair compacts, tie tacks, ashtrays, and other souvenirs fill this sparkling store to the brim.

The Ward-Nasse Gallery, a nonprofit alternative space at 178 Prince Street, is the first of many art galleries on this route, many of which are on the upper levels of the six- and seven-story buildings. Keep your eyes open for gallery signs and walk up the stairs (or take an elevator) for an inside look at the art. The Provincial Offices of the Franciscan Friars is headquartered on the corner of Prince and Thompson, lending the neighborhood a sense of serenity and protection. Caffe Borgia II at 161 Prince Street (Borgia I is at the corner of Bleecker and MacDougal in the Village) has outdoor tables for street-watching while sipping a cappuccino and munching on a cannoli. Across Prince at 160, the historic Vesuvio, a wholesale and retail bakery selling biscuits and bread, is run by second-generation Italian-American Anthony Dapolito, and he hasn't altered the store since it was founded in 1920.

Alex Streeter has been making his unique, handcrafted jewelry at 152 Prince for almost twenty-five years, though his shop looks brand-new next to Vesuvio. Stop and examine the one-of-a-kind gold and silver ornaments from this SoHo pioneer and craftsman, who also makes jewelry to order. A tremendous selection of art postcards are available at Untitled—Fine Art in Print, at 159 Prince Street, a narrow shop that also carries greeting cards (not the Hallmark kind) and a fine selection of art books and monographs.

As you cross West Broadway, you can see to the north for one block and to the south all the way to Canal Street. West Broadway is the center of SoHo, a wide street filled with galleries, clothing shops, crafts emporia, boutique and antique shops, elegant wine bars, restaurants, and upscale coffee shops. The Rizzoli bookstore has an excellent two-story SoHo location on the west side of Broadway between Houston and Prince, as well as a gift shop next door. Continuing east on Prince, stop to admire a unique piece of SoHo's past, now enjoying historic landmark status at 141 Prince Street—a nineteenth-century vault cover, one of the last of the illuminated sidewalks in the country. Patented in 1845 and built to allow sunlight into the basement, this metal-and-circular-glass, stepped-up sidewalk device is best viewed at night when lit from below. Louis K. Meisel Gallery at the top of this sidewalk at 141 Prince always has large-scale art shows in progress. Susan P. Meisel at 133 Prince Street, next door, has a permanent collection of Clarice Cliff pottery displayed in her window and sells a variety of unusual twentieth-century antiques, ranging from handmade airplane models of wood and metal to 1950s Schwinn bicycles, unique folk-art pieces and attractive groupings of popular Art Deco furniture and accessories. James Danziger, Jose Freire Fine Art, and a number of other galleries are located in one building at 130 Prince.

Harriet Love (126 Prince Street) is the grand doyenne of the antique clothes business in New York, as well as a SoHo and Village pi-

The Moondance Diner on the edge of SoHo on Sixth Avenue and Grand Street

oneer, originally offering in her Thirteenth Street shop Victorian linen underwear, gowns, and other delicate summer clothing. She opened on West Broadway in a tiny shop and sold exquisite little suits from the 1940s to people like Meryl Streep and Catherine Deneuve. Recently she moved to Prince, where she sells, in addition to selected vintage dresses, gowns, suits, blouses, scarfs, and other accessories, a small selection of fine men's clothing and a complete line of new apparel in the retro style. In the vintage department everything is in perfect condition, ready to wear out into the streets of SoHo or an evening out at a Village night spot.

The Leslie Lohman Gay Art Foundation at 127 Prince Street exhibits group and individual shows of gay, often erotic, art in its below-street-level gallery. Dean & DeLuca has a tile-floored European-style coffee shop at 121 Prince Street, with a spacious and airy room in the rear. Stop for a cappuccino break and read a copy of *Le Figaro* or *The New York Times*, and eavesdrop on the money-minded real-estate, art, or literary conversations all around. A small charcuterie across the street, Olive's, at 120 Prince, offers delicious homemade takeout sandwiches and freshly made soups to go. Whole Foods at 119 Prince Street is a natural foods supermarket that is one of the pioneers in organic foods, supplying bulk beans, flour, sugar, vitamins, natural remedies, whole-grain natural breads, juices, vegetables, and coffee to artists living in the area who are sometimes on tight budgets. This is a supermarket with a neighborhood ambience. The big Tweety Bird cartoon character in the window at Too Cute (113 Prince) stands over ten feet tall, and along with equally enormous figures of Sylvester, Betty Boop, Donald Duck, and Mickey Mouse adds color to this shop, which sells casual clothing emblazoned with your favorite Looney Tune, Merry Melodie, or Silly Symphony character. Pick out a tie featuring Yosemite Sam, undershorts with Disney mice running all over them, or a shirt or a pair of jeans with Olive Oyl and Popeye embroidered on the pockets. Replay, at 109 Prince Street, is a two-story clothing emporium that employs pop-culture collectibles as a backdrop for selected vintage and new retro-style items. There is even a room fully stocked with Depression-era dishware as well as a 1920s soda fountain where you can get a cappuccino or croissant. The shop features special memorabilia exhibitions and displays collections such as World War II military knives and Zippo lighters with advertising motifs.

Old Fanelli's Cafe at 94 Prince Street has been at the same location and largely unchanged since 1872. Fanelli's is one of the places open late in SoHo, and during happy hour it's jammed with young business types drinking beer and munching barfood, acting just like Bohemians, if only for the evening. Behind the etched glass door is a mahogany bar with the sign "Ladies and Gents Sitting Room." Tables with red-and-white checkered tablecloths line one wall in the main room, under vintage framed pictures of famous fighters such as Rocky Marciano and Joe Louis, all inscribed to Mike Fanelli, the proprietor for over fifty years. Food, served in the back room, is good and filling, modestly priced in keeping with a place that served artists beer and pasta when there was no other place to eat in the area. Zoe's, a very upscale restaurant up the block toward Broadway at 90 Prince Street, usually features a three-hundred-dollar floral arrangement in the window. Inside, a wood-burning grill, rotisserie, and large ovens cook the delicious food. Main plates include black pepper fettucine with roasted mushrooms, swiss chard, bacon, and shaved goat cheese at $17.50; grilled twelve-ounce Angus ribeye steak with red wine hunter sauce and oak barrel baked potato with truffle butter is $25. Appetizers include pepper-seared tuna carpaccio with a crisp salad of pea shoots, cabbage, radish, and a miso vinaigrette for $11.50 or butternut squash and corn chowder with spicy shrimp dumplings for $7. The minimum here is $20 per person, so make your reservation and dress to the hilt.

The Guggenheim Museum SoHo at 575 Broadway (at Prince) tripled its museum space with its new quarters, opened in 1992 in a landmark, nineteenth-century red-brick industrial building with a cast-iron storefront and detailed cornice. The street-level gift shop, designed by Arata Isozaki (who also designed the new museum and a tea room downstairs called Club Oi), features reproductions from the museum's holdings and an extensive selection of art books and artists' monographs. Artists represented in SoHo Guggenheim's first downtown show included the pop-art greats such as Jim Dine, Jasper Johns, Roy Lichtenstein, Claes Oldenburg, Robert Rauschenberg,

SoHo art by Roy Lichtenstein

James Rosenquist, George Segal, Coosje van Bruggen, and Andy Warhol.

Dean & DeLuca is the supermarket of the gourmet foodshops in New York, and its main store on the southeast corner of Prince and Broadway stretches a full block. The front vegetable and fruit department is loaded with giant mangos from the Philippines, hand-picked raspberries from Oregon's Cascade Mountains, giant California artichokes, and an infinite variety of lettuces. Gourmet coffees can be purchased right out of the shipping bag across a tiled aisle from a display of tempting and rich cakes, tortes, and chocolate truffles; roasted on the premises are capons, chickens, turkeys, beef, pickled pork, and fine pasta salads all prepared for takeout. You can stock up on Italian salamis and cheeses or gourmet mustards and vinegar, prepared specialty jams and jellies, and imported crackers and cookies, as well as a choice of fresh jumbo shrimp, octopus, or giant scallops. The store also stocks the latest in pots and pans and has a choice selection of gourmet cookbooks.

Past Broadway on Prince, being careful as you cross, look north, where you can see the Chrysler Building uptown on Forty-second Street, and then look south where you can see the Woolworth Building in lower Manhattan. The eastern section of Prince Street, actually out of the Cast Iron District, takes you to a number of fascinating and unique antique shops, mostly located in a one-block area on Lafayette Street, two blocks east of Broadway. Paula Rubenstein at 65 Prince Street (between Crosby and Lafayette) displays along one wall a selection of quilts, bedcoverings, 1930s cotton-duck pillows, and 1930s and 1940s floral drapery and furniture fabrics while the rest of the high-ceilinged, square shop is artfully cluttered with antique Cowboyana and one-of-a-kind folk and pop-culture items. Large, colorful 1930s mixing-bowl sets are displayed with rare Mexicana Harlequin dish sets featuring cups, bowls, and teapots. The giant corner store (270 Lafayette), Second Hand Rose, is an important source for distinctive and far-out pièces-de-résistance for decorators and connoisseurs featuring elaborate chandeliers, large-scale 1930s, 1940s, and 1950s designer furniture ensembles, giant framed mirrors, and vintage linoleum in Art Deco patterns. Don't ask Suzanne, the glamorous proprietor, for her Hopalong Cassidy linoleum; it's her last roll and she's saving it for posterity. She'll give you a fair price for her matching lounge chairs and sofa from the ocean liner *Normandie*, offering a full background and history of the Deco set. Second Hand Rose will ship its huge vanity sets or iron grillework anywhere.

James Elkind, of Lost City Arts across the street at 275 Lafayette, has an enormous collection of pop-culture artifacts from an actual Coney Island bumber car (expensive) to a giant, red-enameled neon metal sign of the Mobil Gas Company's flying Pegasus, Mr. Elkind's

favorite icon (also expensive). Lost City Arts also carries small treasures such as 1939 World's Fair memorabilia and other fun collectibles from the Depression era, at reasonable prices. Cynthia
Beneduce and Brian Windsor, at 281 Lafayette Street, exhibit a flair
with selected folk art pieces, and Urban Archaeology at 285 Lafayette
Street, a salvaging company with an eye for the unique, will sell you
anything from a massive Medusa-head pediment to the revolving
doors of the demolished Biltmore Hotel.

Continue north on Lafayette Street, cross tiny Jersey Street, an alley, and take in the magnificent Puck Building at 295 Lafayette (between Jersey Street and Houston), built in 1885 by Albert Wagner for
the Ottman Lithographic Company. The magazine *Puck* was printed
here from 1887 to 1916. Now a commercial building with gallery
and exhibition space and two ballrooms for special events, it was restored in 1983 by Peter, Paul and Puck, Ltd. Cross to the west side of
Lafayette and visit the Pop Shop (Lafayette at Jersey Street), covered
entirely in Keith Haring's distinctive comic pop-art-style drawings.
Inside you can buy Harings's jumpy designs on anything from pin-
back buttons, posters, and T-shirts to backpacks, umbrellas, hats,
jackets, radios, and much more.

Walk west along Jersey Street one block and turn left on Crosby
Street. Crosby is still an undeveloped back street, its west side lined
with the freight entrances of the cast-iron industrial buildings facing
Broadway; the east side features warehouses and empty lots used for
parking. The Flynn Gallery is located at 113 Crosby Street, Foster
Peet Gallery at 62 Crosby Street, and A.I.R. Gallery at 63 Crosby
Street (the latter two just below Spring). Turn right on Spring, heading west for a return swing through SoHo. The first stop is 83 Spring
Street, between Crosby and Broadway, at the New York Open Center,
which is a prototype of the urban holistic learning center, this one
with a worldwide reputation. Walter Beebe, the founder, expresses
the Center's point of view in a brochure: "Encompass the inner,
outer, intellectual and physical aspects of life." The Center offers
workshops, lectures, and films of every kind from yoga and dance to
spiritual psychology and integrative therapy. There's a "wellness"
center on the premises as well as a fully stocked bookstore featuring
such titles as *Gloria Steinem on Self-Esteem*; *Other Lives, Other Selves*
by Roger Woolger; *The Energetics of Western Herbs* by Peter Holmes;
Getting Through the Day by Nancy Napier; and *How to Live Between
Office Visits* by Bernie Siegel. Audiotapes, videos, incense, tarot card
decks, meditation cushions, spiritual greeting cards, jewelry, and New
Age gifts are also available. Sit awhile on a couch in the lounge, enjoy
the astral music, and relax.

After a refreshing rest stop at the Open Center, continue west on
Spring, cross Broadway again, and stop in at New Republic Clothing

at 93 Spring Street, for elegant 1930s- and 1940s-style haberdashery with a flair. The selected clothing and accessories from this store turn up in all the national fashion magazines. Next door at Arizona, 91 Spring Street, you can purchase the finest Italian leatherware in cowboy style, from chaps to fancy, fringed jackets. Across the street on the seventh floor at 96 Spring Street is the Illustration House, which specializes in original illustrative art, cozily exhibited in an informal series of showrooms. You can find original drawings and cover illustrations from magazines dating back one hundred years or more. Book artists and other illustrators are represented as well. Illustration House has frequent special exhibitions featuring specific artists, and yearly house-cleaning sales, too.

The Spring Street Market at 111 Spring Street flourishes today just as it did before SoHo was discovered. The wooden floorboards lead you to a well-stocked cooler for beer and soda and the deli counterman will make you a delicious sandwich. Run by second-generation owners, its rustic old-world grocery store ambience is worth a look. Penny Whistle Toys at 132 Spring Street offers creative, safe, and unusual toys for tots, as well as children's furniture ensembles and playground equipment. The widest selection of American arts and crafts furniture in the United States is available for sale at Peter Roberts Antiques at 134 Spring Street. On the corner of Spring and Wooster is a seven-day-a-week outdoor market set up in an empty corner lot. Twenty vendors sell new items, primarily clothing, practically all year round, closing only during the most severe cold spells or when it's raining or snowing.

E. Buk Antiques is on the second floor at 151 Spring Street, just above the street-level picture window, which is carefully arranged like a miniature museum box with unusual antique items rescued from the early industrial age. Ring the bell or call for an appointment to see his old telescopes and antiquated patent machines. Spring Street Books and Magazines at 169 Spring Street carries a full line of new books and magazines, with a special emphasis on poetry and art books. At Ben's Pizza (try a slice), turn right on Thompson Street for a visit to Palma (90 Thompson Street, between Spring and Prince). Yogi, the elegant blond owner, has a background in vintage clothing and designs a classic line of skirts, slacks, and tops in different materials with mixes of prints and colors that create unique ensembles. Yogi has a penchant for the tropics and it's a treat just to sit on the 1930s bamboo, floral-print-covered couches and matching chairs or at her bamboo counter. Yogi's clothing racks include a select line of vintage men's sweaters and shirts.

Right: The Spring Street Market, a typical cast-iron building, at 111 Spring Street

Return to Spring and continue west, turning right again (for a quick side trip) to Melampo Imported Foods at 105 Sullivan Street for a made-to-order Italian sandwich that is sure to satisfy. SoHo and TriBeCa celebrities like Robert De Niro and Al Pacino come here for their afternoon nosh. The tiny Melampo also attracts Hollywood actors in town for Broadway play auditions as well as neighborhood regulars. Back on Spring, Nick and Eddie's Restaurant and Bar (203 Spring Street at the corner of Sullivan) hosts the in-crowd most evenings, hanging out at the bar or dining on the light, varied, and reasonably priced food. Nick and Eddie's is one of the old SoHo spots, a post-Prohibition tavern in business since the 1930s. SoHo Fish and Chips (204 Spring Street) is the best place for English fish and chips—you can also get takeout Japanese sushi. The Spring Street subway stop (C or E line) is on the corner of Spring and Sixth Avenue. Across Sixth Avenue, just to the right of the entrance to the large Janovic-Plaza store on the northwest corner, a plaque informs that this is the site of Richmond Hill—Washington's headquarters during the Revolution and later the home of Vice President John Adams and his wife, Abigail, when New York was the country's capital. To get back to where you started on your jaunt through SoHo, round the corner on Sixth Avenue, walk north one block, and you're there, at Father Fagan Square.

Village Stages and Screens

Theater

Village Theater Scene Off and Off-Off

The Village

In the Village in '65
15¢ tokens pizza slices
To survive
My Sister Eileen's apartment
For rent
Ceiling's too low
Looking to be alive
Somewhere to go
In the Village in '95
> *—Steve Davis, off-off Broadway actor who*
> *appeared in Tom Eyen's original*
> *productions of* Why Hanna's Skirt Won't
> Stay Down, *opposite Helen Hanft, and*
> The Dirtiest Show in Town

The origin of off-Broadway theater (differentiated from Broadway proper by the size of the house and union rules) can be traced back to the Provincetown Playhouse on MacDougal Street, which was home to the Provincetown Players in the 1920s. Here, productions of O'Neill's early works, such as *Emperor Jones,* written in 1921 while he was living on Milligan Place, the tiny courtyard off Sixth Avenue near Tenth Street, and avant-garde plays by the likes of e. e. cummings, who lived on Patchin Place, were produced. A youthful Bette Davis appeared in 1928 in *The Earth Between* at the Provincetown.

In the 1920s, as a sideline to "serious" theater, you could go to *The Greenwich Village Follies* (a new revue each year) and see the Dolly Sisters or comic Fred Allen (later of radio fame), and if you had attended *The Greenwich Village Follies* of 1924, you might have heard "I'm in Love Again," a famous tune by Cole Porter. Eva Le Gallienne founded the Civic Repertory Theater in 1926 on Fourteenth Street west of Seventh Avenue, which lasted through 1933 with productions in repertory of *Camille, Cradle Song*, and *Romeo and Juliet*. Edna St. Vincent Millay worked with the Provincetown Players until 1924, when she founded the Cherry Lane Theater, which was devoted to experimental theater.

The Living Theater, under the leadership of Julian Beck and his wife, Judith Malina, opened in 1951 and had a direct lineage to the experimental theater fostered by the Provincetown and the Cherry Lane groups. Located at Fourteenth Street and Seventh Avenue, the Becks originally presented the works of Gertrude Stein, T. S. Eliot, W. H. Auden, and later Jack Gelber and Ken Brown. The Circle in the Square, originally located in Sheridan Square on West Fourth Street (now on Bleecker Street near Thompson), was formed by Ted Mann, Leigh Connell, and Jose Quintero. Its off-Broadway revival of Tennessee Williams's *Summer and Smoke*, which introduced the luminous Geraldine Page as Alma, and the 1950s revival of O'Neill's *The Iceman Cometh* caused sensations in the Village and all over town. Colleen Dewhurst and George C. Scott began their stormy marriage when they were acting at the Circle in the Square. The Theater de Lys on Christopher Street (now named the Lucille Lortel, after the owner) presented *The Threepenny Opera* and offered audiences Norman Mailer's *The Deer Park* in the early off-Broadway days. The Provincetown and the Cherry Lane theaters and the Lucille Lortel

New York Theater Strategy playwrights, left to right, front row: Robert Heide, Leonard Melfi, Julie Bovasso, Paul Foster; second row: Megan Terry, Charles Ludlam, Ed Bullins, Jean Claude van Italie, Rochelle Owens, Murray Mednick, Ronnie Tavel, Rosalyn Drexler; third row: Ken Bernard, John Ford Noonan (with beard), Tom Eyen (in dark glasses), Maria Irene Fornes, William M. Hoffman .

continue to operate as off-Broadway houses.

Due to the demands of unions and many other factors, the cost of producing an off-Broadway show skyrocketed in the 1950s and 1960s. Ticket prices also jumped sky-high and today are comparable to Broadway's. The Great White Way has almost outpriced itself save for that special outing that people manage to afford to see overproduced musical extravaganzas such as those written by Andrew Lloyd Weber and Tim Rice, usually imported from England.

Bernadette Peters in George Haimsohn's Dames at Sea, *directed by Robert Dahdah at the Caffe Cino in 1966*

In the 1960s, off-off Broadway emerged as a reaction to the stranglehold of commercial theater. Increasingly, experimental and new writers could not compete in the off-Broadway arena, where revivals of established playwrights' work were produced and avant-garde drama came mostly out of Europe's Theater of the Absurd, mainly the plays of Ionesco, Genet, or Beckett. Not till Edward Albee paired his one-act play *The Zoo Story* with Beckett's *Krapp's Last Tape* was anyone interested in the new American playwrights.

Inspired by Albee and the European absurdists, many younger writers began to experiment with the one-act form in storefront coffeehouse theaters, in church basements and lofts, in the dingy anterooms of seedy hotels like the Jane West on the West Village waterfront, and in other hard-to-reach locations. The earliest and first coffeehouse theater was the Caffe Cino at 31 Cornelia Street, which began in earnest in 1959. The Cino was the first off-off Broadway theater.

Cafe La Mama, under the aegis of Ellen Stewart, and including Paul Foster, a lawyer-playwright, and Jim Moore, a businessman—all inspired by the Caffe Cino—opened their own coffeehouse

Playwright Robert Patrick

theater in 1962 in a dirt-floor basement in a tenement building at 321 East Ninth Street. Later Ellen Stewart moved her Cafe La Mama to a loft at 122 Second Avenue where she presented new plays and cooked soup for the actors and writers so they would not starve.

As Joe Cino eventually deteriorated under the influence of drugs, Ellen Stewart and La Mama grew and became more professional, applying for and receiving grants and funding from the Rockefeller Foundation, the Ford Foundation, the National Arts Council, the Kaplan Fund, and the New York State Council on the Arts. Paul Foster and Jim Moore, members of the La Mama corporation, used their skills to help in the drawing up of union contracts, in building and equipment matters, and in the production of plays. In 1966, Actors Equity pounced on La Mama for using Equity actors, and through complicated legal maneuvers put all kinds of limits on La Mama and other off-off Broadway houses. The union limited the number of performances actors could give, meaning a production or play could not run beyond a certain limit. This became a hardship for writers, who could no longer build a play into a success. If the actors had to leave, the production was in effect stopped. La Mama did its best, but with Equity breathing down its neck, the theater's creative spirit suffered. The question persisted, Could a union tell an artist, a painter, for instance, not to give himself exposure by hanging his artworks in a coffee shop or restaurant? The truth is that most Equity actors are unemployed and the union can do nothing to find work for them.

Joe Cino at the Caffe Cino

On April 2, 1969 (two years to the date following Joe Cino's death at St. Vincent's Hospital), Cafe La Mama became La Mama ETC and soon had a European traveling troupe under the direction of Tom O'Horgan and a new larger theater complex at 74 East Fourth Street. La Mama ETC (Experimental Theater Club) changed its focus from a purely playwrights' theater to a directors' theater, usually featuring actor groups and troupes in vast numbers performing stylistic, gymnastic hijinks. This style culminated in the 1968 Broadway rock musical *Hair*, directed by Tom O'Horgan, who also directed Rochelle Owens's *Futz* and Paul Foster's *Tom Paine*, both of which opened in

Ondine and Jacque Lynn Colton at the Caffe Cino in A Christmas Carol, *written by Soren Angenoux, adapted from Charles Dickens*

off-Broadway houses in 1968. La Mama and its founder, Ellen Stewart, are now regarded as international theatrical institutions.

Ann and George Harris and their children are a theatrical family troupe of long standing in the Village, performing at Judson Church, La Mama, Theater for the New City, and other off-off Broadway theaters over the past three decades. George Harris, Jr., known as Hibiscus, first appeared as Jeff Weiss's younger brother in *A Funny Walk Home* in 1966 at the Caffe Cino. Out of his experiences at the Cino, he went on to form in the early 1970s a glitter group he called the Angels of Light, which consisted of young men in beards and full-face makeup and girls covered with glitter dust who sang Depression-era songs such as "Keep Your Sunny Side Up," "Let a Smile Be Your Umbrella," and "Somewhere Over the Rainbow." When Hibiscus and his lover, Angel Jack (Jack Coe), brought their revue to Greenwich Village at the Jane West Hotel, it played to sold-out houses before going on tour all over Europe. The Angels of Light were really all about gay liberation, drag liberation, and "anything goes" liberation, and had an important influence on avant-garde theater and social changes in America. Hibiscus later formed a rock 'n' roll group with his three sisters, MaryLou, Jane, and Eloise, calling it Hibiscus and the Screaming Violets, and for a long time a glittering billboard on Sheridan Square over the United Cigar promoted this group. Hibiscus died of AIDS in 1982.

The Harris Sisters continue to perform in the Village and elsewhere on their own, often singing Andrews Sisters songs such as "Boogie-Woogie

Hibiscus and Angel Jack

Ellen Stewart of Cafe La Mama

Bugle Boy of Company B." Brother Walter Harris, who was a member of the original cast of *Hair* on Broadway, wrote a musical tribute to Hibiscus with songs provided by mother Ann. This was presented at La Mama in 1993, directed by off-off Broadway veteran and founder of La Mama West (in Los Angeles), Jacque Lynn Colton. Brother Fred, now with a family of his own, was active in off-off Broadway groups such as Ron and Harvey Tavel's Theater for the Lost Continent, which produced plays at the Jane West Hotel before Theater for the New City took it over. Lost Continent produced *Kitchenette, Boy in a Straight Back Chair, Life of Juanita Castro*, all by Ronnie Tavel, as well as *The Trojan Women*, the Greek tragedy produced by Donald Brooks and starring Jackie Curtis and Harvey Fierstein.

The Judson Poets Theater at the Judson Memorial Church on Washington Square South presented plays and musicals under the leadership of Al Carmines. This program emerged out of the Judson Gallery, where Claes Oldenburg, Allan Kaprow, and Jim Dine had staged their Art Happenings. The Judson Theater opened in 1961 with *The Great American Desert* and *Breasts of Tiresias* by Joel Oppenheimer and Guillaume Apollinaire, directed by Lawrence Kornfeld. *Gorilla Queen*, by Ron Tavel, was a big hit at Judson, as was *Home Movies* by Rosalyn Drexler and *Red Cross* by Sam Shepard. The Judson produced many successful musicals, some with "books" by Gertrude Stein or Village playwright Marie Irene Fornes.

Diane DiPrima and Alan Marlowe founded the New York Poets Theater in 1962, producing the plays of LeRoi Jones, Michael McClure, Frank O'Hara, Robert Duncan, and others. They were also the sponsors of exhibits of the photography of Jack Smith and the early pop-art

Crystal Field

collage work of Ray Johnson, who referred to himself as a Zen scavenger. A disciple of John Cage, Johnson took to the streets and garbage bins, where he and girlfriend Dorothy Podber collected dead rats and mice. They presented these to friends and outraged strangers as a new type of "happening" theater which took place on the street, in a restaurant, or on an unplanned visit to a friend's apartment. One such friend re-

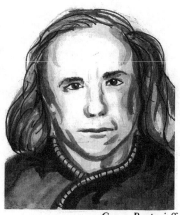

George Bartenieff

ceived a dead rat inside a large Mickey Mouse clock for a birthday present. Apparently, Podber and Johnson, an odd couple, were hurt when their friend refused the "gift."

For several seasons, the New York Theater Strategy presented first-rate productions, such as Ron Tavel's *The Ovens of Anita Orange Juice*, loosely based on the homophobic ravings of singer Anita Bryant. Julie Bovasso hired her friend Robert De Niro to act in her play at the Manhattan Theater Club, and for a time playwrights had a field day just doing their own thing with no one telling them what to do or how to do it. The New York Theater Strategy was initially formed by Marie Irene Fornes in 1972, with Julie Bovasso and several other playwrights, to produce their own plays, which they did at festivals at the Manhattan Theater Club and at the Westbeth Theater Center in the Village. Fornes said that she and the others had tired of the autocratic system in which theater artists were treated like little babies by theater managers or off-off Broadway entrepreneurs who seldom even bothered to read scripts.

The Theater for the New City was founded by Crystal Field and George Bartenieff (a husband and wife acting team), Theo Barnes, and Lawrence Kornfeld. All had emerged out of the Judson Poets Theater. Originally producing works like *Eunichs for the Forbidden City* by Charles Ludlam and *Evidence* by Richard Forman, they later presented new plays at Westbeth, at the Jane West Hotel, at 162 Second Avenue (at Tenth Street), and now in a permanent home at 155 First Avenue (at Tenth Street). Theater for the New City presented the first production of Sam Shepard's *Buried Child*, which went on to receive a Pulitzer Prize. The first act of Harvey Fierstein's *Torch Song Trilogy* was introduced at TNC in 1976 on the two hundredth anniversary of the American Revolution at a festival of Village plays by Village writers. A Cino committee was formed at TNC in 1993 to build a new Joe Cino Theater there. In 1994, the Cino Theater opened in honor of "the first off-off Broadway shrine" with the idea of continuing the new, innovative kind of theater that was a hallmark of the original Caffe Cino Theater on Cornelia Street.

Theater Genesis at St. Marks Church-in-the-Bowery (at Tenth Street and Second Avenue) was founded in 1964 by Ralph Cook and became a second home to Tony Barsha, Sam Shepard, Leonard Melfi, Walter Hadler, Murray Mednick, and David Scott Milton. Tom Sankey had a following at the Genesis with a 1966 folk-rock musical called *The Golden Screw*.

The Circle Repertory Theater thrived at 99 Seventh Avenue South (between Bleecker and West Fourth Street) on Sheridan Square before it moved to Circle in the Square on Bleecker. Circle Rep was formed by Rob Thirkield, the heir to Ben-Gay, Marshall Mason, and Lanford Wilson, who is its primary resident writer. Wilson's *Talley's Folly* (a Pulitzer Prize–winning work), *Fifth of July*, and *The Mound Builders* were first produced at this theater under the direction of Marshall Mason. William M. Hoffman's play about AIDS, *As Is*, was first presented at the Circle Rep prior to its successful Broadway triumph. Lanford Wilson and Marshall Mason, both Midwesterners, first met at the Caffe Cino, where Mason directed Wilson's early work. Inspired by "the magic" that they found at the Caffe Cino, they went on to form the Circle Repertory and to develop their professional careers in the theater. Though both are veterans of the commercial Broadway arena, they always return to their home base in the Village to hone their craft and sharpen their skills.

Eugene Ionesco once said he would have preferred that the tag "Theater of the Absurd," a label he, Beckett, Genet, and other theatrical writers labored under, be rephrased as "Theater of Derision." Following the example of these European "absurdists," John Vaccaro and his young protégé Charles Ludlam came up with the "Theater of the Ridiculous" to describe their own particular common vision of a new theater movement.

Everett Quinton and Charles Ludlam in The Mystery of Irma Vep

When Charles Ludlam, playwright, director, and performer, split off from his mentor-director Vaccaro, he called his new group the Ridiculous Theatrical Company. Vaccaro was then directing Ludlam's *Conquest of the Universe*, which he owned the rights to, and Ludlam decided to do his own version of this same

Charles Ludlam

play, calling it *When Queens Collide*. This latter title was an intentional jab by Ludlam over the ongoing feud he was having with Vaccaro about who had the right to the term *Ridiculous*. It was a ridiculous real-life feud that could have been a plot for a Ludlam play.

In the long run it was Ludlam who superseded his mentor. He originally presented his various productions at several different Village locations, and his earliest successes were camp versions of *Camille* and *Bluebeard*, in which he played to perfection the title roles. Another in this series was *Stage Blood*. The Ridiculous Theatrical Company, under Charles Ludlam's autocratic control and direction, was founded in 1967, and the permanent home for this madcap company became 1 Sheridan Square. The basement space previously at 1 Sheridan Square once housed the Cafe Society, where Billie Holiday sang, and in another incarnation was a gay bar. *Reverse Psychology*, *Secret Lives of the Sexist*, and *Love's Tangled Web* were other early Ludlam hits. In 1978, he wrote and presented *Utopia, Incorporated* and *The Enchanted Pig*, the latter being a great success for the group. In 1983, *Le Bourgeoise Avant-Garde* opened, and critic David Kaufman, who has written the definitive biography of Ludlam for Crown Publishers, considers this play to be one of his best. *Gallas*, based on the life of Maria Callas, with Ludlam as a ridiculous diva in the title role, was another big hit. The topsy-turvy gender-bender plays that found impresario-actor Ludlam in and out of drag reached their

zenith with *The Mystery of Irma Vep* in 1984. *Irma Vep* has been produced more often than any other Ludlam play in new productions all over the globe. The final plays of the 1986–87 season, written by and starring Charles Ludlam before he succumbed to AIDS, were *The Artificial Jungle* with the brilliant Black-eyed Susan, a regular Ridiculous performer, which offered a great non-drag deadpan virtuoso performance by Ludlam; and *Salammbo*, in which Ludlam, in high drag again, dominated a stage filled with undressed

Ron Link in Robert Heide's play Statue, *at Cafe La Mama*

musclemen who had previously performed only at the Sheridan Square Gym.

The Ridiculous Theatrical Company became a "theater at large" in June 1995, when landlord difficulties forced them out of 1 Sheridan Square on the tiny block between West Fourth Street and Washington Place that has been renamed Charles Ludlam Lane. The company is now under the leadership of Everett Quinton, Ludlam's lover, who has revived several of Ludlam's classic plays starring himself, as well as writing and starring in some of his own works. Following in the footsteps of his mentor, Quinton has also presented new "ridiculous" plays by such writers as H. M. Koutoukas and Georg Osterman, and he has been acclaimed for some of his own "performance art" solo pieces. As time goes by, the Charles Ludlam legend takes its place alongside those of other great leading "ladies" of the American stage, such as Tallulah Bankhead and Katherine Cornell, whose dominant personalities always overshadowed their roles. It will be difficult to take the place of an authentic genius such as Ludlam, but many hopefuls are out there trying. Too often, the "ridiculous" results are a burlesque parody in high heels rather than the intelligence, wit, and satire with which Ludlam treated his many and varied subjects.

One of the foremost developers of drag avant-garde theater in the 1960s and 1970s in the Village was director Ron Link, who first introduced a brownette Candy Darling (a.k.a. James Slattery) in Tom Eyen's *Give My Regards to Off-Off Broadway* and also featured the pre-Warhol Candy with Melba LaRose, Jr., in *Glamour, Glory and Gold* by and with Jackie Curtis, both at Bastiano's Cellar Theater on Washington Place. Robert De Niro had his first acting role in this play. Ron also directed the "for real" and nondrag Roz Kelly (although audiences remained confused about Roz's gender) in a revival of *Rain*, which featured Sylvester Stallone in his very first role. Roz went on to play the role of Pinky Trocadero in *The Fonz*, the "Happy Days" TV series. Likewise, Barry Bostwick, who starred in *The Rocky Horror Picture Show* and who also played George Washington on TV, appeared in the nude in Gregory Rozakis's (all-male) *Whores of Broadway*, directed by Link. Rozakis was a well-known actor who had appeared as the young Kazan in the director's film *America, America* (1963) and appeared opposite Kim Stanley on Broadway in *Natural Affection*. Later Link presented Divine of John Waters's *Pink Flamingos* and *Female Trouble* fame in the off-Broadway production of Tom Eyen's *Women Behind Bars*, a campy prison farce, and Eyen's *Neon Woman*, again starring Divine, with Lady Hope Stansbury playing Divine's hysterical daughter.

Village Theaters

The following is a list of functioning off-Broadway theaters and off-off Broadway theaters and performance spaces in the Village, where the live art of theater continues to thrive. Economic realities often plague smaller theaters but as long as playwrights need to create, and audiences need to see live drama, the theater will persist.

Cherry Lane Theater,
  38 Commerce Street

Variety Arts Theater,
  110 Third Avenue

Ridiculous Theatrical Company
  (at large)

Classic Stage Company,
  136 East Thirteenth Street

Theater for the New City,
  155 First Avenue

Westbeth Theater, 151 Bank Street

Actors Playhouse,
  100 Seventh Avenue South

St. Marks Theater Project,
  131 East Tenth Street

Joseph Papp Public Theater,
  425 Lafayette Street

La Mama, E.T.C.,
  74 A East Fourth Street

La Mama La Galleria,
  6 East First Street

Nuyorican Poets Cafe,
  236 East Third Street

Dixon Place, 258 Bowery

Here, 145 Sixth Avenue (SoHo)

The Planet Q Theatre,
  94 St. Marks Place

Jewish Repertory Theater,
  344 East Fourteenth Street

Living Theater,
  272 East Fourth Street

Performance Space 122,
  150 First Avenue

Circle in the Square,
  159 Bleecker Street

Lucille Lortel,
  121 Christopher Street

Orpheum Theater, Second Avenue
  and St. Marks Place

Minetta Lane, 18 Minetta Lane

Players Theater,
  115 MacDougal Street

Provincetown Theater,
  133 MacDougal Street

Sullivan Street Playhouse,
  181 Sullivan Street

Astor Place Theater,
  434 Lafayette Street

New York Theater Workshop,
  79 East Fourth Street

Perry Street Theater,
  31 Perry Street

Tony n' Tina's Wedding, St. John's
  Church, 81 Christopher Street

The Pearl Theater Company,
  80 St. Marks Place

WOW Café, 59 East Fourth Street

Cinema

Greenwich Village in the Movies

The Village has long been a popular setting for movies, whether actually filmed in the Village or on a Hollywood set. Some of these include *Greenwich Village* (1944) with Carmen Miranda, Don Ameche and, the Cherry Blonde, Vivian Blaine with Tony and Sally De-Marco, William Bendix, Judy Holliday, Betty Comden, and Adolph Green; *My Sister Eileen*; *Bell, Book and Candle* with Kim Novak; *The Seventh Victim*, Val Lewton's film noir about witchcraft in the Village starring Kim Hunter; *Cruising* with Al Pacino (a film about the sleazier side of gay life in the Village); *Rose of Washington Square* (with Alice Faye playing Fannie Brice, Tyrone Power as Nick Arnstein, and Al Jolson); and *Alexander's Ragtime Band*, the Irving Berlin musical (Alice Faye and Ethel Merman both sing their version of "Blue Skies" in a Village speakeasy while Tyrone Power and Don Ameche listen admiringly). Portions of *Manhattan* (1979), *Annie Hall* (1977), *Bullets Over Broadway* (1994), and other Woody Allen films take place in the Village, as do, of course, *Next Stop Greenwich Village* (1975) and *The Pope of Greenwich Village* (1984) with Daryl Hannah and Geraldine Page.

A weird, cult film-noir movie, *Scarlet Street* (1946), stars Joan Bennett as a lazy, laid-back pseudo-artist who manipulates Edward G. Robinson, a frustrated bank clerk with a nagging wife, into supporting her and her sleazy boyfriend, played to perfection by Dan Duryea. In the movie, Robinson plays a painter who is exploited by Joan Bennett, an impostor who gains fame as an artist by signing her own name to his paintings. Robinson kills her in a jealous rage when he hears her make fun of him after making love with her pimp-boyfriend. It ends with Robinson wandering around Washington Square as a disillusioned bum, letting Duryea take the rap for the murder.

Funny Face (1956), the Paramount musical with Fred Astaire, has Audrey Hepburn playing a radical-feminist who works in a Greenwich Village bookshop and is selected by *Quality* magazine's editor (played by Kay Thompson) to be the "Quality Girl" model for a Paris fashion show.

Jane Fonda at the Washington Arch in Barefoot in the Park

In *Call Her Savage* (1933), Clara

20th Century–Fox film Greenwich Village, 1944 lobby card

Bow visits a gay bar in the Village and there are plenty of "limp-wrist" gags in one particular scene.

In *Daisy Kenyon* (1947), Joan Crawford plays a fashion designer with two men in her life, Henry Fonda and Dana Andrews, who both romance her in her studio, which looks out on Greenwich Avenue and the neon-lit marquee of the Greenwich Theater. With Ruth Warrick, Martha Stewart, and Peggy Ann Garner.

The original intent was to shoot *Rear Window* (1954) on location in Greenwich Village to keep costs down, but it be-

Bleecker Street was the real place used for Woody Allen's film Bullets Over Broadway, *set in 1928*

came impractical and Hitchcock had to build a Hollywood replica of a Greenwich Village courtyard with over thirty apartments, twelve of them completely furnished. This elaborate and expensive set made for an artificial but gripping murder mystery with Jimmy Stewart and Grace Kelly looking out the "rear window" through a telescope.

Set on Washington Square in the 1890s, *The Heiress* (1949) has Olivia de Havilland taking revenge on her lover, played by Montgomery Clift. This bitter family drama, costarring Ralph Richardson and Miriam Hopkins, was taken from a stage success based on a story by Henry James.

Other Greenwich Village and East Village movies include:

Author! Author! (1982), with Al Pacino, Dyan Cannon, Bob Dishy, and Tuesday Weld

Back Street (1932), with Irene Dunne and John Boles, based on the best-selling Fannie Hurst novel

Back Street (1941), a remake with Margaret Sullavan and Charles Boyer

Back Street (1961), directed by Ross Hunter, with Susan Hayward and John Gavin

Barefoot in the Park (1967), based on the Neil Simon Broadway play with Jane Fonda and Robert Redford

The Boys in the Band (1970), from Mart Crowley's play with Leonard Frey and Cliff Gorman

Carlito's Way (1994), with Al Pacino and John Leguizamo

Desperately Seeking Susan (1985), with Madonna, Aidan Quinn, and Ann Magnuson

Dog Day Afternoon (1975), with Al Pacino, Penny Allen, Judith Malina, John Cazale, Charles Durning, Chris Sarandon, Sully Boyar, and James Broderick

Godfather II (1974), with Al Pacino, Robert De Niro, Lee Strasberg, Diane Keaton, Troy Donahue, and Talia Shire, directed by Francis Ford Coppola and winner of the Best Picture Academy Award

The Group (1966), from the Mary McCarthy novel, directed by Sidney Lumet, with Candice Bergen, Kathleen Widdoes, Joanna Pettet, Joan Hackett, Shirley Knight, and James Broderick

Moonstruck (1987), with Cher, Nicholas Cage, Olympia Dukakis, and off-off Broadway actresses Helen Hanft and Julie Bovasso

Parting Glances (1986), directed by Bill Sherwood with John Bolger and Adam Nathan

Serpico (1973), directed by Sidney Lumet, with Al Pacino and Biff McGuire

Smithereens (1982), directed by Susan Siedelman, with Susan Berman and Brad Rinn

Alice Faye plays a Fanny Brice–like character in Rose of Washington Square. *Tyrone Power is her bad boy, Nickie Arnstein. Film has Faye in a super Greenwich Village–Washington Square number*

*Olivia de Havilland as
the spinster and
Montgomery Clift as her
fortune-hunting suitor in*
The Heiress, *based on the
Henry James book*
Washington Square

Cinema Listings

Film Forum, 209 West Houston

Angelika Film Center, 18 West Houston

Cineplex Odeon Art Greenwich, Greenwich Avenue and Twelfth Street

Anthology Film Archives, Second Avenue and Second Street

Cineplex Odeon Waverly, Sixth Avenue and Third Street

Movieland 8th Street, Eighth Street and University Place

Public Theater, 425 Lafayette Street

Loews East Village Theater, Third Avenue at Eleventh Street

City Cinemas Village East, Second Avenue at Twelfth Street

Cinema Village 12th Street, Twelfth Street east of Fifth Avenue

The Quad, Thirteenth Street west of Fifth Avenue

Village Hangouts

Bars

Landmark Pubs

The Lion's Head (at 59 Christopher Street) is where writers and journalists like to gather to drink, talk shop, and just plain yak. Norman Mailer, Pete Hamill, Jimmy Breslin, and others have been known to shoot the literary and political bull in this lively setting. Lanford Wilson, the Pulitzer Prize–winning playwright, also likes to down a few at the Lion. Book jackets from old and recent novels line the walls. Attractive waitresses (one who worked here was Jessica Lange) serve hamburgers, chicken potpies, salads, and various pasta dishes, prepared by chef Richard Flavin for writers, editors, and agents who are always cooking up book deals.

Chumley's at 86 Bedford Street has no sign and there is another "secret" entrance (or exit) out of Pamela Court on Barrow Street. Leland Stanford Chumley opened the speakeasy restaurant in 1928 and dust jackets of novels of that time line the walls. The room is plain and dimly lit with carved and initialed wooden tables and booths. In the corner is a 1920s oak telephone booth now used for storing crockery. "Lee" Chumley died of a heart attack at fifty in 1935, and his widow, Henrietta, then took over, holding court at this center of Bohemia for over twenty-five years, later passing it on to her nephews. Edna St. Vincent Millay read her poetry here, and other notables who came were Mary McCarthy, Orson Welles, J. D. Salinger, Eugene O'Neill, Upton Sinclair, and Anaïs Nin.

White Horse Tavern

The White Horse Tavern (567 Hudson Street at West Eleventh) is the third-oldest bar in New York City, dating from 1880, and is still one of the Village's liveliest bars and hangouts. Dylan Thomas was a regular at the White Horse Tavern until his death from acute alcoholism, and Norman Mailer, who liked to hold court with a group of intellectuals, formed the idea for the *Village Voice* at his table in the back room.

McSorley's Old Ale House (15 East Seventh Street between Second and Third Avenues) is the oldest tavern in New York, dating from 1858, and is the East Village counterpoint to the White Horse, an historic must for all who guzzle ale and relish old-time pubs. Other old-timers not to be missed are the Kettle of Fish, which moved a few years ago intact from MacDougal Street to its present location at 130 West Third Street (between Sixth Avenue and MacDougal), and the famed Cedar Tavern (82 University Place between Eleventh and Twelfth Streets), at the same location for over thirty years. Prior to that, the Cedar was on University between Eighth and Ninth Streets. Abstract painters like Jackson Pol-

Portrait of Dylan Thomas hangs in the White Horse Tavern. Customers drank ale out of white-crockery mugs with "The White Horse Tavern—Hudson & 11th St., N.Y.C." imprinted right on them.

lock and Franz Kline were regulars at the old Cedar, as were poets Allen Ginsberg, Jack Kerouac, Frank O'Hara, and Kenneth Koch.

Other Village landmark pubs not to be missed on a bar run of "olde" taverns include the Corner Bistro at 341 West Fourth Street at Jane, and McBell's at 359 Sixth Avenue between West Fourth Street and Washington Place. Two old-time East Village bars have been right next door to each other for over fifty years. Verkhovyna has a bar on the right and booths on the left, with a pool table in the back. It's at

McBell's on Sixth Avenue between West Fourth Street and Washington Place

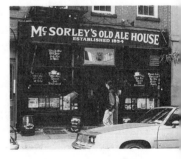

The oldest tavern in New York

81 East Seventh Street. The Blue and Gold Bar at 79 East Seventh Street has a bar on the left and tables on the right as well as wonderful old painted murals—and a pool table. A few bars far from historic but certainly for the adventurous include, in the West Village:

Art Bar, 52 Eighth Avenue (between Jane and Horatio)

Hudson Bar & Books, 636 Hudson Street (between Horatio and Jane)

Knickerbocker, 33 University Place

Scrap Bar, 116 MacDougal Street

Tortilla Flats, 767 Washington Street

Hogs & Heifers Saloon, 859 Washington Street (corner of Thirteenth Street)

and in the East Village:

Mars Bar, 25 East First Street (loud jukebox)

Acme Bar & Grill, 9 Great Jones Street

Alcatraz, 132 St. Marks Place

Bandito's, 153 Second Avenue

Max Fish, 176 Ludlow Street

Ludlow Cafe, 165 Ludlow Street

Sidewalks, 94 Avenue A

Telephone Bar, 149 Second Avenue

The St. Marks Bar, 132 First Avenue

Vasac Hall, Seventh Street and Avenue B

Wally's Bar, Seventh Street and Avenue A

Doc Hollidays, 141 Avenue A

Tenth Street Lounge, 212 East Tenth Street

No-Tell Motel, 167 Avenue A

Flamingo East, 219 Second Avenue

Sports Bars

Sports bar is a euphemism for "swinging singles," whose patrons include College Joes, Secretary Janes, office workers, legal wheeler-dealers, young real-estate yuppies, the "bridge and tunnel" Jerseyites and Long Islanders, BBQs (Brooklyn, Bronx, Queens), and others on the make who like to sit in a bar with five television sets tuned into baseball, football, or hockey games while a CD jukebox is blaring anything from Country Joe to the Frank Sinatra/Nelson Riddle songbook to Villager Bob Dylan's old folk-rock tunes. Sportswear outfits

Caliente Cab Company, Bleecker Street at Seventh Avenue South

Caliente Cab Company

for the guys and teased-up "mall" hairdos for the gals fill the bill, but almost everyone is welcome in the loud, brash, heavy drinkers' sports arena bars. Try:

Boxers, 190 West Fourth Street
Brother's Bar-B-Que, 228 West Houston
Googie's, 237 Sullivan Street
Dew Drop Inn, 57 Greenwich Avenue
Caliente Cab Company, 61 Seventh Avenue South
Riviera, 225 West Fourth Street
Gulf Coast, 489 West Street
Rock Ridge Saloon, 144 Bleecker Street
Fuddruckers, 87 Seventh Avenue South
Burp Castle, 41 East Seventh Street
Manhattan Brewing Company,
    42 Thompson Street
Babyland, 81 Avenue A

The Riviera Cafe and Sports Bar, Sheridan Square

Eerie Pubs

A new tradition of the old in Greenwich Village are the Eerie Pubs, based on the English pubs of the nineteenth century. These bars, which serve seventy-five to one hundred different varieties of connoisseur ales and beers, fit perfectly into the winding streets and historic houses that comprise Greenwich Village. Jekyll and Hyde is set in a fantasy of Dr. Jekyll's weird laboratory, while Jack the Ripper Pub features a life-size replica of the cutthroat killer and other gruesome images. The Slaughtered Lamb Pub is dedicated to the lore of werewolves, half-men-half-beast schizophrenics that preyed upon innocent victims in ye-olde-times-gone-by in merry olde blood-thirsty England.

Jekyll and Hyde, 91 Seventh Avenue South
Jack the Ripper Pub, 228 West Fourth Street
The Slaughtered Lamb Pub, 182 West Fourth Street

The Slaughtered Lamb on West Fourth Street

Gay and Lesbian

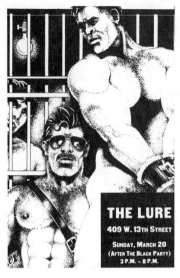

THE LURE
409 W. 13TH STREET
SUNDAY, MARCH 20
(AFTER THE BLACK PARTY)
3 P.M. – 8 P.M.

Gay bars have been a staple of life in the Village since the speakeasy days. Before that time, they operated illegally in dark and dingy dens with no city permits to serve liquor. In fact, no liquor license was the case right up to the Battle of Stonewall (the Stonewall had no liquor license and, like other gay bars in the sixties, was constantly raided by police in search of bigger payoffs). The 1970s gay bar scene was fueled by the sexual revolution and the gay liberation movements of that decade. Bars and sex clubs of every kind, including all-nighters, flourished. Some, such as the Mine Shaft, the International Stud, or the Anvil, hosted wild orgiastic scenes whose excess will probably never be seen again. By the mid-1980s, all of this came to an end with the advent of what was at first called "The Gay Plague," GRID (Gay-Related Immune Deficiency Syndrome), and then AIDS (Aquired Immune Deficiency Syndrome). By the late 1980s and early 1990s, gay bars and the streets (the bath houses all closed) calmed down and phrases like conservatism, monogamy, and "safe sex" entered the gay vocabulary. Now, rather than a bowl of chips, pretzels, popcorn, or peanuts at the gay watering holes, you will find a bowl of packaged condoms. However, even in the midst of what *Time* magazine described as "The Age of the Virulent Virus," gay life goes on—sometimes with added determination, sometimes with a vengeance. There must be a time and a place for fun, fetishisms, or whatever gets a body through the night; but it is also a time to be careful. A sixties song by Petula Clark, whose lyric promises that you can forget all your troubles and cares when you go *Downtown*, is still a perennial favorite on most gay bar jukeboxes in the Village and is sung in the gay cabarets as well.

Gay bars in the West Village include:

Boots & Saddles, 76 Christopher Street

Dugout, 185 Christopher Street

The Hangar, 115 Christopher Street

Julius, 159 West Tenth Street (at Waverly)

Keller's, 348 West Street (at Barrow)

One Potato, 518 Hudson Street

Sneakers, 392 West Street (between
   Christopher and West Tenth Street)

The Monster, 80 Grove Street

Pieces, 8 Christopher Street

Stonewall, 53 Christopher Street

Uncle Charlie's, 56 Greenwich Avenue

Orbit, 46 Bedford Street

Two Potato, 145 Christopher Street

Ty's, 114 Christopher Street

The Lure, 409 West Thirteenth Street

Bulge, 135 Christopher Street

Nuts & Bolts Lounge, 101 Seventh Avenue South

Lesbian bars include:

Taboo, 40 West Eighth Street

Crazy Nanny's, 21 Seventh Avenue South (at Leroy)

Henrietta Hudson, 438 Hudson Street (at Morton)

The Cubby Hole, 281 West Twelfth Street

Rubyfruit Bar & Grill, 531 Hudson Street

Orbit, 46 Bedford Street

Henrietta Hudson on Hudson Street, a women's bar

Gay bars in the East Village include:

The Bar, 68 Second Avenue (at Fourth Street)
Crowbar, 339 East Tenth Street (near Avenue B)
Dick's Bar, 192 Second Avenue (at Twelfth Street)
Tunnel Bar, 116 First Avenue (at Seventh Street)
Wonder Bar, 505 East Sixth Street (off Avenue A)
The Boiler Room, 86 East Fourth Street

Sheridan Square's pride and joy, the Monster (80 Grove Street), is one of the hottest in the West Village for disco dancing and they have a cabaret with a piano player as well. Marie's Crisis (59 Grove Street) is the place for a gay sing-along, and for those into leather, uniforms, rubber, and so on, try the Lure at 409 West Thirteenth, which has a weekend leather dress code strictly enforced. Other "recreational" clubs in the far northwest section of Greenwich Village include the Cellblock (28 Ninth Avenue at Fourteenth Street) and the Vault (at the same address) and Mike's (432 West Fourteenth Street (between Ninth and Tenth Avenues). Several clubs like Jackie 60 (434 West Fourteenth Street), Mr. Fuji's Tropicana (at Fifth Avenue and Thirteenth Street), Flamingo East (219 Second Avenue between Thirteenth and Fourteenth Streets), the Boy Bar (at 15 St. Marks Place), the Grand at 76 East Thirteenth Street, and the Pyramid (101 Avenue A) offer special weekly gay dance parties on different nights of the week. Cards for "special evenings" at clubs are usually distributed at gay clothing shops and at some gay bars, and give-away magazines list all the week's activities on the gay circuit.

The Wonder Bar was founded by Jeff Geiger and is located in the East Village at 505 East Sixth Street (at Avenue A).

Clubs

The Five Oaks and Other Cabaret and Nightclub Spots

The Five Oaks at 89 Grove Street at the corner of Bleecker Street is a bar/nightclub/restaurant that includes pianist/singers and customers who stand up and sing with the piano player, some of whom may be in the chorus of a Broadway show and others who mostly sing in the shower (and should probably keep on doing it there). The great Marie Blake entertained here and at other spots in Sheridan Square for over forty years. This slide pianist and scat singer sang special versions of "Down in the Depths on the 90th Floor," "Rapture" (the Blondie song), and "Ragmop." The cellar room with its chocolate-brown walls and chocolate-brown tablecloths, intimate booths, and small, ship-style horseshoe bar was Marie's exclusive headquarters for the past twenty years. With her death in 1993, a new generation of talent is emerging and the Five Oaks is still one of the most fun places in the Village—or anywhere else for that matter. A smart, sophisticated group of gays mix here with straight couples who all gather to have a helluva good time. Steven Miller is your host, assisting owner Ginger Regan; bartender Barbara Ross, a sassy Joan Blondell looka-like, mixes up cocktails. When Lise Hall, a dead ringer for Ida Lupino in *The Man I Love*, gets out from behind the bar to sing her version of George Gershwin's "The Man I Love," she changes the

Marie Blake of the Five Oaks in 1993

Ruby Rims after her show at Eighty Eights, "In The Can" across Tenth Street at the Sixth Precinct

The Harris Sisters—Eloise, Mary Lori, and Jayne Anne

lyric of the song so that the unattainable man she loves turns out to be gay. Others dishing out the fun at the Five Oaks include piano players and singers Jay Bradley, Benny Martini, Jim Keefe, Laurel Watson, and a yellow-haired glam-rocker called Satyr.

Continuous entertainment, piano playing, and singing are the order of the night at the hotspots on the cabaret/club circuit.

The Five Oaks, 89 Grove Street
Marie's Crisis, 59 Grove Street
Duplex Cabaret, 61 Christopher Street
Eighty-Eight's, 228 West Tenth Street

All That Jazz (The Clubs)

Jazz joints and classy jazz clubs have always been the thing downtown; and some of these jumping jive or "real cool" "in" places feature top bands, combos, trios, and pop-jazz vocalists.

Sweet Basil, 88 Seventh Avenue South
The Blue Note, 131 West Third Street
The Fez, 380 Lafayette Street
Bradley's, 70 University Place

Knickerbocker's, 33 University Place
Arthur's Tavern, 57 Grove Street
Village Vanguard, 178 Seventh Avenue
Smalls, 183 West Tenth Street

Rock 'n' Roll Clubs and Folk-Rock Joints

Rock clubs that feature live entertainment like CBGB, the Continental, and the Pyramid Club attract the young crowd who want to experience an electronic buzz and a loud thump.

Cafe Wha?, 115 MacDougal Street
Lion's Den, 214 Sullivan Street
The Back Fence, 155 Bleecker Street
CBGB, 315 Bowery
CBGB's Gallery, 313 Bowery

Don Hill's, 511 Greenwich Street
Webster Hall, 125 East Eleventh Street
Fez under Time Cafe, 380 Lafayette
The Bitter End, 147 Bleecker Street
Kenny's Castaways, 157 Bleecker Street
Rock 'n' Roll Cafe, 149 Bleecker Street
Under Acme, 9 Great Jones
The Continental, Third Avenue at St. Mark's Place
The Pyramid Club, 101 Avenue A
Mercury Lounge, 217 East Houston Street

Coffeehouses

There is a Greenwich Village coffeehouse tradition wherein espresso, cappuccino, other exotic coffees, fine teas, and soft drinks are served along with light fare and with pastries and rich cakes to customers who want to sit in a cafe for a long time, relax, have a conversation, or read a book or newspaper. While a cup of coffee or cappuccino may seem expensive at these emporia, it should be understood that what the customer is paying must be commensurate with the rent the proprietor must pay each month to stay in business. These places, just like a bar, have to have a certain atmosphere, charm, and personality to survive in the Village. Many intimate coffee-cafes are operated just as they were in the nineteenth century by Italians who know how to use an espresso machine to make the perfect coffee drink. Some, like the Cornelia Street Cafe (29 Cornelia Street), next door to where the famous Caffe Cino coffee shop theater used to be, also serve food with their cappuccino as well as wines and liquors, and hosts Robin Hirsch, Raphaela Pivetta, Judith Kallas, and Charles McKenna encourage poetry and play readings—what life in the Village is all about. Others, like the Bleecker Street Pastry & Cafe at 245 Bleecker Street or Rocco's Pastry Shop right next door at 243 Bleecker Street, are primarily bakeries with tables where you can enjoy your exotic coffees with fresh croissants, cannoli, napoleons, or fancy cream puffs—or you might want to take home one of their many fancy cakes.

Cornelia Street Cafe

Cafes and Pastries

Among the most prominent and atmospheric coffeehouses in the Village and East Village are:

Caffe Donatello and Gelateria, 207–211 Waverly Place

The Cornelia Street Cafe, 29 Cornelia Street

Caffe Dell'Artista, 46 Greenwich Avenue

Bleecker Street Pastry, 245 Bleecker Street

Rocco's Pastry, 243 Bleecker Street

Rumbul's Cafe, 128 East Seventh Street
    559 Hudson Street
    20 Christopher Street

Caffe Dante, 81 MacDougal Street

Caffe Picasso, 359 Bleecker Street

Le Figaro, 184 Bleecker Street

Cafe Borgia, 185 Bleecker Street

Caffe Lucca, 228 Bleecker Street

Caffe Vivaldi, 32 Jones Street

Espresso Bar, 82 Christopher Street

Patisserie Lanciani, 271 West Fourth Street

French Roast Cafe, 458 Sixth Avenue

Reggio, 119 MacDougal Street

De Robertis Pasticceria, 176 First Avenue

Veniero's Pasticceria, 342 East Eleventh Street

The Peacock, 24 Greenwich Avenue

The Antique Cafe, 388 Bleecker Street

New World Coffee, 449 Sixth Avenue
    412 West Broadway

Dalton Coffee Ltd., 70 Greenwich Avenue
    36 St. Marks Place

Black Medicine, 554 Hudson Street

Michael and Zoë's Cafe and Bakery,
    101 Second Avenue

Greenwich Cafe, 75 Greenwich Avenue
    (24 hours)

Le Figaro Cafe
The Garden Spot of the Village

Village Restaurants

Quick Bites

Greek Diners (West Side)

The basic Greek restaurant diner is a staple for Villagers who can order anything from coffee, eggs, and toast to lobster Newburg served with a cocktail or a glass of wine. Most of them are open twenty-four hours and they all offer good food at inexpensive prices, though not all have bars. Manatus at 340 Bleecker Street (between Christopher and West Tenth Street) is decorated in faux Art Deco and when the lights are lowered in the evening and the table candles lit, the place fills up with theatrical types and you could imagine you're in a much more expensive setting. Many people can be found after all-night barhopping having breakfast at Tiffany's on West Fourth Street or one of the many other Greek emporia. Incidentally, you can have your breakfast—eggs and bacon—at any time of the day in these eateries in keeping with the Village tradition of morning into night and vice versa. The following are all in the West Village:

Manatus, 340 Bleecker Street

Tiffany II, 222 West Fourth Street

Sheridan Square Restaurant, 72 Grove Street

Homer's, 121 West Tenth Street

The Village Star, 33 Seventh Avenue

The Washington Square Restaurant, 150 West Fourth Street

The Waverly, 19 Waverly Place

The Village Den, 225 West Twelfth Street

Polish/Ukrainian/German (East Side)

Cheap Polish restaurants offering wholesome food are the mainstay of East Village residents, and not a few West Villagers walk across town to these numerous eateries, most of them on First and Second Avenues. Ukrainian restaurants as well as Jewish delis, some serving kosher, dot the area. Some of the best in the East Village are:

B & H Dairy, 127 Second Avenue

Kiev, 117 Second Avenue

Odessa, 117 Avenue A

Second Avenue Deli, 156 Second Avenue

Teresa's Coffee Shop, 103 First Avenue

Ukrainian East Village, 140 Second Avenue

Veselka, 144 Second Avenue

Little Poland Restaurant, 200 Second Avenue

Polonia, 110 First Avenue

Christine's, 208 First Avenue

Leshko's, 111 Avenue A

Margaret's, 23 Avenue A

KK Restaurant, 192–194 First Avenue

Katz's Delicatessen of Houston Street, 205 East Houston Street (at Ludlow)

They Want Pizza

Villagers and tourists who come out in search of a delicious, savory slice of America's favorite food, which originated in Italy, are always in for a special treat. The very best pizza in the world can be found in the Village at:

John's, 278 Bleecker Street

Ray's (the *real* original place), 465 Sixth Avenue (at Eleventh Street)

Stromboli's, 112 University Place (and at 83 St. Marks Place)

Pizza Box, 174 Bleecker Street

Two Boots to Go, 36 Avenue A

Two Boots to Go-Go, 74 Bleecker (at Broadway)

Two Boots to Go West, 201 West Eleventh Street

Joe's Pizza, 233 Bleecker Street (at Carmine)

Rivoli Pizza I, 180 Seventh Avenue South

St. Marks Pizza, 23 Third Avenue

Pizza One, 535 Hudson Street

Goodfellas Pizza, Fourteenth Street and Seventh Avenue

LaBella Pompeii Pizza, 59 Greenwich Avenue

Arturo's, 106 West Houston Street

Joe's Pizza, Carmine and Bleecker Streets

The restaurant that is rated the very best anywhere in the land for Pizza Pie (or "tomato pies," as they were originally called) is John's on Bleecker Street, where brick-oven charcoal pizza must be ordered by the whole pie (no slices) at sit-down tables. John's was established in 1934 and is being managed by the founder's son, Peter Castellotti, who has opened up a John's at 408 East Sixty-fourth Street, 48 West Sixty-fifth Street, and 2390 Tamiami Trail in Port Charlotte, Florida. Two Boots at 37 Avenue A is another good sit-down pizza restaurant where you can order other Italian dishes. Arturo's Restaurant at 106 West Houston (at Thompson) is a coal-brick-oven pizza place with an atmospheric bar and live entertainment that has been a favorite in the Village for many years.

Tex-Mex and Juicy Burgers

Cowtown in the West Village

The Wild West is riding high again in the nineties in New York's own little Cowtown, nestled on Hudson Street in the West Village (between West Tenth and Charles Street). There are a couple of shops selling Western gear, including Mervin Bendewald's Whiskey Dust for cowboy boots and hats and the latest from the West and Southwest. But the real fun in Cowtown is at the bar and picturesque rooms of the Cowgirl Hall of Fame Restaurant. Here dudes from the East can meet cowgirls from the West, or vice versa. It's not hard to get romantic surrounded by the nostalgic trappings of the Old West, and once a year there's a gender-bending Patsy Cline look-alike contest that attracts real gals and drags all imitating the inimitable Patsy. Have a margarita at the bar and a brick of deep-fried onions, then chow down a big ranch dinner, and if you're lucky, you might catch Patsy Montana (the original) singing some of her country-western hits—or you could meet the cowgirl (or cowboy) of your movie dreams.

Western, Southwestern, Spanish

Cowgirl Hall of Fame, 519 Hudson Street

Caribe, 117 Perry Street

Mexican Village, 224 Thompson Street

Cottonwood Cafe, 415 Bleecker Street

Mesa Verde, 531 Hudson Street

Violeta's Mexican Restaurant, 220 West Thirteenth Street

Bandito, 153 Second Avenue

Burrito Loco, 166 West Fourth Street

Harry's Burritos, 91 East Seventh Street

Benny's Burritos, 112 Greenwich Avenue

　Avenue A and Sixth Street

Flying Burrito Brothers, 165 West Fourth Street

El Paso Restaurant, 134 West Houston Street

National Cafe (Cuban), 210 First Avenue (at Twelfth Street)

El Faro Restaurant, 823 Greenwich Street (at Horatio)

Sevilla, 62 Charles Street

Rio Mar, 7 Ninth Avenue at Little West Twelfth Street

Two Gastronomic Legends

The Pink Teacup   *The Pink Teacup at 42 Grove Street (between Bleecker and Bedford) has been dishing out good American soulfood for almost forty years, the first twenty-five around the corner on Bleecker Street. It was pink then, it's pink now, including the ceiling, walls and floor, the tables and chairs and long wooden benches, even the table linen. Mary Raye Stokes founded the place after learning the business from Adele Speare, who ran Mother Hubbard's on Sheridan Square. The current owner, Serita Ford, is the niece of Mary's husband, Charles Raye, and she carries on the Southern tradition, serving honey-dip fried chicken with fritters, baked pork with collard greens, grits, eggs, and a mouth-watering choice of home-baked pies and cakes.*

Pennyfeathers   *For a broader view, Pennyfeathers (95 Seventh Avenue South) glassed-in front offers a protected panorama of Sheridan Square. This is the "in" place for show-*

biz celebs, writers, and popular journalists like Cindy and Joey Adams, who call it their favorite Village hangout. The charming owner-hostess, Angelina Boone, features breakfast, late lunches, or wild boar ravioli, salmon steak, or rack of lamb for dinner. This intimate place also features a bar and late-night suppers.

Best Burgers

Nothing is more satisfying than sinking your teeth into a great American hamburger, and you will find a number of good burger joints in the Village. If you *must* have a McDonaldburger, the best is the Greenwich Village McDonald's on Third Street (at Sixth Avenue), which features an enclosed glass observation dining area on its second floor. Wimpy, the obsessive hamburger overeater, heartily, and hungrily, recommends:

Cedar Tavern and Roof Garden, 82 University Place

Boxers, 190 West Fourth Street

The Bagel, 168–70 West Fourth Street

Woody's Restaurant/Bar, 140 Seventh Avenue South

Elephant & Castle, 68 Greenwich Avenue

The Lion's Head, 59 Christopher Street

Chumley's, 86 Bedford Street

The White Horse Tavern, 567 Hudson Street

Corner Bistro, 341 West Fourth Street

McBell's, 359 Sixth Avenue (between West Fourth Street and Washington Place)

Speciality Dining

American Fare

Grove, 314 Bleecker Street

The Grange Hall, 50 Commerce Street

Cornelia Street Cafe, 29 Cornelia Street

Ye Waverly Inn, 16 Bank Street

Dix et Sept, 181 West Tenth Street

The Little Cafe, 183 West Tenth Street

Home, 20 Cornelia Street

Universal Grill, 44 Bedford Street

The Derby Steak and Seafood Grill, 109 MacDougal Street

ıe Street Seafood Cafe, 31 Eighth Avenue

Elephant & Castle, 68 Greenwich Avenue

The Bagel, 168–170 West Fourth Street

Brothers Bar-B-Que, 228 West Houston

Woody's Restaurant/Bar, 140 Seventh Avenue South

A Stray Cafe, 59 Horatio Street

Marylou's, 21 West Ninth Street

Knickerbocker Bar and Grill, 33 University Place

Old Homestead, 56 Ninth Avenue

Marion's Continental Restaurant and Lounge, 354 Bowery

Cub Room, 131 Sullivan Street

Caffe Passione, 159 Christopher Street

Papi Luis, 34 East Second Street

Savoy, 70 Prince Street

Pamela's Cafe, 683 Broadway

Amsterdams Grand Bar & Rotisserie, 454 Broadway

Ludlow Cafe, 165 Ludlow Street

2A, Avenue A and Second Street

Aggie's, 146 West Houston Street

Baby Jake's, 14 First Avenue

7A, Seventh Street and Avenue A

9, 110 St. Marks Place

Soups Cafe, 210 West Tenth Street

SoHo Kitchen and Bar, 103 Greene Street

Zoe, 90 Prince Street

The Markham Cafe, 59 Fifth Avenue

Anglers & Writers, 420 Hudson Street

One If by Land, Two If by Sea, 17 Barrow Street

Sazerac House Bar and Grill, Charles and Hudson Streets

Italian

Minetta Tavern, 113 MacDougal Street

Pó, 31 Cornelia Street

The Grand Ticino Restaurant, 228 Thompson Street

Mary's, 42 Bedford Street

Arturo's, 106 West Houston Street

John's, 278 Bleecker Street

Gus' Place, 149 Waverly Place

Monte's, 97 MacDougal Street

Lanza, 168 First Avenue

Fedora, 239 West Fourth Street

Carmella's Village Garden, 49 Charles Street

Casa Di Pré, 283 West Twelfth Street

Beatrice Inn, 285 West Twelfth Street

Trattoria Spaghetto, 232 Bleecker Street

Tutta Pasta, 26 Carmine Street

    504 La Guardia Place

Porto Bello, 208 Thompson Street

Cucina Della Fontana, 368 Bleecker Street

Adolph's Asti Restaurant, 13 East Twelfth Street

Villa Mosconi, 69 MacDougal Street
Caffé Cefalù, 259 West Fourth Street
La Focaccia, 51 Bank Street
Fanelli's Cafe, 94 Prince Street
La Casalinga, 120 First Avenue

French

Village Atelier, 436 Hudson Street
The Paris Commune, 411 Bleecker Street
La Ripaille, 605 Hudson Street
La Métairie, 189 West Tenth Street
Tartine, 253 West Eleventh Street
Bistro Jules, 65 St. Marks Place
Restaurant Florent, 69 Gansevoort Street
L'Ecole Bar Restaurant, 462 Broadway
L'Auberge du Midi, 310 West Fourth Street
Chez Michallet, 90 Bedford Street
Chez Ma Tante, 189 West Tenth Street
Chez Jacqueline, 72 MacDougal Street

THE PARIS COMMUNE

Asian, Middle Eastern, Indian

Cuisine de Saigon, 154 West Thirteenth Street
Can (French-Vietnamese), 482 West Broadway
Marnie's Noodle Shop, 466 Hudson Street
Bayamo (Cuban-Chinese), 704 Broadway
Shanghai Bar (Kelley and Ping Asian Grocery), 127 Greene Street
Sung Tieng, 343 Bleecker Street
Jade Mountain, 197 Second Avenue
Ginger Toon, 82 Bank Street
Satsuki Japanese Restaurant,
    133 Seventh Avenue South
Sapporo East, 245 East Tenth Street
Kun Paw, 39 Greenwich Avenue
Lucky Cheng's, 24 First Avenue
Dojo, 24–26 St. Marks Place
    14 West Fourth Street
Mamoun's Falafel Restaurant, 119 MacDougal Street

Lucky Cheng's
Delicious & Beautiful
Asian-California Cuisine
Graciously
served To you
by Asian
Drag-Queen
"Waitresses"

Mustafa Restaurant, 48 Greenwich Avenue

Divan Kebab House, 102 MacDougal Street

Sahara East, 184 First Avenue

The Magic Carpet Restaurant, 54 Carmine Street

Rectangles (Yemenite & Israeli), 159 Second Avenue

Olive Tree Cafe, 117 MacDougal Street

Yaffa Cafe, 97 St. Marks Place

Prince of India, 342 East Sixth Street

Natural/Health Food

Souen, 210 Sixth Avenue

   28 East Thirteenth Street

Spring Street Natural, 62 Spring Street

Angelica Kitchen, 300 East Twelfth Street

Village East Natural, 2 St. Marks Place

Life Cafe, 343 East Tenth Street

Village Natural, 46 Greenwich Avenue

Whole Wheat'n Wild Berrys, 57 West Tenth Street

Melanie's Natural Cafe, 445 Sixth Avenue

Caravan of Dreams, 405 East Sixth Street

Henrietta's Feed & Grain Company, 444 Hudson Street

Whole Earth Bakery & Kitchen, 130 St. Marks Place

   70 Spring Street

Village Shops

Books and Records

The Small Bookstore

Small bookstores are a mainstay in the Village. While some are tiny and intimate, other larger ones still strive to maintain an intimate atmosphere in terms of selection and presentation of books. The used or antiquarian bookstores of old are as scarce as hen's teeth these days, so it is a special treat to go into such a shop, talk to the owner, and browse or buy. The message is, "Support your small bookstore," lest they disappear and become yet another movie-video or porn-video outlet.

Bookleaves, 304 West Fourth Street (off Bank Street)

Pageant Book & Print Shop, 114 West Houston Street

Three Lives, 154 West Tenth Street

Strand Bookstore, 828 Broadway

Creative Visions, 548 Hudson Street

Oscar Wilde Memorial Bookstore, 15 Christopher Street

Biography Bookshop, 400 Bleecker Street (at Eleventh Street)

Mercer Street Books and Records, 206 Mercer Street

St. Marks Bookshop, 31 Third Avenue

Nicholas Davies & Co., 23 Commerce Street

Three Lives bookstore, Waverly and Tenth Street

Spring Street Books, 169 Spring Street
Shakespeare & Co., 716 Broadway
Untitled (Fine Art in Print), 159 Prince Street
A Photographer's Place, 133 Mercer Street
East/West Books, 78 Fifth Avenue
   67 Cooper Square (Third Avenue and Eighth Street)
Tompkins Square Books and Records, 111 East Seventh Street
Pathfinder Bookstore, 167 Charles Street (corner West Street)
Partners & Crime, 44 Greenwich Avenue

Comic book shops carry some wonderful books as well:

Village Comics, 163 Bleecker Street
Jeff's Comics, 150 Second Avenue
All Comics, 44 Carmine Street (between Bleecker and Bedford)
The Science Fiction Shop, 168 Thompson Street
Forbidden Planet, 821 Broadway

Some of the best "big" bookstores include:
Posman Books, 1 University Place
B. Dalton, Sixth Avenue at Eighth Street
Barnes and Noble, 4 Astor Place
Rizzoli Bookstore, 454 West Broadway
Tower Books, 383 Lafayette Street

Records, Tapes, CDs, and Videos

Bleecker Bob's, 118 West Third Street
Village Jazz Shop, 163 West Tenth Street
Record Runner, 5 Jones Street
Strider Records, 22 Jones Street
Second Coming Records, 235 Sullivan Street
Generation Records, 210 Thompson Street
Nostalgia . . . and All That Jazz, 217 Thompson Street
House of Oldies, 35 Carmine Street
Culture Records, 31 Carmine Street
Watu Records, 41 Carmine Street
The Golden Disc, 239 Bleecker Street
Rebel-Rebel, 319 Bleecker Street
Footlight Records, 113 East Thirteenth Street

Smash CD, 33 St. Marks Place
Tower Records, 692 Broadway at Fourth Street
Venus, 13 St. Marks Place
Kim's Underground Video, 144 Bleecker Street
World of Video, 178 Seventh Avenue South

Tchotchkes

Antiques and Collectibles

Second Childhood, 283 Bleecker Street
Dullsville, 143 East Thirteenth Street
Rene Kerne, 322 Bleecker Street
Susan Parrish, 390 Bleecker Street
Back Pages, 125 Greene Street
The Quilted Corner, 120 Fourth Avenue
Mood Indigo, 181 Prince Street
Atomic Passion, 430 East Ninth Street
Lost City Arts, 275 Lafayette Street
Radio Hula, 169 Mercer Street
Depression Modern, 150 Sullivan Street
Secondhand Rose, 270 Lafayette Street
Paula Rubenstein, Ltd., 65 Prince Street
E. Buk, 151 Spring Street
Antique Addiction, 436 West Broadway
Galileo, 167-1/2 Seventh Avenue South
Niall Smith Antiques, 344 Bleecker Street
Gallagher Paper Collectibles, 126 East Twelfth Street (basement)
The Rural Collection, 117 Perry Street

Jewelry and Gifts

Gifts, 86 Christopher Street
Bellardo, Ltd., 100 Christopher Street
R. J. White, Inc., 107 Christopher Street
Stick, Stone & Bone, 111 Christopher Street
Gallery II, 175 Bleecker Street
The Den of Antiquity, 108 MacDougal Street

Scarab, 104 MacDougal Street
The Silversmith, 184-3/4 West Fourth Street
Lou Fichera and Ron Perkins, 50 University Place
Scent from Heaven, 333 Bleecker Street

Threads and Boutiques

Clothing

Harriet Love, 126 Prince Street
Greenwich Village Army/Navy, 328 Bleecker Street
Don't Panic, 98 Christopher Street
Too Cute!, 113 Prince Street
Lee's Mardi Gras, 400 Ninth Avenue
Rockit Rags, 33 St. Marks Place
Sam Wagner Activewear, 169 Thompson Street
X-Large Store, 151 Avenue A
XTC Studio, 88 Christopher Street
The World, 75 Christopher Street
The Loft, 89 Christopher Street
Streetwise, 113 Christopher Street
Patricia Field, 10 East Eighth Street
Amalgamated, 19 Christopher Street
New Republic Clothier, 93 Spring Street
Screaming Mimi's, 382 Lafayette Street
Trash and Vaudeville, 4 St. Marks Place
Religious Sex, 7 St. Marks Place
Diesel, 154 Prince Street

Ladies Boutique on West Tenth Street

Replay Country Store, 109 Prince Street
O.M.G. Inc., the jeans store, 555 Broadway
Whiskey Dust, 526 Hudson Street

Leather:

The Leather Man, 111 Christopher Street
The Cockpit, 595 Broadway
Red Rock, 502 La Guardia Place
Arizona, 91 Spring Street

Children's:

Peanut Butter and Jane, 617 Hudson Street

Olympia

Vintage Clothing:

O Mistress Mine, 143 Seventh
    Avenue South

Dorothy's Closet, 335 Bleecker
    Street

Star Struck, 270 Bleecker Street

47 Greenwich Avenue

Andy's Chee-Pees, 16 West
    Eighth Street

Stella Dallas,
    218 Thompson Street

The Usual Suspects,
    337 East Ninth Street

Rose Is Vintage, 147 First Avenue
    350 East Ninth Street
    96 East Seventh Street

Interesting and Offbeat Shops

Little Rickie, 49-1/2 First Avenue

Greetings, 45 Christopher Street

Howdy Do, 72 East Seventh Street

Alphabets, 115 Avenue A
    47 Greenwich Avenue

Abracadabra, 10 Christopher Street

Altar Egos Gallery, 110 West Houston Street

Witchcraft, 238 East Sixth Street

Love Saves the Day, 119 Second Avenue

Village Chess Shop, Ltd., 230 Thompson Street

Jerry Ohlinger's Movie Material Store, 242 West Fourteenth Street

Animation, 34 West Thirteenth Street
Animated Classics, 399 Bleecker Street
The Candle Shop, 118 Christopher Street
Kate's Paperie, 8 West Thirteenth Street
   561 Broadway
Uplift Lighting, 506 Hudson Street

Sex:
Pink Pussy Cat Boutique, 167 West Fourth Street
The Pleasure Chest, 156 Seventh Avenue South
Condomania, 351 Bleecker Street

PINK PUSSY
CAT BOUTIQUE

Dogs and Cats (Pets):
Beverly Hills LaunderMutt, Ltd., 45 Grove Street
Whiskers, 235 East Ninth Street
J. B. J. Discount Pet Shop, 151 East Houston Street
Pets Kitchen, 116 Christopher Street

Edibles

Specialty Foods

Balducci's (since 1916), 424 Sixth Avenue
Bonsignour, 35 Jane Street
Jack David Caffe & Ice Cream Bar, 330 Bleecker Street
Yonah Schimmel, 137 East Houston Street
Olive's, 120 Prince Street
Dean & DeLuca, 560 Broadway
Spring Street Market and Deli, 111 Spring Street
Bella's Mini Market, 109 First Avenue
First Avenue Pierogi & Deli, 130 First Avenue
Russo's Mozzarella and Pasta Corp., 344 East Eleventh Street
Medina Natural Food Market, 51 Avenue A
Pete's Spice, 174 First Avenue
Li-Lac Chocolates, 120 Christopher Street
Fancy Grocery, 329 Bleecker Street
Dowel Indian Grocery, 91 First Avenue

DEAN & DELUCA

Porto Rico Importing Company, 201 Bleecker Street
    40 1/2 St. Marks Place
McNulty's Tea & Coffee Company, 109 Christopher Street

Bakeries

Chez Claude, 187 West Fourth Street
Once Upon a Tart, 135 Sullivan Street

Lafayette Bakery on Bleecker Street

Lafayette French Pastry Bakers,
    298 Bleecker Street

Taylor's, 523 Hudson Street

Bruno Bakery,
    506 LaGuardia Place

New 1st Avenue Bakery,
    121 First Avenue

Bleecker Street Pastry & Cafe,
    245 Bleecker Street

Zito & Sons Bakery,
    259 Bleecker Street

Patisserie Lanciani,
    271 West Fourth Street

De Robertis Pasticceria,
    176 First Avenue

Rocco's Pastry Shop and Cafe, 243 Bleecker Street
Jon Vie, 492 Sixth Avenue

Choice Meats

Florence Meat Market, 5 Jones Street
O. Ottomanelli & Sons, 285 Bleecker Street
Katz's Delicatessen, 205 East Houston Street
First Avenue Meat Products, 140 First Avenue
Kurowycky Meat Products, 124 First Avenue
E & S Meat Market, 111 First Avenue
East Village Meat Market, 139 Second Avenue
Faicco Pork Store, 260 Bleecker Street

Faicco Pork Stores, Inc.
"THE FINEST IN ITALIAN PORK SAUSAGE"

Village Miscellaneous

Parking Garages

Brevort, 21 East 12th Street (University Place)
Edison Park Fast, 215 East Houston (Essex Street)
Edison Park Fast, 174 Center Street (Canal Street)
Broome-Thompson Street Garage, 520 Broome Street (Thompson)
Minetta, 122 West Third Street (MacDougal)
Travelers, 160 West Tenth Street (Seventh Avenue South)
Washington Square, 2 Fifth Avenue (West Eighth Street)

Hospitals and Clinics

St. Vincent's Hospital and Medical Center of New York,
    153 West Eleventh Street (16 clinical departments and a doctor's
    directory—24-hour service: 1-800-999-6266)
St. Vincent's Hospital Outpatient, Edward and Theresa O'Toole Building,
    30 Seventh Avenue (with 57 clinics)
Cabrini Medical Center Stuyvesant Polyclinic, 137 Second Avenue
New York Eye and Ear Infirmary, 310 East 14th Street

Special Events

Halloween Prade—October
Gay Pride Prade—June
Ukranian Festival (East Seventh Street)—May
Washington Square Art Show—May and September
Feast of Saint Anthony of Padua—June
Bastille Day (Gansvoort Street)—July
Feast of San Gennaro—September

AMERICAN HAMBURGER

a play in one act by Robert Heide

CHARACTERS:

Village Tourist

George Washington

Maxwell Bodenheim

SCENE: A park in the Village near McDonald's

American Hamburger, Robert Heide's one-act play, was presented during a two-week event called "Village Writers on the Village," which was produced by Theater for the New City at the Jane West Hotel Theater to commemorate the two hundredth anniversary of American independence on November 11, 1976. Other writers, all presenting works about the Village, included Allen Ginsberg, Kenneth Patchen, Joel Oppenheimer, Harvey Fierstein, Ron Tavel, Victor Lipton, Harvey Tavel, Amlin Gray, Joan Durant, Maria Irene Fornes, Helen Duberstein, and H. M. Koutoukas. *Village Voice* critic David Finkle called Heide's *American Hamburger* and Ginsberg's *Kaddish* "already a worthy part of Village literature."

VILLAGE TOURIST: I don't live that far away from the Village . . . I'm from Jersey . . . just across the river . . . a little factory town called Kearny. Not much happens there . . . there's a sameness, a repetition. I teach school . . . history . . . but my main concern . . . my obsessions . . . are mostly erotic . . . I come here on my Indian motorcycle to cruise . . . look for a sexual encounter. As a child, I had sexual fantasies about George Washington . . . I guess I thought he was a perfect father figure . . . other than that . . . I love the costume freaks in the Village. One night I thought I saw Martha Washington or was it Betsy Ross on roller skates carrying a wand like Glinda the Good . . . from Oz.

MAXWELL BODENHEIM: The old Village in the twenties was a tough, exciting place to be . . . we commingled . . . in those days with thugs, sneak thieves, pimps, gamblers, voluptuous whores . . . waterfront sailors . . . in fact, later in my more dissolute forgetful years, my own life was taken by a tightass sexual sailor—longshoreman, he actually was, although legend persists that it was a group of sailors that killed myself and my wife that night. At some point I guess one ought to go with the legend, it must have been perpetuated for good reason . . . well . . . it was after a bar-to-bar drinking binge . . . murdered . . . you see, I too liked to lurk about, to " cruise," as you call it . . . feelings of hopelessness . . . despondency would overtake me, you see . . . and . . . the phantom of night would move into my very being . . . overtake me.

GEORGE WASHINGTON: I camped around here . . . myself . . . Greenwich Village . . . I think it was called Green Village then . . . my headquarters were around King and Vandam below Houston . . . during the Revolution . . . of course as legend has it for me, I slept around a good deal. Everywhere you go . . . a sign is posted "George Slept Here." Indeed. I couldn't have slept in all those places. Could I?

BODENHEIM: Maxwell Bodenheim is my name, General . . . who would fail to know you, General Washington . . . I am honored. I represent the old Village Bohemia that is with us no more . . . things come and go . . . change quickly . . . it is strange to have the sense of having been here before . . . is it not? To appear and then disappear . . . like a retrogressive photographic image. Death . . . to have been through that ultimate orgasmic experience . . . but that really is past—beyond . . . why look at it . . . as if staring into a maze of mirror-infinity.

WASHINGTON: What is this, some sort of trick poetry? This is unbelievable, sir, that I should find myself at a common meeting ground with the likes of you . . . what does this mean? I have always been regarded as a pinnacle of virtue . . . a soldier who fought in the name of—*truth*. Even in the order of things past, I deserve better than this.

TOURIST: I run into more costume freaks! Why, on Christopher Street I saw the Statue of Liberty with green hair and green skin . . .

BODENHEIM: Each of us has his own truth to deal with . . . his own inclinations . . . anyone can meet anyone in the Village. Also, this man could be an impostor, a costume freak as you called him, in a powdered wig and I a bag-of-tricks poet . . .

WASHINGTON: You would certainly have been regarded as riffraff in my day . . . your kind . . . certainly would not be welcome in discreet polite . . . society . . . formality never bred contempt.

TOURIST: I travel around America a lot, during my school vacations . . . It's funny . . . all of the towns . . . are beginning to look the same . . . McDonald's . . . Arthur Treacher's Fish and Chips . . . Tico Taco . . . are mushrooming everywhere. My thing is raunchy, stainless-steel 1950s diners with pink mirrors . . . it's hard to escape the fast-food ethic, polysorbate 80, sturbestrome Colonel Saunder's chicken injected with female hormones . . . boy! I do like Nathan's hot dogs though . . . but eating there is like eating in a pig trough . . . everyone just gobbling it up . . . do you remember the battle of The Stonewall?

WASHINGTON: No.

TOURIST: On Christopher Street. Sexual liberation. That's what it was all about. Now the Stonewall is a bagel restaurant. Can you believe it?

WASHINGTON: Things change. Yes. I hear there is even a hamburger chain called Minutemen.

TOURIST: Yes, in New Jersey, and Roy Rogers, Pat Boone—and Johnny Carson—have hamburger stands turning up everywhere.

BODENHEIM: I liked to hang out at a place . . . in my day . . . called the Hell Hole . . . over on the corner . . . southeast . . . on Sixth Avenue and Fourth Street. Actually it was called the Golden Swan—a sign with a golden swan hung out front . . . but we who frequented it knew it as a true-hell inferno.

WASHINGTON: Rubbish.

BODENHEIM: We would drop a nickel into a player piano that would pound out garish melodies, "brazen agonies," I would call those tunes . . . usually Irish ditties like "My Wild Irish Rose"—"the sweetest flower that grows" . . . awful. The walls, covered with photos of boxers . . . all Irish . . . and race horses. The place was mostly all us men but painted whores came in through the family entrance. I wrote poetry there. The stench of beer mixed with the odor of alcoholic piss and tobacco was foul. Ha-ha. I can still smell it.

WASHINGTON: Sir, you disgust me . . . your language.

TOURIST: Nobody takes the Bohemia of the 1920s too seriously nowadays. The idea they had of avant-garde seems juvenile, unenlightened by today's standards . . . as an off-off playgoer . . .

BODENHEIM: Oh, we had nudity . . . in the Ziegfeld Follies, but no serious artist paid much attention to it. It was words that moved us then. Words.

WASHINGTON: Your words couldn't move a sow . . . I loathe Bohemians.

BODENHEIM: I heard your true skin color, that you cover with white powder and dry French rouge, is a sallow yellow and that your complexion is pitted with worm holes.

WASHINGTON: Why bring up that?

BODENHEIM: . . . that your teeth are wooden. You Puritan.

TOURIST: Yes. I read that in a historical biography . . . It is true . . . but I would never teach that to my students at Kearny High School or they might never take George Washington or this country seriously again.

WASHINGTON: Slander . . . I will not abide these insults.

BODENHEIM: We all know that men of your time and your position . . . fornicated . . . with their slaves.

TOURIST: To me the battle of The Stonewall is the most important battle fought in this country. Hundreds of screaming queens having it out with the police—wam! "We want to be liberated. Down with oppressive straight pigs. Yeah!" Now it's just a memory, like a forgotten dream. All bills for sexual freedom wind up in politicians' wastepaper baskets . . . no bronze plaque even on the building itself . . . saying . . . "Here was fought the Battle of Stonewall."

WASHINGTON: Stonewall?

TOURIST: A memory. Things change so fast.

BODENHEIM: It is all memory when you are dead.

WASHINGTON (ASIDE):   Like dry rouge on a pitted cheek. Made up as if by a mortician. Covering up the underlying truth. What is lacking inside.

BODENHEIM: Like one of the whores from the Hell Hole.

WASHINGTON: I beg your pardon.

TOURIST: We're all just tourists in this country. We think we know it and we don't. We don't even know ourselves . . . in America.

BODENHEIM: Confusion was everywhere . . . still . . . we did have a good time of it . . . in our confused state . . . at the Hell Hole. We always *yearned* for something better. Eugene O'Neill was one of the drunks that I befriended there. He respected me, as an artist. He was a dark, lugubrious black Irishman with a gift for gab. He would sit for hours talking to a cutthroat gang called the Hudson Dusters . . . hijackers, thieves whom everyone else was terrified of. Not him. One thing we were not—in the old Village—was pansies. Some of us may have been queer but we were tough.

TOURIST: There are the legions of leather and denim today on the street.

BODENHEIM: Conformists. Yearning for conformity even within nonconformity.

WASHINGTON: What is happening to the land I knew?

BODENHEIM: We thought nothing of sitting elbow to elbow —artists and writers—with killers and scum. The worst enticed us, brought out the best in our imagination.

WASHINGTON: No wonder you were killed by a sailor. A piteous victim.

BODENHEIM: I became a Village character . . . a viable personality . . . my outward identity loomed much larger than my work. Now I belong mostly to folklore . . . the old Bohemia . . . a memory. What difference does it make?

WASHINGTON: I never thought of taking up pen. I was always content to be just myself—what are those men doing over there in the park? Smoking . . .

TOURIST: Oh . . . black beauties, speed and grass. They sell it . . . drugs . . . to passersby . . . mood-changers.

OFFSTAGE VOICES: Black beauties, loose joints, uppers, downers, get your mood-changers here.

WASHINGTON: Oh yes, we would smoke on certain occasions—Ben Franklin, myself, and the others. It wasn't uncommon.

BODENHEIM: And didn't you die of a sexual disease, Mr. Washington?

WASHINGTON: Don't say it . . .

BODENHEIM: Of a venereal complication . . .

WASHINGTON: No . . . don't mention it . . .

TOURIST: History does have the last word, they say. The force of history can be pretty tremendous at times. Truth does emerge . . . somehow . . . it comes out of nowhere . . . sweeps us up . . . into change . . .

BODENHEIM: Sometimes things change for the worse . . . like peace or hopeful prosperity interrupted by gunshot fire into . . .

TOURIST: Like hamburger and chicken restaurants cropping up everywhere . . . money. The almighty fucking dollar. Yeah.

WASHINGTON: America is changing and change is good . . is progress . . when it comes.

TOURIST: It changes but it all looks the same . . . just one giant hamburger.

WASHINGTON: Just one hot dog . . .

BODENHEIM: . . . in America . . . things covering up . . . to conspire . . . to evade . . .

WASHINGTON: I remember crossing the river into Trenton. With my troops.

TOURIST: There are a great many eat-in diners in Trenton now. McDonald's has a stronghold there.

WASHINGTON: Is he a general, this McDonald? ·

TOURIST: McDonald's is a capitalist organization that sells hamburgers to millions of hungry Americans . . . They can't get enough to fill their fat faces.

WASHINGTON: So it's all hamburger then?

TOURIST: All hamburger. Hamburger is spreading everywhere—it is our favorite.

WASHINGTON: America always had good taste.

BODENHEIM: Yum. Yum. Let's all go to McDonald's and get ours.

WASHINGTON: A good idea.

TOURIST: The fast-food ethic is contagious. I'm getting hungry. Boy. I'd even choose a hamburger over sex anytime. And sex is . . . was . . . one of my favorite obsessions. Mmmmm.

BODENHEIM: Me too. Yumm.

WASHINGTON: I prefer peanuts.

TOURIST: You can get a peanut burger in certain places . . . like the South.

WASHINGTON: Tell me. How is it that you have joined us, young man, since we are, well, sort of, you might say, free-floating spirits?

TOURIST: Oh, yeah . . . well . . . I forgot to mention to you guys . . . that . . . see . . . well. The other night . . . I had had . . . well, a couple of drinks as well as . . . ha-ha . . a couple of tranquilizers . . Librium . . . I'm . . . ah . . . kind of a nervous type . . . teaching school and all . . . and my father . . . he hated my guts . . . but that was beside the point. I lived with my folks in Jersey . . . he despised my being gay . . . he saw me once in the garage . . . I was only nine . . . with my friend Arnold . . . he beat the shit outa me . . . so what about it . . . anyhow it was after doing my usual Friday evening rounds, Hotel Keller Bar, Peter Rabbit, Boots and Saddles, I took a walk down by the docks near the trucks . . . a lot was going on down there, it seemed . . . I felt kind of way out there . . . see . . . music was blaring from the bars. Anyhow I was between two stationary trucks . . . I don't know what it is that I was looking for . . . see . . . anyhow . . . I wasn't too drunk to notice several young guys . . . teenagers . . . in the dark . . . they looked like kids from my American history class—one had a knife—I went toward them . . . I said "Stop!" "Help!" But no one came . . . I didn't even feel the jab of the knife. I was scared. Why is this happening to me? I asked and . . . and . . . well . . . so what I'm trying to say is I've experienced the death trip myself. It's sort of new to me all this. It's only been a couple of days. Quite a heavy . . . next day . . . Saturday or Sunday . . I was dragged out of the river . . . must have been dumped there. Funny, I don't feel any different than when I was alive . . . it's confusing . . . not being sure if you're alive . . . or dead.

BODENHEIM: Many people are alive in life and act as if they are dead, so what's the difference? At least we know we have passed on. Hamburger to hamburger. Is it so intolerable really? I spent my earthly existence pondering the metaphysics of the other world . . . death . . to no end. I might have dropped the whole question in favor of my fervor for . . . lustful ambiguity. Well, we should examine this hamburger situation.

TOURIST: I sure could use a Big Mac. I sure could. I know that would give me a sense of the "real" somehow.

BODENHEIM: We'll head toward the building near where the old Hell Hole used to be.

(TO WASHINGTON) Are you with us, General?

WASHINGTON: How can I avoid it? It seems to be inevitable.

TOURIST: Having kicked over we still need the Big Hamburger.

WASHINGTON: Strange. The last word is "hamburger."

END

A giant hamburger appears in the sky (photoprojection), two golden arches on either side. Organ music ("You Deserve a Break Today"). Characters look beatific, as if preparing to enter the golden gates of heaven.

Author's note: The Stonewall on Christopher Street mentioned in *American Hamburger* went from an inn catering to wedding parties and banquets to a gay bar (the original scene of the 1960s Stonewall Riots) to a bagel restaurant to a clothing store (1970s and 1980s) to a second incarnation as a gay bar called the Stonewall. A plaque was placed on the building in 1994 commemorating the twenty-fifth anniversary of the riots.

ROBERT HEIDE, born in Irvington, New Jersey, received his formal education at Northwestern University in Evanston, Illinois, where he studied with the great theater teacher Alvina Krause. Following this exercise in academia, he moved to Greenwich Village, studying the theater (acting, directing, playwrighting) with Stella Adler, Uta Hagen, and Harold Clurman. A seminal playwright of the off-off Broadway movement of the late 1960s, 1970s, and 1980s, Heide had his many plays produced at the Cherry Lane, New Playwrights, Caffe Cino, Cafe La Mama, Theater for the New City, Westbeth Theater, New York Theater Strategy—all in the Village. His works were produced in cities across America as well. The scenarios for his play *The Bed* and the original filmscript *The Death of Lupe Velez* were filmed by Andy Warhol. He was a member of Edward Albee's Playwrights Group at the Van Dam Theater. His plays were published in the collections *The Best of Off-Off Broadway* (E. P. Dutton; Michael Smith, editor), *The Off-Off Broadway Book* (Bobbs-Merrill; Albert Poland, Bruce Mailman, editors), *New American Plays*, Volume 4 (Hill & Wang; William M. Hoffman, editor), as well as in acting editions (Breakthrough Press), and he is, with John Gilman, the author of a number of books on American popular culture—ranging in subject matter from cowboys to the Great Depression and Mickey Mouse. *Moon*, with the original Cino cast, along with *The Bed*, with John Patterson, was presented in 1993 at Theater for the New City. A play about Andy Warhol is in the works.

JOHN GILMAN is a photographer and writer and the author, with Robert Heide, of ten books on popular culture in twentieth-century America. He spent his childhood years in Honolulu and San Francisco; as a young man, he came to Greenwich Village and stayed. As an actor, he appeared in Village productions at the Caffe Cino, Judson Church, Cafe La Mama, and Theater for the New City. He worked at several publications in New York, including the *Village Voice*, and was also Executive Director of the American Society of Magazine Photographers. He is a contributor to several publications, including the *New York Daily News*, *Collectors' Showcase*, and the *Village Voice*.

Books co-authored by Robert Heide and John Gilman include *Home Front America*, *Disneyana*, *O'New Jersey*, *Popular Art Deco*, *Box-Office Buckaroos*, *Starstruck*, *Cartoon Collectibles*, *Cowboy Collectibles*, and *Dime-Store Dream Parade*.

Greenwich Village